New Testament

Who's WHO

ILLUSTRATED EDITION

New Testament

Who's WHO

ILLUSTRATED EDITION

A Comprehensive Guide to the People in the New Testament

Richard J. Allen

Front Cover Images (clockwise from top left): *The Ascension* by Harry Anderson © Intellectual Reserve, Inc. Courtesy of the Church History Museum; *Hope* © Liz Lemon Swindle. Used with permission from Foundation Arts. For print information, go to www.foundationarts.com or call 1-800-366-2781; *In Humility* © Simon Dewey. Courtesy of Altus Fine Art. For print information, visit www.altusfineart.com; *Gethsemane* © Joseph Brickey. For more information, visit www.josephbrickey.com; *Suffer the Children* © J. Kirk Richards. For more information, visit www.jkirkrichards.com; *Mary Heard His Word* © Walter Rane. For more information, visit www.walterrane.com; *Judas Betrays Christ* by Ted Henninger © Intellectual Reserve, Inc.; *In Favor with God* © Simon Dewey. Courtesy of Altus Fine Art. For print information, visit www.altusfineart.com; *The Doubting Thomas* by Carl Heinrich Bloch. Courtesy of Ugerløse Kirke, Ugerløse, Denmark; *Nicodemus Came Unto Him by Night* © Walter Rane. For more information, visit www.walterrane.com; *Why Weepest Thou* © Simon Dewey. Courtesy of Altus Fine Art. For print information, visit www.altusfineart.com; *To Fulfill All Righteousness* © Simon Dewey. Courtesy of Altus Fine Art. For print information, visit www.altusfineart.com; *The Transfiguration* by Carl Heinrich Bloch. Courtesy of Det Nationalhistoriske Museum på Frederiksborg, Hillerød; *Raising of the Daughter of Jairus* © Jeffery Hein. For more information, visit www.jeffreyhein.com.

Back Cover and Spine Images: *Raising Lazarus* by Carl Heinrich Bloch. Courtesy of Det Nationalhistoriske Museum på Frederiksborg, Hillerød.

Cover and book design © 2010 by Covenant Communications, Inc.

Published by Covenant Communications, Inc.
American Fork, Utah

Copyright © 2010 by Richard J. Allen

Printed in China
First Printing: October 2010

16 15 14 13 12 11 10   10 9 8 7 6 5 4 3 2 1

ISBN-13 978-1-60861-072-3

PREFACE

The events portrayed in the New Testament happened long ago—but their impact on our lives is of eternal consequence. The Atonement of Jesus Christ, established before the foundation of the world and carried out during the meridian of time according to the will of the Father, constitutes the power that sustains every moment of our life. King Benjamin reminds us, "I say unto you that if ye should serve him who has created you from the beginning, and is preserving you from day to day, by lending you breath, that ye may live and move and do according to your own will, and even supporting you from one moment to another—I say, if ye should serve him with all your whole souls yet ye would be unprofitable servants" (Mosiah 2:21). To know the work of the Lord and embrace His example and counsel with devotion is to become profitable in spiritual matters, helping us to recognize and be grateful for the blessings He bestows upon us.

The individuals who surrounded the Savior on the stage of life during His mortal ministry are personalities of a bygone era—but they, too, live on as a vital force and have a continuing presence in the lives of all who look back with humble thanksgiving at the mission of salvation and exaltation the Lamb of God as Redeemer and Savior of the world completed. Said He, "All things are present with me, for I know them all" (Moses 1:6). Using that same pattern, we can strive to look back at the people of the New Testament—the Savior and His disciples, the succeeding leaders of the Church, the Saints of that era, and the individuals and groups who both supported and condemned the cause of truth—and let these personalities come alive in our present day as a means to teach us lessons and help guide us in making wise decisions on the pathway of life. The examples of valor and obedience will teach us lessons of light, and the examples of those who were blinded by worldly concerns and failed to recognize the Messiah among them will teach us what to avoid as we move forward steadfastly toward the destination of eternal life and salvation.

The record of the Savior's mortal ministry of mercy and atonement is sacred evidence of the scope and power of infinite love and redemption. This priceless chronicle is of inestimable worth as a means to reinforce and strengthen personal commitment to honor one's covenants with unshakable faith and enduring devotion. The greatest story ever told did not emerge without roots or context. It was the fulfillment of a divine plan originating in the premortal realm before the foundations of the world. "Here I am, send me" (Abraham 3:27) were the words that inaugurated the mission of salvation for all mankind. From the moment God the Father approved and activated the holy commission for His Only Begotten, "full of grace and truth," (John 1:14) to bring about the eternal plan of happiness, the pathway toward the ultimate triumph of light over darkness, good over evil, life over death, was established with irreversible momentum and infinite power. The Beloved Son of God was to become the "author of eternal salvation unto all them that [would] obey Him," Paul expressed (Hebrews 5:9). He was to ensure the perpetuity of life beyond death. He was to be "the light and the life of the world" (Alma 38:9; D&C 10:70; 11:28). That is the message of the New Testament.

"For unto us a child is born, unto us a son is given," declared Isaiah with the voice of prophecy (Isaiah 9:6). This same child, born of Mary in the stable, was even Jehovah of the Old Testament, signifying "the Unchangeable One," "the Eternal I Am." He was the Lord of ancient scripture (*Adonai* in Hebrew), even the Son of God—the Only Begotten Son of God in the flesh, Alpha and Omega. This little child born beneath the light of the new star was the Messiah or the Christ (in the Greek formulation), meaning the "Anointed"—the one divinely commissioned, authorized, and foreordained to complete the divine mission of the Atonement. This little child, who "grew, and waxed strong in spirit, filled with wisdom," having the "grace of God . . . upon him" (Luke 2:40), was the Great Creator, the Word of God, the Giver of life, the Light of the World. This young child, who would grow into manhood and immerse himself in the ministry of salvation, was Emmanuel (or Immanuel), meaning "God among us" in Hebrew, the Only Begotten, with a mortal mission of divine sanctification as the Messenger of the Covenant to condescend to come among us as the Good Shepherd without fearing betrayal or death. This Son of God, "full of grace and truth" (2 Nephi 2:6; D&C 66:12; 93:11; Moses 1:6, 32; 5:7; 6:52; 7:11) was Jesus, the Savior—"God is help"—even the Redeemer, the one chosen to bring about the infinite sacrifice and Atonement on behalf of mankind, the Lamb of God, the Bread of Life. Passing through the Crucifixion and Resurrection, according to the will of the Father, He became the Life of the World, even the great King, Judge, Mediator, Advocate, and Bridegroom—the same who is to come again in glory to inaugurate the millennial reign and serve as our Law Giver, the Prince of Peace, and the Covenant Father of all who shall believe on Him and overcome in faith and righteousness.

The New Testament tells this story of salvation and hope through the mouths of personal witnesses who labored with Jesus in the ministry, suffered with Him as He wrought the infinite Atonement, gloried with Him in the Resurrection, obeyed His commandment to take the message of the gospel unto all the world (Matthew 28:19–20), and in many cases, sealed their testimonies with their lives. Others who did not know Him personally carried on His mission of love and redemption under the auspices of the Abrahamic Covenant. *New testament* means, in effect, the "new covenant" or the covenant between God and His children that binds them to Him with sacred promises to be fulfilled on the basis of everlasting principles and powers inherent in God's design to "bring to pass the immortality and eternal life of man" (Moses 1:39). This covenant or testament was ordained of God and foretold by His prophets:

> Behold, the days come, saith the Lord, that I will make a new covenant with the house of Israel, and with the house of Judah:
>
> Not according to the covenant that I made with their fathers in the day *that* I took them by the hand to bring them out of the land of Egypt; which my covenant they brake, although I was an husband unto them, saith the Lord:
>
> But this *shall* be the covenant that I will make with the house of Israel; After those days, saith the Lord, I will put my law in their inward parts, and write it in their hearts; and will be their God, and they shall be my people. (Jeremiah 31:31–33)

Can we write the message of the New Testament in our hearts and become the "children of the prophets" and the "children of the covenant" (3 Nephi 20:25–26)? Can we follow in the footsteps of the Savior and become as He commanded, "even as I am" (3 Nephi 27:27)? The answer given by the New Testament and confirmed by the resurrected Savior to the ancient American Saints is a resounding "yes"—if we will but honor our covenants and mold our daily lives in the spirit of meekness and righteousness after the patterns set by our Lord and Master. In this current volume, I have attempted to present in the portraits included evidence of the patterns, principles, and precepts of salvation that are formulated in the New Testament as the record of Christ's ministry of hope and life and are confirmed by all the holy scriptures. We are told that "the government shall be upon his shoulder: and his name shall be called Wonderful, Counsellor, The mighty God, The everlasting Father, The Prince of Peace" (Isaiah 9:6). We are assured "that there shall be no other name given nor any other way nor means whereby salvation can come unto the children of men, only in and through the name of Christ, the Lord Omnipotent" (Mosiah 3:17). In that spirit, I hope this volume will help the reader in the process of understanding and applying the scriptures prayerfully and inviting the Spirit to confirm these truths and sustain every noble effort to come unto Christ and follow in His footsteps.

The approach used in this volume is to place central emphasis on the scriptural account itself. Some historical, linguistic, and cultural elements are included, but the prevailing compass to navigate through the landscape presented in this volume—populated by more than 350 personalities—is *the word of God*. For that reason, many scriptural passages are provided, not only from the King James Version of New Testament but also from relevant passages in the other books of the sacred canon: the Old Testament, the Book of Mormon, the Doctrine and Covenants, and the Pearl of Great Price. What happens in the New Testament is part of the broader flux of events constituting the unfolding of the divine plan of salvation on behalf of humankind—from the beginning of time until the ultimate completion of the work at the end of the millennial era—hence the need to look at things from a higher perspective by seeking and exploring the connections, patterns, promises, prototypes, fulfillments of prophecies, and the key doctrines and principles that hold everything together in harmony and light. Thus, in support of this process, the most enlightening scriptural passages are included, wherever possible, and the readers are encouraged to "liken the scriptures" unto themselves, as Nephi counseled, "that ye may have hope" (1 Nephi 19: 23, 24).

Background materials used in the preparation of the present *New Testament Who's Who* include the previous volumes in this series, authored by Ed J. Pinegar and Richard J. Allen: *Book of Mormon Who's Who* (2007), *Doctrine and Covenants Who's Who* (2008), and *Old Testament Who's Who* (2009). Also helpful have been the commentary volumes by these same authors: *Latter-Day Commentary on the Old Testament* (2001), *Teachings and Commentaries on the Book of Mormon* (2003), *Teachings and Commentaries on the Doctrine and Covenants* (2004; soft-cover reprint 2008), *Teachings and Commentaries on the Old Testament* (2005; soft-cover reprint 2009), *Teachings and Commentaries on the New Testament* (2006), and *Commentaries and Insights on the Book of Mormon*, vol. 1 (2007) and vol. 2 (2008).

In addition, the following sources have been especially useful: Bruce R. McConkie, *Doctrinal New Testament Commentary*, 3 vols. (Salt Lake City: Bookcraft, 1965-1973); James E. Talmage, *Jesus the Christ* (Salt Lake City: Deseret Book, 1983); and Richard Neitzel Holzapfel, Eric D. Huntsman, and Thomas Wayment, *Jesus Christ and the World of the New Testament* (Salt Lake City: Deseret Book,

2006). The last named volume gives an up-to-date scholarly perspective on the historical, cultural, and linguistic dimensions of the New Testament record, including the LDS point of view. Also helpful as a cross-check on prevailing opinion and interpretation have been the online reference sources for *Easton's Bible Dictionary* and *Smith's Bible Dictionary*.

I wish to express appreciation for the undeviating support of the staff members of Covenant Communications and their devoted interest in this project. Special thanks go to managing editor Kathryn Jenkins and to Margaret Weber and Samantha Van Walraven for their extraordinary commitment to excellence in editing and design. Gratitude is also due to the artists and illustrators whose work enlivens the discourse and opens up the world of visual illumination throughout the volume.

Special thanks goes to Carol Lynn Allen, my wife, for her support and encouragement as this work progressed to its completion.

Richard J. Allen

Table of Contents

New Testament Who's Who Entries: List

(The numbers in parentheses indicate the number of individuals of that name or title who are included in the New Testament.)

ABBREVIATIONS

DCE: Hoyt W. Brewster Jr., *Doctrine and Covenants Encyclopedia* (Salt Lake City: Bookcraft, 1996)

DNTC: Bruce R. McConkie, *Doctrinal New Testament Commentary*, 3 vols. (Salt Lake City: Bookcraft, 1965–1973)

HC: Joseph Smith, *History of The Church of Jesus Christ of Latter-day Saints*, 7 vols., introduction and notes by B. H. Roberts (Salt Lake City: The Church of Jesus Christ of Latter-day Saints, 1932–1951)

JCWNT: Richard Neitzel Holzapfel, Eric D. Huntsman, and Thomas Wayment, *Jesus Christ and the World of the New Testament* (Salt Lake City: Deseret Book, 2006)

JD: *Journal of Discourses*, 26 vols. (London: Latter-day Saints' Book Depot, 1854–1886)

MD: Bruce R. McConkie, *Mormon Doctrine*, 2nd ed. (Bookcraft, 1966)

TPJS: Joseph Smith, *Teachings of the Prophet Joseph Smith* (Salt Lake City: Deseret Book, 1976)

WJS: Joseph Smith, *The Words of Joseph Smith: The Contemporary Accounts of the Nauvoo Discourses of the Prophet Joseph*, comp. and ed. Andrew F. Ehat and Lyndon W. Cook, 2nd ed. (1996)

Aaron

As a companion to his younger brother Moses, Aaron was a pivotal figure in the Lord's cause to free the Israelites from Egyptian bondage, shape their spiritual preparation, and lead them to the Holy Land (see Exodus 4:10–16, 27–31; 5:1–12:50). Upon Aaron was conferred the administrative keys and powers for the operation of the lesser priesthood, perpetually named in his honor following Sinai. He and his worthy progeny among the Levites were those designated to perform sacred rites and services on behalf of Israel down through the generations (see Numbers 18:20–24; 25:10–13; 1 Chronicles 23:13). As the Apostle Paul confirmed, Aaron's priesthood calling by revelation and installation under the authority of prophetic leadership became the exemplum of the pattern of how divine commissions are conveyed and inaugurated: "And no man taketh this honour unto himself, but he that is called of God, as was Aaron" (Hebrews 5:4; see also Hebrews 7 for a comparison between the priesthood after the order of Aaron and the higher priesthood after the order of Melchizedek). Stephen, prior to his martyrdom, censured his persecutors by invoking, among other things, the disobedience of the Israelites at the foot of Mount Sinai when

MOSES CONFERS THE LESSER PRIESTHOOD ON AARON.

the Israelites refused the fulness of the Lord's offering of glory unto them and induced Aaron to allow them to build a golden calf to worship (see Acts 7:37–41). Aaron is also mentioned one other time in the New Testament in confirming the descendants of Zacharias and Elisabeth through the lineage of Aaron (see Luke 1:5).

Through the generations, Aaron has been upheld in honor and dignity for the devoted service he performed as a priesthood leader and for his office as holder of the keys of the lesser priesthood.

ABBA

In the Garden of Gethsemane, on the eve of His crucifixion, the Savior prepared Himself for the ultimate sacrifice: "And he went forward a little, and fell on the ground, and prayed that, if it were possible, the hour might pass from him. And he said, Abba, Father, all things are possible unto thee; take away this cup from me: nevertheless not what I will, but what thou wilt" (Mark 14:35–36). The word *abba* is a personal and affectionate form of the word *father* in Aramaic, the language used by Jesus. In a renowned passage about the destiny of the faithful, the Apostle Paul used this same word:

> For as many as are led by the Spirit of God, they are the sons of God.
>
> For ye have not received the spirit of bondage again to fear; but ye have received the Spirit of adoption, whereby we cry, Abba, Father.
>
> The Spirit itself beareth witness with our spirit, that we are the children of God:
>
> And if children, then heirs; heirs of God, and joint-heirs

with Christ; if so be that we suffer with him, that we may be also glorified together. (Romans 8:14–17; see also Galatians 4:6)

ABEL

Abel was a righteous son of Adam and Eve, born into an environment of gospel instruction from his parents, who heeded the voice of the Lord when "he gave unto them commandments, that they should worship the Lord their God, and should offer the firstlings of their flocks, for an offering unto the Lord. And Adam was obedient unto the commandments of the Lord" (Moses 5:5). Abel, "a keeper of sheep" (Moses 5:17), was not the oldest child, he and Cain having come into mortality after Eve had already born unto Adam other "sons and daughters" (Moses 5:2). However, Abel is singled out for his devotion and righteousness as one "who walked in holiness before the Lord" (Moses 5:26).

Abel is mentioned four times in the New Testament, initially in a reference by the Savior in His censure of the scribes and Pharisees (see Matthew 23:34–35; Luke 11:51). The Apostle Paul also invoked the memory of Abel in teaching about the principle of faith (see Hebrews 11:4). Finally, Paul refered to the death of Abel, the first martyr, in teaching about the shedding of the blood of the Redeemer as an act of divine atonement to empower the plan of eternal life and exaltation for all those who come "to Jesus the mediator of the new covenant, and to the blood of sprinkling, that speaketh better things than that of Abel" (Hebrews 12:24). In this latter reference, Abel is remembered as one whose blood was shed in the cause of righteousness, while the death of the Lamb of God and the shedding of His blood is of infinite consequence, bringing as it does the assurance of immortality for all and eternal life for the obedient.

ABIATHAR (MEANING: FATHER OF EXCELLENCE OR ABUNDANCE.)

Abiathar (pronounced uh-by'-uh-thahr) is mentioned only one time in the New Testament, in connection with a response by Jesus to the Pharisees, who had accused His disciples of breaking the Sabbath (see Mark 2:23–28).

ABRAHAM (MEANING: FATHER OF A MULTITUDE.)

Abraham—father of Isaac, grandfather of Jacob, and great-grandfather of Joseph—was the exemplary patriarch whose descendants were commissioned to carry forth the cause of the Abrahamic Covenant to spread the blessings of the gospel of salvation and the priesthood of

God to the world (see Genesis 17:1–8; Abraham 2:9–11; 3 Nephi 20:25–27)—a commission that continues today under the ensign of the restored gospel. The Lord promised Abraham, "In thy seed after thee . . . shall all the families of the earth be blessed, even with the blessings of the Gospel, which are the blessings of salvation, even of life eternal" (Abraham 2:11). According to this royal covenant, Israel was assured a homeland upon the earth with the blessings of the fulness of the gospel truth and an inheritance in the mansions of heaven with salvation and exaltation for the faithful and obedient. They were also promised a bounteous earthly progeny and, in keeping with the new and everlasting covenant of marriage, eternal increase in the hereafter. By divine decree, the obligation under this magnificent covenant was that Israel was to convey priesthood blessings to the entire world and spread the gospel of

ABRAHAM HOLDS HIS LONG-AWAITED SON, ISAAC.

saving ordinances to the receptive children of God in all lands. In the context of this divine covenant, Abraham is among the most admired and celebrated of the Lord's chosen prophets, being mentioned frequently in all the standard works of the Church, including sixty-nine times in the New Testament, beginning with the opening verses of that canon: "The book of the generation of Jesus Christ, the son of David, the son of Abraham. Abraham begat Isaac; and Isaac begat Jacob; and Jacob begat Judas and his brethren" (Matthew 1:1–2).

By invoking the memory of Abraham, the Savior and His followers were able to teach important lessons about gospel truths. For example, John the Baptist confronted the Pharisees and Sadducees by reminding them that the Abrahamic lineage was in itself—absent good works—insufficient for salvation: "And think not to say within yourselves, We have Abraham to our father: for I say unto you, that God is able of these stones to raise up children unto Abraham" (Matthew 3:9; see also Luke 3:8). He then announced the coming of the Savior: "I indeed baptize you with water unto repentance: but he that cometh after me is mightier than I, whose shoes I am not worthy to bear: he shall baptize you with the Holy Ghost, and with fire" (Matthew 3:11). Later on, the Savior Himself, marveling that the faith of one of the centurions exceeded that of the people of Israel, declared, "And I say unto you, That many shall come from the east and west, and shall sit down with Abraham, and Isaac, and Jacob, in the kingdom of heaven. But the children of the kingdom shall be cast out into outer darkness: there shall be weeping and gnashing of teeth" (Matthew 8:11–12).

Clearly the canopy of the Abrahamic lineage was perceived by the Jewish leaders as a primary source of their authority and power—a perception that the Savior consistently placed in juxtaposition with the authentic plan of salvation and exaltation, or the new covenant, that He was restoring through His ministry.

Following the Crucifixion, Peter also incorporated references to Abraham in his discourse (see Acts 3:13). He taught the people about the true nature of the Abrahamic Covenant as it related to them (see Acts 3:25; see also 3 Nephi 20:25–26). Prior to his martyrdom, Stephen repeatedly made reference to Abraham in bearing witness of the divinity of the Savior (see Acts 7:2, 8, 16, 17, 32). Paul referred to his audience as "children of the stock of Abraham" (Acts 13:26) and "the seed of Abraham" (Romans 9:7; 2 Corinthians 11:22), and to Abraham, the man of faith, as "the father of us all" (Romans 4:16).

ADAM (MEANING: MAN OR MANY.)

From holy writ we know that Adam was the first man (see Moses 1:33–34; Genesis 1:27; D&C 84:16). Adam and Eve were taught the gospel from the beginning and in turn instructed their children in the principles of faith, repentance, baptism, and receiving the gift of the Holy Ghost (see Moses 6:51–63). Modern revelation speaks of "Michael, or Adam, the father of all, the prince of all, the ancient of days" (D&C 27:11).

Adam has a pervasive presence throughout the holy scriptures. Possibly the most well-known reference to Adam in the New Testament confirms the verity of the Resurrection brought about through the Atonement of Jesus Christ: "For since by man came death, by man came also the resurrection of the dead. For as in Adam all die, even so in Christ shall all be made alive" (1 Corinthians 15:21–22; see also Romans 5:14–

ADAM AND EVE LEAVE THE GARDEN OF EDEN.

15). In another reference by Paul, Adam is used as an emblem for the spiritual consequences of the Atonement (see 1 Corinthians 15:45, 47). Adam is also listed as the last in a sequence of progenitors of the Savior (see Luke 3:38), as an example (along with Eve) of how the man and woman should cultivate a holy relationship (see 1 Timothy 2:12–15), as the ancestor of Enoch (see Jude 1:14), and as the great warrior (Michael) prevailing over the devil (see Jude 1:9; Revelation 12:7–9).

AENEAS (MEANING: TO PRAISE OR PRAISEWORTHY.)

Aeneas was a man living in Lydda (known as Lod in the Old Testament), a commercial town located some ten miles southeast of the seaport of Joppa on the road leading to Jerusalem. In visiting Lydda during his ministry, Peter healed the paralytic Aeneas in the name of the Savior, leading to the conversion of those who learned

of the miracle: "And it came to pass, as Peter passed throughout all quarters, he came down also to the saints which dwelt at Lydda. And there he found a certain man named Æneas, which had kept his bed eight years, and was sick of the palsy. And Peter said unto him, Æneas, Jesus Christ maketh thee whole: arise, and make thy bed. And he arose immediately. And all that dwelt at Lydda and Saron [the surrounding district] saw him, and turned to the Lord" (Acts 9:32–35).

AGABUS

Agabus was a man who prophesied of a coming famine: "And in these days came prophets from Jerusalem unto Antioch. And there stood up one of them named Agabus, and signified by the Spirit that there should be great dearth throughout all the world: which came to pass in the days of Claudius Cæsar" (Acts 11:27–28). Later, at Caesarea, Agabus also warned Paul of his impending captivity should he follow through with his plan to go to Jerusalem (see Acts 21:10–11). In confirmation of his intention to do the will of the Lord, whatever the outcome, Paul responded to his concerned compatriots: "What mean ye to weep and to break mine heart? for I am ready not to be bound only, but also to die at Jerusalem for the name of the Lord Jesus" (Acts 21:13). Thereupon he left for Jerusalem, where he was indeed persecuted by the people and arrested by the authorities (see Acts 21:33).

AGRIPPA (HEROD AGRIPPA II)

It was before this Agrippa (Herod Agrippa II, son of Herod Agrippa I, brother of Bernice and Drusilla, and great-grandson of Herod), that Paul, confined in Caesarea because of accusations against him by the Jewish leaders, pled his innocence and delivered his celebrated speech about his conversion through a vision of the Savior while on the road to Damascus (see Acts 25:13–27; 26:1–32). So convincing was Paul that Agrippa declared at the end of the delivery the well-known words: "Almost thou persuadest me to be a Christian" (Acts 26:28).

ALEXANDER

1. Alexander was the son of Simon of Cyrene and the brother of Rufus, Simon being the man whom the authorities compelled to bear the cross of Jesus en route to Golgotha (see Mark 15:21).

2. Alexander was an individual in the circle of Annas the high priest and those others who arrested Peter and John and attempted to undermine their apostolic ministry in the cause of Christ (see Acts 4:6).

3. Alexander was a Jew in Ephesus selected by his Jewish countrymen to testify before the angry local citizens during an uproar against Paul, occasioned by those of the silversmith trade who claimed that Paul's message was undermining their profitable business making silver shrines in honor of the goddess Diana (see Acts 19:33). Apparently, this Alexander was supposed to appease the local population by denying that the Jewish segment of the population had any connection to Paul's teachings.

4. Alexander was an individual identified by Paul as unfaithful and blasphemous (see 1 Timothy 1:20).

5. Alexander was an individual (perhaps the same as in item 4) mentioned by Paul in his continuing counsel to Timothy: "Alexander the coppersmith did me much evil: the Lord reward him according to his works" (2 Timothy 4:14).

ALPHAEUS

1. Alphaeus was the father of the Apostle Levi: "And as he [Jesus] passed by, he saw Levi the son of Alphæus sitting at the receipt of custom, and said unto him, Follow me. And he arose and followed him" (Mark 2:14). Levi was also called Matthew (see Matthew 9:9; Luke 5:27, 29).

2. Alphaeus was the father of the Apostle James (see Matthew 10:3; Mark 3: 8; Luke 6:15; Acts 1:13). According to the Bible Dictionary, some scholars identify Alphaeus with Cleopas (see Luke 24:18) and Cleophas (see John 19:25).

ANANIAS

1. Ananias was a disciple of the Church who sold some personal land for the benefit of the Church but secretly kept back a portion for himself, misrepresenting the matter to the Apostles. When Peter confronted Ananias concerning this deception, asking, "Why hast thou conceived this thing in thine heart? thou hast not lied unto men, but unto God" (Acts 5:4), the man immediately perished (see Acts 5:5). His wife, Sapphira, who had been complicit in the deal, subsequently lied about the matter and likewise died (see Acts 5:10). The actions of the couple were a violation of the commandment against lying and a serious breach of the mutual covenant of support among the Saints of that day.

2. Ananias was, in the words of Paul, "a devout man according to the law, having a good report of all the Jews which dwelt there [in Damascus]"

ANANIAS IS STRUCK DEAD AFTER LYING TO THE LORD.

(Acts 22:12). It was to Ananias that the Lord sent Paul after Paul's miraculous vision and conversion on the road to Damascus (see Acts 9:10–18). Ananias restored Paul's sight and arranged for him to be baptized (see Acts 9:18; 22:13–16).

3. Ananias was the high priest before whom the accused Paul was brought at the direction of Claudius Lysias, the chief captain over the Roman troops in Jerusalem (see Acts 23:1–5; see also Acts 21:31–40). When the chief captain learned that Paul was a Roman citizen, he secretly sent him to Caesarea to appear before Felix, the procurator or governor (see Acts 23:23–35). During the hearing before Felix, Ananias served as Paul's accuser (see Acts 24:1). According to the historical account, Ananias, a Roman sympathizer, was later killed by his compatriots at the beginning of the first Jewish-Roman war (AD 66–73).

ANGEL/ANGELS (MEANING: MESSENGER/MESSENGERS.)

Angels are ministering servants of the Lord. In a revelation given through the Prophet Joseph Smith at Nauvoo on February 9, 1843, the Lord declared, "There are two kinds of beings in heaven, namely: Angels, who are resurrected personages, having bodies of flesh and bones— For instance, Jesus said: Handle me and see, for a spirit hath not flesh and bones, as ye see me have. Secondly: the spirits of just men made perfect, they who are not resurrected, but inherit the same glory" (D&C 129:1–3).

The holy scriptures contain a rich treasure of information about angels—what Paul referred to as "ministering spirits, sent forth to minister for them who shall be heirs of salvation" (Hebrews 1:14). The word *angel* or *angels* appears 540 times in the scriptures, including 178 times in the New Testament. The first such reference in the New Testament was the appearance of an angel to

AN ANGEL CALLS MOSES TO BE A DELIVERER.

Joseph in a dream, directing him to accept Mary as his wife, for she would bring forth the child Jesus (see Matthew 1:20–21). The same angel, Gabriel, visited Mary to announce the divine commission of her future son (see Luke 1:26–38). At the birth of Jesus, an angel of the Lord, accompanied by "a multitude of the heavenly host" (Luke 2:13), proclaimed "good tidings of great joy, which shall be to all people" (Luke 2:10). Later, the angel of the Lord directed Joseph to flee to Egypt with Mary and the newborn child. Then, after the death of Herod, the angel directed the holy family to return home again (see Matthew 2:13, 19). Angels ministered unto Christ after He had withstood the temptations of the devil in the wilderness (see Matthew 4:11; Mark 1:13). In the Garden of Gethsemane, the Savior was comforted by a heavenly ministrant (see Luke 22:43). After the Resurrection of the crucified Lord, an angel was on guard at the tomb and announced to the two visiting Marys, "He is not here: for he is risen" (Matthew 28:6; "angels" as in Luke 24:23; "two angels" as in John 20:12).

The Savior spoke frequently of angels and their role in the designs of heaven (see Matthew 13:39, 41, 49; 16:27; 18:10; 22:30; 24:31, 36; 25:31; 26:53; Mark 8:38; 12:25; 13:27, 32; Luke 9:26; 12:8, 9; 15:10; 16:22; 20:36; John 1:51). Likewise, Peter referred to angels in his teachings (see 1 Peter 1:12; 3:22; 2 Peter 2:11), as did Paul (see 2 Thessalonians 1:7; 1 Timothy 5:21; Hebrews 1:4–7, 13; 12:22). For example:

- "Though I speak with the tongues of men and of angels, and have not charity, I am become as sounding brass, or a tinkling cymbal" (1 Corinthians 13:1).
- "And without controversy great is the mystery of godliness: God was manifest in the flesh, justified in the Spirit, seen of angels, preached unto the Gentiles, believed on in the world, received up into glory" (1 Timothy 3:16).
- "Thou madest him a little lower than the angels; thou crownedst him with glory and honour, and didst set him over the works of thy hands" (Hebrews 2:7; see also verses 9 and 16).

Angels continued to play an active role in the unfolding of the gospel following the Resurrection. An angel delivered Peter and John from prison on one occasion (see Acts 5:19), and on a later occasion, Peter was again freed from imprisonment in the same way (see Acts 12:7–15). An angel gave Philip directions for missionary work (see Acts 8:26), just as an angel directed Cornelius, a Gentile, to send for Peter in order to learn the truths of the gospel (see Acts 10:1–7, 22; 11:13). Moreover, an angel comforted Paul during his perilous sea voyage en route to be brought before Caesar (see Acts 27:23). In terms of instruction and revelation, an angel helped unfold the mysteries of God unto John the Revelator (see Revelation 1:1). Recording an amazing panoply of angelic ministrations to John, the book of Revelation refers to an "angel" or "angels" frequently. Perhaps the most well-known of these references for members of the Church today is the following: "And I saw another angel fly in the midst of heaven, having the everlasting gospel to preach unto them that dwell on the earth, and to every nation, and kindred, and tongue, and people" (Revelation 14:6, in reference to Moroni).

Not all angels are heavenly in character. The Savior spoke of the devil and his angels (see Matthew 25:41). Paul warned that Satan can appear as "an angel of light" (2 Corinthians 11:14). Peter also spoke of the angels cast "down to hell" (2 Peter 2:4; see also Jude 1:6). The ultimate defeat of Satan and his angels was shown to John in vision (see Revelation 12:7–9).

ANNA (MEANING: GRACE.)

Anna was a widow of some eighty-four years who had served in the temple at Jerusalem night and day all her life. She happened to arrive at the temple during the time Joseph and Mary were there to present their new child, according to Mosaic practice, and just at the moment the aged Simeon was expressing his words of praise and prophecy concerning the new Messiah (see Luke 2:25–35). The only reference to Anna in the New Testament brings that moment to life and refers to Anna as a prophetess (see Luke 2:36–38).

Only three others of noble character were given the appellation "prophetess" in the scriptures: Miriam, sister of Moses (see Exodus 15:20); Deborah the judge (see Judges 4:4); and Huldah at the time of Josiah (see 2 Kings 22:14; 2 Chronicles 34:22).

ANNAS (MEANING: HUMBLE; VARIANT OF THE NAME ANANIAS.)

Annas was a man of high stature among the priestly leaders of the Sanhedrin, or ruling assembly, having the title of "high priest." As reported by Luke, John the Baptist began his ministry in the days of Annas and his son-in-law Caiaphas (see Luke 3:2). It was to Annas that the arrested Lord was first delivered (see John 18:12–13). Annas inquired of Jesus concerning His doctrine, whereupon the Lord declared that His teachings had always been given in public: "Why askest thou me? ask them which heard me, what I have said unto them: behold, they know

what I said. And when he had thus spoken, one of the officers which stood by struck Jesus with the palm of his hand, saying, Answerest thou the high priest so? Jesus answered him, If I have spoken evil, bear witness of the evil: but if well, why smitest thou me?" (John 18:21–23).

Annas then sent Jesus to Caiaphas to stand trial (see John 18:24; Matthew 26:56–68), the next step in the process leading to the Crucifixion. Later, following the Crucifixion, Annas and Caiaphas presided at an examination of Peter and John in connection with their healing of a lame man at the temple gate called Beautiful, and it was before them that Peter pronounced his powerful witness of the Savior (see Acts 4:8–12).

When Annas and Caiaphas ordered Peter and John to desist from spreading the news about the miracle, they answered boldly, "Whether it be right in the sight of God to hearken unto you more than unto God, judge ye. For we cannot but speak the things which we have seen and heard" (Acts 4:19–20). Fearing the will of the people, who were witnesses to the healing and believers in the testimony of the recovered man, Annas and Caiaphas then reluctantly released the Apostles. Historically, Annas had been appointed high priest by the Roman legate Quirinius in AD 7 but was deposed in AD 15 by Valerius Gratus, procurator of Judea, in favor of another individual. During the period AD 18–36 Joseph Caiaphas, son-in-law of Annas, served as high priest, but Annas retained his title of high priest and his station of influence in the Sanhedrin.

ANTI-CHRIST

The term *anti-Christ* was used by John to describe someone who stands in direct opposition to Christ and the truths of the gospel (see 1 John

2:22-23; 4:1-3; 2 John 1:7). The supreme exponent of anti-Christian opposition is Lucifer (Satan), who was the arch-anti-Christ from the beginning (see Revelation 12:7-8). Similar terms to *anti-Christ* were used by Jesus in His references to "false Christs" and "false prophets" (Matthew 24:5, 23-24), by Paul in his warnings against the hypocritical deceptions of the "man of sin" (see 2 Thessalonians 2:3-10), and by John in describing the "beast" and his confederates warring against the Lamb (see Revelation 17).

ANTIPAS

1. Antipas. (See entry for Herod Antipas.)

2. Antipas was a "faithful martyr" mentioned in Revelation 2:13. Nothing more of him is known.

APOLLOS

Apollos was an Alexandrian Jew and contemporary of the Apostle Paul who was known for his eloquence and scriptural mastery (see Acts 18:24-25). Aquila and Priscilla, who were coworkers with Paul, took him aside "and expounded unto him the way of God more perfectly" (Acts 18:26), apparently unfolding to him the fuller knowledge about the ministry of the Savior. Apollos, then convinced of the divine mission of the Savior, journeyed to the Grecian province of Achaia with a recommendation from the Church leaders at Ephesus, and while at Corinth he proclaimed the gospel message (see Acts 18:28).

Members of the Church admired Apollos for his eloquence in proclaiming and upholding gospel truths, but he evidently became the unwitting cause of a degree of dispute among some of them, as confirmed in the appeal of Paul unto them for unity: "Now this I say, that every one of you saith, I am of Paul; and I of Apollos; and I of Cephas; and I of Christ. Is Christ divided? was Paul crucified for you? or were ye baptized in the name of Paul?" (1 Corinthians 1:12-13). Apollos, well-meaning and devout, became therefore an emblem for the syndrome of spiritual partisanship reflected in the lives of some Saints who choose to focus more fully on their mortal gospel heroes rather than on the Savior.

Paul later refers once again to Apollos in a caring way: "Bring Zenas the lawyer and Apollos on their journey diligently, that nothing be wanting unto them" (Titus 3:13). Some modern-day scholars have taken the position that Apollos may have played a role in the writing of the epistle to the Hebrews, although such cannot be confirmed.

APOSTLE (MEANING: MESSENGER.)

The word *apostle* derives from the Greek word *apostolos*, meaning "messenger" or one who has been sent. References to "apostle," "apostles," and "apostleship" are found frequently in the scriptures. The first such reference occurs relative to the calling of the twelve disciples by Jesus Christ:

> And when he had called unto him his twelve disciples, he gave them power against unclean spirits, to cast them out, and to heal all manner of sickness and all manner of disease.
>
> Now the names of the twelve apostles are these; The first, Simon, who is called Peter, and Andrew his brother; James the son of Zebedee, and John his brother;

Philip, and Bartholomew; Thomas, and Matthew the publican; James the son of Alphæus, and Lebbæus, whose surname was Thaddæus [probably the same as Judas mentioned in Luke 6:16]; Simon the Canaanite, and Judas Iscariot, who also betrayed him." (Matthew 10:1–4; see also Luke 6:13–16; 9:1–2; Mark 3:14; 6:7)

The commission of Jesus to His Apostles is summarized in the following passages:

• "Ye are my friends, if ye do whatsoever I command you. Henceforth I call you not servants; for the servant knoweth not what his lord doeth: but I have called you friends; for all things that I have heard of my Father I have made known unto you. Ye have not chosen me, but I have chosen you, and ordained you, that ye should go and bring forth fruit, and that your fruit should remain: that whatsoever ye shall ask of the Father in my name, he may give it you. These things I command you, that ye love one another" (John 15:14–17).

• "Go ye therefore, and teach all nations, baptizing them in the name of the Father, and of the Son, and of the Holy Ghost: Teaching them to observe all things whatsoever I have commanded you: and, lo, I am with you alway, even unto the end of the world. Amen" (Matthew 28:19–20; see also Mark 16:14–16).

During His mortal ministry, the Savior used a special symbolic reference in relation to the calling of the Apostles: "And he saith unto them,

Jesus washes Peter's and the other Apostles' feet.

CHRIST ORDAINS THE ORIGINAL TWELVE TO THE OFFICE OF APOSTLE.

Follow me, and I will make you fishers of men" (Matthew 4:19; see also Mark 1:17). He empowered them to be fishers of men by giving them special authority and keys (see Matthew 16:19).

Was Paul a member of the Twelve? Paul was called and commissioned of the Savior in a remarkable vision (see Acts 9:1–6). Paul is identified as an Apostle in several passages (see Romans 1:1; 1 Corinthians 1:1; 9:1–2; Galatians 1:1; 1 Timothy 2:7). Besides Paul, two others not of the original Twelve were identified as Apostles: Barnabas (see Acts 14:14; see also 1 Corinthians 9:6) and "James the Lord's brother" (Galatians 1:19). Concerning the calling of Paul, James, and Barnabas as Apostles, the Bible Dictionary reads, "The New Testament does not inform us whether these three brethren also served in the council of the Twelve as vacancies occurred therein, or whether they were apostles strictly in the sense of being special witnesses for the Lord Jesus Christ" ("Apostle," 612). In the latter days, the Lord spoke of Paul as "Paul mine apostle" (D&C 18:9).

The office of Apostle relates in a fundamental way to the organizational foundation of the Church (see 1 Corinthians 12:28; Ephesians 2:19–21; 4:11–12).

Joseph Smith stated, "We believe in the same organization that existed in the Primitive Church, namely, apostles, prophets, pastors, teachers, evangelists, and so forth" (Articles of Faith 1:6).

Who was and is the ultimate Apostle? "Wherefore, holy brethren, partakers of the heavenly calling, consider the Apostle and High Priest of our profession, Christ Jesus; Who was faithful to him that appointed him, as also Moses was faithful in all his house" (Hebrews 3:1–2).

Following the Ascension of the resurrected Lord, Peter summarized the calling of the Apostles as witnesses of the Resurrection (see Acts 1:21–22; see also Acts 4:33).

What was the fate of the original Apostles? Beyond the suicidal death of Judas Iscariot (see Matthew 27:5; Acts 1:16–18), the divine commission of John to remain on earth as a translated ministering servant of the Lord until the Second Coming (see John 21:20–23; 3 Nephi 28:6; D&C 7), and the martyrdom of James (see Acts 12:1–2), we have no scriptural report of the deaths of the other Apostles. However, according to tradition and historical accounts, all the others, including Paul, were martyred.

AQUILA (Meaning: eagle.)

Aquila (Akyla in the Greek form) and his wife Priscilla (Priska in the Greek form, meaning "ancient") are noteworthy examples of devout Saints who served as missionaries of the gospel and made their home available for Church meetings (see 1 Corinthians 16:19). The first mention of Aquila and Priscilla tells that they came to Corinth from Italy (see Acts 18:1-3). After a season, they moved to Ephesus, accompanied by Paul (see Acts 18:18), where the couple met Apollo, an articulate spokesperson from Alexandria who was visiting there to discourse on gospel themes (see Acts 18:26). Thanks to Aquila and Priscilla, Apollo, a Jew who was accepting of the ministry of John the Baptist, was able to grasp the full measure of the Savior's atoning mission and carry the message to others. Subsequently, Aquila and Priscilla returned to Rome (see Romans 16:3-5). Apparently, they later returned to Ephesus because Paul asks Timothy to greet them (see 2 Timothy 4:19).

ARABIA/ARABIANS

Arabia, the vast territory to the east of the holy land, bounded by the Red Sea on the west, the Indian Ocean on the south, and the Persian Gulf and Euphrates River on the east, was occupied over generations by a variety of peoples, and the Israelites had diverse types of contacts with the Arabian people. At Pentecost there were Arabians present in Jerusalem (see Acts 2:11), and Paul spent some time in Arabia following his conversion (see Galatians 1:17).

ARCHELAUS (Meaning: ruler of the people or prince of the people.)

Archelaus was a son of Herod the Great by Malthace, a Samaritan woman. He is mentioned only once in the scriptures, in connection with the return of Joseph, Mary, and the baby Jesus from Egypt (see Matthew 2:19-23).

Archelaus—ethnarch (governor) over Judea, Samaria, and Idumea—was the brother of Herod Antipas.

AREOPAGITE

An Areopagite is a member of the Areopagus (see Acts 17:19), the chief council or legislative court of justice in Athens that met in the open on Mars' Hill—the site of Paul's celebrated discourse concerning Jesus and the Resurrection (see Acts 17:32-34). The word *areopagus* derives from the Greek words *pagos* ("hill") and *Ares* (the god Mars), hence "Mars' Hill." Though most of Paul's listeners rejected his message, some were touched by it: "Howbeit certain men clave unto him, and believed: among the which was Dionysius the Areopagite, and a woman named Damaris, and others with them" (Acts 17:34).

ARETAS

Aretas was the father-in-law of Herod Antipas, son of Herod the Great by Malthace, a Samaritan woman. Paul was able to escape the threatening forces of Aretas, who is mentioned by name in only one passage of the New Testament (see 2 Corinthians 11:32-33).

Aristarchus (Meaning: best ruler.)

Aristarchus was a native of Thessalonica (see Acts 20:4) and a faithful companion of Paul (see Acts 19:29; 27:2). Paul called him his "fellowprisoner" (Colossians 4:10; Philemon 1:24).

Aristobulus

In Romans 16, Paul salutes various individuals, as in this phrase: "Salute them which are of Aristobulus' household" (Romans 16:10). Aristobulus, the Roman mentioned, is possibly a grandson of Herod the Great.

Assyria/Assyrians

In the crucible of human endeavor, the fledgling Israelite state sprouted and took shape in accordance with its intended destiny—always in the midst of the formation of mighty empires emerging on all sides. Countless tribes and cultures interacted with the children of Abraham over the generations—more often than not with aggressive designs and preemptive motivation. At the highest level of stature and power were the three grand empires of Egypt, Assyria, and Babylonia—each with its own hour of predominance and hegemony. Egypt, the fountainhead of the Exodus during the days of Moses, lay to the southwest of the holy land. Assyria and Babylonia, constant rivals between themselves, were Mesopotamian cultures. Babylonia (or Shinar—see Genesis 10:10) lay in the southern region between the Tigris and Euphrates, and Assyria (or Asshur—see Genesis 10:22) to the north between those two rivers. The southern capital was Babel or Babylon; the northern capital was Nineveh (see 2 Kings 19:36; Isaiah 37:37), located on the western side of the Tigris, across from Mosul. The language of both cultures was Semitic, that is, belonging to the language family thought to originate through the line of Noah's son, Shem (see Genesis 10:22), and spoken by the biblical ancestors of the Arabs, Aramaeans, Assyrians, Babylonians, Chaldeans, Hebrews, and other related groups.

Augustus (Meaning: venerable.)

1. Augustus was the first Roman emperor, who reigned from 27 BC until his death in AD 14. Though also called Julius Caesar or Julius Caesar Augustus, he is usually known as Augustus. "And it came to pass in those days, that there went out a decree from Cæsar Augustus, that all the world should be taxed" (Luke 2:1).

2. Augustus (Tiberius Caesar Augustus) was the second Roman emperor, who reigned from AD 14 until AD 37. He is usually known as Tiberius. Except for Luke 2:1, Tiberius is the Caesar mentioned in the Gospels of the New Testament.

3. Augustus (Gaius Caesar Augustus Germanicus) was the third Roman emperor, who reigned from AD 37 until his assassination in AD 41. He is usually known as Gaius but sometimes as Caligula, meaning "military boot." He is not directly mentioned in the New Testament but exerted considerable influence in political matters in Judea during his reign.

4. Augustus (Tiberius Claudius Caesar Augustus Germanicus) was the succeeding Roman emperor, who reigned from AD 41 until AD 54. He is usually known as Claudius. He expelled the Jews from Rome as a result of uprisings and disputes concerning Christ. It was at that

time that the Jewish Christians Aquila and Priscilla left Rome to resettle in Corinth, where they met Paul (see Acts 18:2). Claudius is also mentioned by Luke: "And there stood up one of them named Agabus, and signified by the Spirit that there should be great dearth throughout all the world: which came to pass in the days of Claudius Cæsar" (Acts 11:28).

5. Augustus (Nero Claudius Caesar Augustus Germanicus) was the succeeding Roman emperor, who ruled from AD 54 until AD 68. He is usually known as Nero.

Note: The ministry of Paul extends from around AD 35 to around AD 65; thus his ministry encompasses the later years of the reign of Tiberius, all of the reigns of Gaius and Claudius, and most of the reign of Nero.

BAAL (MEANING: LORD OR POSSESSOR; PRO-
NOUNCED BAYL OR BAH-AL.)

Baal (plural Baalim) was the supreme male god in the Phoenician pagan culture (see 1 Kings 16:31). The female counterpart was Ashtoreth (plural Ashtaroth). Concerning this ancient Phoenician god, there is only one reference in the New Testament: where Paul confirms that some of the Lord's chosen lineage have remained true to their covenants, as the Lord said to Elias (i.e., Elijah): "I have reserved to myself seven thousand men, who have not bowed the knee to the image of Baal. Even so then at this present time also there is a remnant according to the election of grace" (Romans 11:4–5). The study of Baalism and its sinister effects among the peoples of the Old Testament is a fascinating exploration of the cosmic conflict between good and evil, the eternal battle between false worship and true worship. Paul invoked this conflict in his statement given in Romans 11:4–5. The conflict still rages today. Though modern gods do not carry the name of Baal or any of its linguistic variations, there are nevertheless countless human obsessions in our time that, in the absence of a balanced and dignified pattern of righteous living, cause people to turn from the true God and place their confidence in influences and philosophies that are powerless to yield the blessings of eternity. It is only the gospel of Jesus Christ that can supplant such misguided patterns of life and provide the spiritual power essential for salvation and exaltation.

BABYLON

An emblematic expression denoting a worldly culture antithetical to eternal principles and practices, one that will be destroyed according to the designs of the Almighty as His everlasting kingdom is unfolded: "And after these things I saw another angel come down from heaven, having great power; and the earth was lightened with his glory. And he cried mightily with a strong voice, saying, Babylon the great is fallen, is fallen, and is become the habitation of devils, and the hold of every foul spirit, and a cage of every unclean and hateful bird" (Revelation

BABYLON FALLS IN SIN.

18:1-2; see also Revelation 14:8; 16:9; 17:5; 18:10, 21).

BABYLONIA/BABYLONIANS

Babylonia was one of the great empires—along with Egypt and Assyria—that defined the broad geographical and cultural environment in which the people of Israel emerged as a chosen nation.

BALAAM

When Peter was warning the Saints against false teachers, he invoked the memory of Balaam (pronounced bay'-lum), saying that such teachers "have forsaken the right way, and are gone astray, following the way of Balaam the son of Bosor, who loved the wages of unrighteousness; But was rebuked for his iniquity: the dumb ass speaking with man's voice forbad the madness of the prophet. These are wells without water, clouds that are carried with a tempest; to whom the mist of darkness is reserved for ever" (2 Peter 2:15-17). Balaam is an exemplar of one with a grand potential but a lowly agenda. The Lord did not reach out to him as His mouthpiece but graciously listened and responded when supplicated. The word of the Lord through Balaam served the divine interests of preparing the way for the people of Israel. The Lord blesses His chosen people as they act in righteousness; those who act in His name in honor are enabled to proclaim the blessings of the covenant and uphold the divine purposes of heaven. Those who associate too closely with groups and individuals of an idolatrous cast, as did Balaam, will suffer the same fate as their masters. The Savior said: "Ye cannot serve God and mammon" (Matthew 6:24; see also Luke 6:13; 3 Nephi 13:24).

Peter used Balaam as an emblem of acute warning for his associates, as did Jude (see Jude 1:11). See also the word of the Lord unto John the Revelator about depraved patterns of Balaam-like behavior in his days (see Revelation 2:14).

BAR

Bar is the Aramaic word for "son," occurring a number of times in the New Testament at the beginning of names such as Barabbas, Bar-jesus, Bar-jona, Barnabas, Barsabas, and Bartholomew.

BARABBAS (MEANING: SON OF THE FATHER.)

Barabbas was a "notable prisoner" (Matthew 27:16) who was released in place of Jesus at the hearing before Pontius Pilate during the

Passover season (see Matthew 27:21-26; see also Mark 15:7-15; Luke 23:13-25; John 18:28-40).

From these passages we learn that the prisoner Barabbas was allegedly guilty of robbery, sedition, and murder (see Mark 15:7; Luke 23:19; John 18:40).

BARAK (Meaning: lightning.)

Barak, the son of Abinoam, of the tribe of Naphtali, was commissioned by the prophetess Deborah, judge of Israel, to wage battle against the encroaching Canaanites under the command of Sisera. Barak agreed to gather the forces and attack, provided Deborah would consent to accompany him. That she did, saying, "Up; for this is the day in which the Lord hath delivered Sisera into thine hand: is not the Lord gone out before thee? So Barak went down from mount Tabor, and ten thousand men after him" (Judges 4:14). That day the Canaanites, with their much larger force, were annihilated, along with their king, whose name was Jabin (see Judges 4:23-24). Thereafter, Deborah and Barak joined in singing a glorious anthem of praise to the Lord (see Judges 5). The final line of this poem carries the moral of the story: "So let all thine enemies perish, O Lord: but let them that love him be as the sun when he goeth forth in his might. And the land had rest forty years" (Judges 5:31). Paul briefly invokes the memory of Barak in his notable discourse on faith (see Hebrews 11:32).

BAR-JESUS (Meaning: son of Jesus.)

Bar-jesus (also named Elymas) was a Jewish man who attempted to dissuade Sergio Paulus, the Roman proconsul at Cyprus, from hearing the gospel message (see Acts 13:6-8). As a result, Paul, "filled with the Holy Ghost, set his eyes on him, And said, O full of all subtilty and all mischief, thou child of the devil, thou enemy of all righteousness, wilt thou not cease to pervert the right ways of the Lord?" (Acts 13:9-10). Paul then consigned the man to the judgment of God, and thus Bar-jesus was rendered blind. The event enhanced the belief of Sergio Paulus in the "doctrine of the Lord" (Acts 13:12).

BAR-JONA (Meaning: son of Jona or son of John.)

Bar-jona was the surname of Simon Peter (see Matthew 16:17). "And when Jesus beheld him, he said, Thou art Simon the son of Jona: thou shalt be called Cephas, which is by interpretation, A stone" (John 1:42).

BARNABAS (Meaning: son of consolation.)

Barnabas was a convert to the gospel of Jesus Christ, who, like his close associates showed great faith in setting aside worldly possessions for the cause of the kingdom of God (see Acts 4:33-37).

When Paul, following his miraculous conversion, was desirous to join with the disciples at Jerusalem, they were afraid and demurred, with only Barnabas having courage enough to step forward and welcome the former persecutor of the Saints (see Acts 9:27). It was Barnabas that the disciples sent soon thereafter to Antioch to counsel the Saints and converts there (see Acts 11:22-24). Thereafter, Barnabas sought after Paul to join with him, and they tarried a year in Antioch, where the disciples were first called "Christians" (Acts 11:26).

BARNABAS WELCOMES PAUL INTO THE CHURCH AND INVITES HIM TO BE HIS COMPANION IN ANTIOCH.

As a companion with Paul, Barnabas served the Lord with devotion and courage (see Acts 12:25; 13:1-7, 43-52; 14:12-20; 15; 1 Corinthians 9:6; Galatians 2:1, 9-13; Colossians 4:10). Barnabas and Paul separated in their journeying when Paul declined to accept John Mark (nephew or cousin of Barnabas—see Colossians 4:10) into their circle, John Mark having earlier "departed from them from Pamphylia, and went not with them to the work" (Acts 15:38). Though Barnabas is not referred to in the New Testament as a member of the Twelve (in succession), he is identified by Paul as an Apostle (see Acts 14:4, 14; 1 Corinthians 9:6).

BARSABAS (MEANING: SON OF SABBAS—A REAL PERSON—OR PERHAPS SYMBOLICALLY, SON OF SABBATH OR REST.)

1. Barsabas was presented, along with Matthias, as a candidate to replace the traitor Judas Iscariot (see Acts 1:23-26).

2. Barsabas was a select leader sent to Antioch to minister unto the Gentile converts: "Then pleased it the apostles and elders, with the whole church, to send chosen men of their own company to Antioch with Paul and Barnabas; namely, Judas surnamed Barsabas, and Silas, chief men among the brethren" (Acts 15:22). Letters of commendation were sent with these emissaries, naming them "chosen men" and "men that have hazarded their lives for the name of our Lord Jesus Christ" (Acts 15:25, 26). The

BARTHOLOMEW COUNSELS WITH THE OTHER DISCIPLES.

message of assurance delivered by these men was that the Gentiles were not required to abide by the law of circumcision (see Acts 15:32).

BARTHOLOMEW (MEANING: SON OF TOLMAI.)

Bartholomew is listed as one of the original Twelve Apostles (see Matthew 10:3; Mark 3:18; Luke 6:14; Acts 1:13). He is generally identified as Nathanael (see John 1:45–49; 21:2). See the entry for Nathanael.

BARTIMAEUS (MEANING: SON OF TIMAEUS.)

Bartimaeus was a blind man at Jericho who sustained himself by begging along the side of the road. When he heard that Jesus was coming that way, he cried out, saying, "Jesus, thou Son of David, have mercy on me" (Mark 10:47). When those around him ordered him to keep his peace, he cried even louder. At last "Jesus said unto him, Go thy way; thy faith hath made thee whole. And immediately he received his sight, and followed Jesus in the way" (Mark 10:49–52).

The words "thy faith hath made thee whole" is an iconic expression used by the Savior on other occasions involving other individuals of uncommon faith: the suffering woman who touched His garment (see Matthew 9:22; Mark 5:34; Luke 8:48); the grateful Samaritan leper who had been healed (see Luke 17:19); and, generations earlier, the repentant Enos, son of Jacob (see Enos 1:6–8).

BEELZEBUB

The New Testament name Beelzebub (pronounced bee-el'-zuh-bub) is generally the equivalent to the Old Testament Baal-zebub ("lord of the flies")—a linguistic extension of the name Baal, the Phoenician sun god (see 2 Kings 1:1–6; Matthew 12:24–30; Mark 3:25–30; Luke 11:14–26). Beelzebub is a title applied to Satan. The Pharisees disclaimed the divine healing power of the Savior, saying that He was working by the power of "Beelzebub the prince of devils" (Matthew 12:24). What then happened is a memorable demonstration of the discernment of spirits (see Matthew 12:25–30).

BEN

Ben is the Hebrew word for "son" or "son of." Examples include Benjamin, Reuben, Benhadad, and Benoni.

BENJAMIN (MEANING: SON OF MY RIGHT HAND.)

Benjamin was the son of Jacob and Rachel, brother of Joseph. The most famous of the descendants of Benjamin down through the generations were King Saul (see 1 Samuel 9:1; Acts 13:21) and the Apostle Paul (see Acts 13:21; Romans 11:1; Philippians 3:5). Benjamin is also mentioned in the book of Revelation concerning the make-up of the 144,000 sealed leaders to emerge in the final days, 12,000 from each of the twelve tribes of Israel, including Benjamin (see Revelation 7:8).

BERNICE (MEANING: BEARER OF VICTORY.)

Bernice, sister to Agrippa (Herod Agrippa II) and Drusilla, was in attendance when Paul, confined in Caesarea because of accusations against him by the Jewish leaders, pled his innocence before Agrippa and delivered his celebrated speech about his conversion through a vision of the Savior while on the road to Damascus (see Acts 25:13–27; 26:1–32). So convincing was Paul that Agrippa declared at the end of the delivery the famous words: "Almost thou persuadest me to be a Christian" (Acts 26:28).

BISHOP

The office of bishop is a key ecclesiastical calling in the priesthood of God. The word *bishop* derives from the Greek word *episkopos*, meaning "overseer," as in this counsel from Paul: "Take heed therefore unto yourselves, and to all the flock, over the which the Holy Ghost hath made you overseers, to feed the church of God, which he hath purchased with his own blood" (Acts 20:28). The assignment of the Apostles to be overseers, in the general sense, is confirmed in this verse concerning the fallen Judas: "For it is written in the book of Psalms, Let his habitation be desolate, and let no man dwell therein: and his bishoprick let another take" (Acts 1:20; see also D&C 114:1–2). In the specific sense of the word, modern revelation makes clear that the bishop is an ordained office in the Aaronic Priesthood (see D&C 20:67) and that the bishop is the president of the priests quorum (see D&C 107:77–78).

What qualities are bishops to cultivate and apply in their service? The following passages provide the answer:

- "For a bishop must be blameless, as the steward of God; not selfwilled, not soon angry, not given to wine, no striker, not given to filthy lucre; But a lover of hospitality, a lover of good men, sober, just, holy, temperate; Holding fast the faithful word as he hath been taught, that he may be able by sound doctrine both to exhort and to convince the gainsayers" (Titus 1:7–9).
- "This is a true saying, If a man desire the office of a bishop, he desireth a good work. A bishop then must be blameless, the husband of one wife, vigilant, sober, of good behaviour, given to hospitality, apt to teach; Not given to wine, no striker, not greedy of filthy lucre; but patient, not a brawler, not covetous; One that ruleth well his own house, having his children in subjection with all gravity; (For if a man know not how to rule his own house, how shall he take care of the church of God?) Not a novice, lest being lifted up with pride he fall into the condemnation of the devil. Moreover he must have a good report of them which are without; lest he fall into reproach and the snare of the devil" (1 Timothy 3:1–7).

BOANERGES (MEANING: SONS OF THUNDER.)

Boanerges was the surname give by the Savior to James and John: "And James the son of Zebedee, and John the brother of James; and he surnamed them Boanerges, which is, The sons of thunder" (Mark 3:17). The forceful character of John is illustrated in this passage: "And John answered him, saying, Master, we saw one casting out devils in thy name, and he followeth not us: and we forbad him, because he followeth not us. But Jesus said, Forbid him not: for there is no man which shall do a miracle in my name, that can lightly speak evil of me. For he that is not against us is on our part" (Mark 9:38–40; see also Luke 9:49–50). The Savior also used the boldness of James and John on another occasion to teach a lesson about service (Mark 10:35–45).

When the time of the Crucifixion was approaching, James and John wanted to call down fire from heaven to turn the tide: "But he [Jesus] turned, and rebuked them, and said, Ye know not what manner of spirit ye are of. For the Son of man is not come to destroy men's lives, but to save them" (Luke 9:55–56).

BRETHREN OF THE LORD

The word *brethren* as a title in the following passage has reference to the brothers of Jesus who were children of Joseph and Mary after Jesus was born:

> And when he was come into his own country, he taught them in their synagogue, insomuch that they were astonished, and said, Whence hath this man this wisdom, and these mighty works?
>
> Is not this the carpenter's son? is not his mother called Mary? and his brethren, James, and Joses, and Simon, and Judas?
>
> And his sisters, are they not all with us? Whence then hath this man all these things?
>
> And they were offended in

him. But Jesus said unto them, A prophet is not without honour, save in his own country, and in his own house." (Matthew 13:54–57; see also Matthew 12:46; Mark 6:1–4; John 2:12; 7:3; Acts 1:14; 1 Corinthians 9:5)

In a reference by Paul, the word *brother* is used in relation to James: "But other of the apostles saw I none, save James the Lord's brother" (Galatians 1:19). The Lord's affirmative witness about the receptiveness of his mother and brethren to His teachings is given in this passage: "Then came to him his mother and his brethren, and could not come at him for the press. And it was told him by certain which said, Thy mother and thy brethren stand without, desiring to see thee. And he answered and said unto them, My mother and my brethren are these which hear the word of God, and do it" (Luke 8:19–21).

C

CAESAR (SEE THE ENTRY FOR AUGUSTUS.)

CAIAPHAS

Caiaphas (Joseph Caiaphas, who reigned from AD 18 to AD 36) was the Jewish high priest during the ministry of Jesus and one of the leading supporters of the conspiracy to put the Lord to death (see Matthew 26:3-4). Following the betrayal by Judas, Jesus was taken captive and led before a hearing chaired by Caiaphas, who subsequently condemned the Lord for blasphemy and referred Him to Pontius Pilate (see Matthew 26:57-58; 27:1-26). Being irreversibly obsessed with the conviction that Jesus should "die for the people, and that the whole nation perish not" (John 11:50; see also John 18:14), Caiaphas was pleased with the ensuing developments leading to the Crucifixion. Caiaphas, himself a Sadducee, was the son-in-law of the high priest Annas (see John 18:13; Luke 3:2), who had first interrogated the captive Lord before sending Him on to Caiaphas (see John 18:24) prior to the sentencing at the court of Pilate (see John 18:28). Later, it was before Annas, Caiaphas,

and their confederate associates that Peter and John were questioned about their healing of a

CAIAPHAS CONDEMNS JESUS AND SENDS HIM TO PONTIUS PILATE FOR SENTENCING.

23

lame man. When the Apostles refused to recant their position as witnesses of the divine calling of the Savior, their accusers, having no way to restrain them before the law, released them, not wanting to offend the believing public who had witnessed the miracle (see Acts 4:1–22). (See the entry for Annas.)

Cain

Cain is the first example among mortals of the consummate rebel who succumbed to the evil dictates of Satan. When the Lord rejected Cain's offering (see Moses 5:20–21), he became angry and murdered his brother Abel (see Genesis 4:8; Moses 5:32) in compliance with the promptings of Satan, "the author of all sin" (Helaman 6:30; see also Moses 5:29–30). The moment of Cain's accountability before the Lord for this atrocity is chilling in its consequences (see Genesis 4:9–13; see also Moses 5:33–40).

For his actions, Cain became the exemplar of evil and Satanic conspiracy—the opposite of the love of God at the core of the gospel plan: "For this is the message that ye heard from the beginning, that we should love one another. Not as Cain, who was of that wicked one, and slew his brother. And wherefore slew he him? Because his own works were evil, and his brother's righteous" (1 John 3:11–12).

We have in Cain an example of the most blatant rejection of the light of God among mortals (see Jude 1:11). He is the opposite of one with faith, as Paul confirmed: "By faith Abel offered unto God a more excellent sacrifice than Cain, by which he obtained witness that he was righteous, God testifying of his gifts: and by it he being dead yet speaketh" (Hebrews 11:4). Cain was taught by loving parents; he was taught in person by a loving Heavenly Father (see Moses

Cain is punished by God for killing his brother Abel.

5:22–25). But, through his alliance with Satan, he became an author of eternal damnation for those who conspire for evil through obedience to darkness—just as the Savior, Jesus Christ, in stark contrast, "being made perfect . . . became the author of eternal salvation unto all them that obey him" (Hebrews 5:9).

Canaanite (Meaning: low or humbled.)

The word *Canaanite* occurs only twice in the King James Version of the New Testament, both times in connection with Simon, one of the Twelve, who is designated as "Simon the Canaanite" (Matthew 10:4; Mark 3:18). In other translations of the New Testament, the word *Cananaean* is used in these verses, referring to one with an attachment to certain political leanings in favor of an independent Israel in the days of Roman imperial sovereignty. In referring to Simon,

Luke uses the term *Zelotes* (see Luke 6:15; Acts 1:13), apparently in reference to the "Zealots" or followers of the Cananaean persuasion. Thus, "Cananaean" rather than "Canaanite" appears to be the more accurate translation in Matthew 10:4 and Mark 3:18.

CAPTAIN OF THE TEMPLE

This expression is used twice in the New Testament, both times in connection with confrontations of the authorities against Peter and John: "And as they spake unto the people, the priests, and the captain of the temple, and the Sadducees, came upon them" (Acts 4:1). Furthermore, when Peter and John were thereafter arrested and thrown into prison, only to be delivered by an angel of the Lord and directed to preach in the temple, the authorities were stunned: "Now when the high priest and the captain of the temple and the chief priests heard these things, they doubted of them whereunto this would grow" (Acts 5:24). "Captain of the temple" in these instances refers to one placed in charge of the priests and Levites who guarded the temple. When Judas Iscariot turned against Christ, we read, "And he went his way, and communed with the chief priests and captains, how he might betray him unto them" (Luke 22:4). "Captains" in this sense also has reference to those who served as "captain of the temple."

CASTOR AND POLLUX

These two figures from Greek and Roman mythology are mentioned once in the New Testament: "And after three months we departed in a ship of Alexandria, which had wintered in the isle, whose sign was Castor and Pollux"

(Acts 28:11). Evidently, the ship in which Paul journeyed from the island of Melita (the Malta of today) to Syracuse (on the southeast coast of Sicily) while on his way to Rome displayed a representation of the two patrons of the sailors on its prow.

CENTURION

A centurion was a Roman officer who was in command of one hundred men. In the New Testament several centurions are mentioned, usually in a positive light.

1. The centurion who asked Jesus to heal his servant (see Matthew 8:5–13).

2. The centurion who witnessed the Crucifixion (see Luke 23:46–47).

3. The centurion Cornelius, who was the first Gentile to come into the fold (see Acts 10; 11:1–18). (See the entry for Cornelius.)

4. The centurion who took note that Paul, arrested in Jerusalem, was a Roman citizen entitled to special privileges (see Acts 22:25–26).

5. The centurion who was commanded by Felix to keep Paul under watch while the latter's case was being reviewed (see Acts 24:23).

6. The centurion Julius, who was placed in charge of Paul on his journey to Rome (see Acts 27; 28:16). (See the entry for Julius.)

7. Centurions (plural) are mentioned in Acts 21:32; 23:17, 23.

CEPHAS (Meaning: a stone.)

Cephas was the Aramaic name given by Jesus to Simon when he received his calling as a disciple: "And he [Andrew, Simon Peter's brother] brought him to Jesus. And when Jesus beheld him, he said, Thou art Simon the son of Jona: thou shalt be called Cephas, which is by interpretation, A stone" (John 1:42; see also 1 Corinthians 9:5; 15:5; Galatians 2:9). *Petros* is the Greek term corresponding to Cephas. In Doctrine and Covenants section 76, concerning the degrees of glory, those who inherit the telestial kingdom are characterized as rejecting the Savior, though they might profess outward allegiance to some religious leader, such as Cephas, Moses, Paul, or some other cause (see D&C 76:99; see also 1 Corinthians 1:12; 3:22).

CHAMBERLAIN

The title of *chamberlain* designates a private and confidential officer of an eastern king (see 2 Kings 23:11; Esther 2:3, 14, 15; Acts 12:20; Romans 16:23). In some cases, the word is also given the translation "eunuch." (See the entry for Eunuch.)

CHERUB/CHERUBIM/CHERUBIMS

A cherub (Hebrew plural *cherubim*) is an angel of some particular order and rank among the hierarchy of the hosts of heaven. Paul spoke of the Mosaic ordinances as prefiguring the Atonement of Jesus Christ. He referred to the Ark of the Covenant: "And over it the cherubims of glory shadowing the mercyseat" (Hebrews 9:5).

CHLOE (Meaning: verdure or blooming.)

Chloe was a Christian woman whose household members had informed Paul of divisions among the Saints in the Corinthian Church. She is mentioned only one time in the New Testament: "Now I beseech you, brethren, by the name of our Lord Jesus Christ, that ye all speak the same thing, and that there be no divisions among you; but that ye be perfectly joined together in the same mind and in the same judgment. For it hath been declared unto me of you, my brethren, by them which are of the house of Chloe, that there are contentions among you" (1 Corinthians 1:10–11).

CHRIST (See the entry for Jesus Christ.)

CHRISTIAN/CHRISTIANS

The words *Christian* or *Christians*, meaning those of Christ's fold, are used only three times in the New Testament: "And the disciples were called Christians first in Antioch" (Acts 11:26); "Then Agrippa said unto Paul, Almost thou persuadest me to be a Christian" (Acts 26:28); "Yet if any man suffer as a Christian, let him not be ashamed; but let him glorify God on this behalf" (1 Peter 4:16).

CHRISTS, FALSE

The Savior warned His disciples concerning false Christs that would come in the future to deceive: "Then if any man shall say unto you, Lo, here is Christ, or there; believe it not. For there shall arise false Christs, and false prophets, and shall shew great signs and wonders; insomuch that, if it were possible, they shall deceive the very elect" (Matthew 24:23–24; see also Matthew 24:4–5;

Mark 13:21-22; Luke 21:8; 2 Peter 2:1-7; JST 1:21-22; Words of Mormon 1:15). (See also the entry for Anti-Christ.)

CHURCH (FROM THE GREEK WORD *ECCLESIA*, MEANING "AN ASSEMBLY")

The Church comprises the community of the Saints of the Lord, gathered into His fold on the basis of saving principles of truth, organized and directed through priesthood power, and enlightened by the Holy Spirit. Through the dispensations of time, the Lord has ordained and arranged for a divine organization to govern the unfolding of His kingdom as a means to bless and sanctify His people. The structure and organization of the Church, with its various offices and circles of leadership, did not evolve by chance but was a prepared gift from God, given by heavenly design to optimize the process of making saving truths and ordinances available to the sons and daughters of God in their quest to return home once again. The celestial kingdom itself is organized on principles of glory and eternal light. Thus, the earthly kingdom is a type and likeness of what awaits the faithful in the coming world (see D&C 105:5). The words *church* and *churches* do not occur in the King James Version of the Old Testament (*congregation* being the term used), but they are used often in the New Testament. During His earthly ministry, the Lord organized His Church and kingdom according to specific principles and stewardships. In the space of only three years, the Savior put in place a dynamic, empowered, and orderly institution that bore the signature of divine perfection. It was complex yet unified, domestic in its outreach yet authorized directly by Deity, designed for the everyday yet governed by keys extending to heaven. It was structured as a living entity for amplifying and making known the light of the gospel as an ensign of truth (see Matthew 5:16).

How did the Savior reach out to the people of His Church and kingdom with guidance and wisdom? Important elements of the organization of the Church in the meridian of time include:

- governing philosophy for members of the Church (see Matthew 13:31-32)
- revelation (see Matthew 16:17-19)
- sealing powers (see Matthew 17:1-3)
- the commission to teach the gospel (see Matthew 28:18-20)
- the ministry of the Twelve Apostles (see Luke 9:1-2)
- the Seventy (see Luke 10:1-3).
- the authority to act in the name of God (see John 15:16)

The Apostles carried on the work of the Church as organized by Jesus Christ. The words of Paul are instructive in this regard concerning the people of the Church (see Ephesians 2:19-22; 4:11-13; 1 Corinthians 12:12-13; 1 Timothy 3:15; Hebrews 5:4-5).

Succession of apostolic leadership in the Church was carried out by revelation (see Acts 1:23-26). The principles and practices taught and cultivated in the original Church included, among others:

- universal love of the Father confirmed through the Atonement (see John 3:16)
- the reality of the Resurrection as a universal gift of grace to all mankind (see 1 Corinthians 15:22)
- Christ as the head of the Church (see Ephesians 1:22; 5:23; Colossians 1:18)
- the central role of faith (see Hebrews 11:1)

- repentance, baptism, and the gift of the Holy Ghost (see John 3:5; Acts 2: 38; 19:4)
- vicarious baptism for the dead (see 1 Corinthians 15:29)
- gospel preached in the spirit world (see 1 Peter 3:18–20; 4:6)
- degrees of glory in the hereafter (John 14:2; 1 Corinthians 15:40; Hebrews 12:22–23)
- gifts of the Spirit among the Saints (1 Corinthians 12:4–6)
- unity and receptivity (see Acts 15:4; Romans 12:5; 1 Corinthians 12:13; 14:33; Ephesians 4:4–7)
- service as an essential component of the Church (see John 21:15–17; Acts 20:28; James 1:27; 1 Peter 5:2)
- the sacrament (see Matthew 26:26–28)
- missionary work (see Matthew 28:19–20; Mark 16:15–18; Luke 24:46–50; Acts 1:8; 2:47).

It is clear from the New Testament text that the early Christian Church would fall into apostasy (see Matthew 24:24; Acts 20:29; 1 Corinthians 11:18; Galatians 1:6; 2 Thessalonians 2:3; 1 Timothy 1:6; 2 Timothy 3:5; 2 Peter 2:1; 1 John 2:18; 4:1).

On April 6, 1830, an event of singular importance in the history of the world took place in a humble cabin in the small town of Fayette, New York (see D&C 20:1). On that occasion, the Lord's Church was formally organized in this dispensation as a divine blessing for all who would come with broken hearts and contrite spirits and covenant to be His children by taking upon them His name and serving Him forever in righteousness. The Church is indeed the organized and authorized structure through which the Saints are to be perfected, the gospel preached unto all the world, and salvation administered and secured for all the hosts of creation—both living and dead—who become heirs of immortality and eternal life.

CLAUDIUS

1. Claudius was a Roman emperor. (See the entry for Augustus.)

2. Claudius Lysias was the commander of a Roman garrison ("chief captain") in Jerusalem (see Acts 21:31, 32, 33, 37; 22:24, 26–29; 23:10, 15, 17–19, 22; 24:7, 22) who rescued Paul from his detractors upon learning that the latter was a Roman citizen. The letter that Claudius sent to the procurator Felix is instructive (see Acts 23:26–30).

Paul was then escorted to Caesarea to the court of Felix, who heard his defense and arranged to refer him to the authorities upward in the line of leadership—until Paul eventually went to Rome.

CLEMENT

Clement was an admired associate of Paul's in the cause of the gospel, mentioned but once in the New Testament: "And I intreat thee also, true yokefellow, help those women which laboured with me in the gospel, with Clement also, and with other my fellowlabourers, whose names are in the book of life" (Philippians 4:3).

CLEOPAS (MEANING: SON OF A RENOWNED FATHER; SHORTENED FORM OF THE GREEK NAME CLEOPATROS.)

Cleopas was one of two individuals (the other not identified) who encountered the resurrected Lord on the way to Emmaus (see Luke 24:13–18).

When Cleopas and his companion recounted unto Jesus the miraculous happenings of the day, He expounded unto them the prophecies of old concerning the Crucifixion and Resurrection of the Messiah, after which they besought him to sup with them (see Luke 25:30–32). Then Cleopas and his companion went directly to Jerusalem to join the gathering of the eleven Apostles. After learning that the risen Lord had appeared to Simon Peter, they shared their confirming news that "he [Jesus] was known of them in breaking of bread" (Luke 24:35). Thus, Cleopas and his companion are witnesses of the power of the Lord to open up His word to believers and to make Himself known through the sacramental process, a reminder of the promises of the sacramental prayer that partakers "may eat in remembrance of the body of thy Son, and . . . always remember him . . . that they may always have his Spirit to be with them" (D&C 20:77; see also verse 79). Nothing more of Cleopas is known, though some surmise that he may be the same as Cleophas, an individual mentioned in John 19:25.

CLEOPHAS

Cleophas (Clopas in the Aramaic form) is mentioned in only one verse in the New Testament, concerning the witnesses at the cross: "Now there stood by the cross of Jesus his mother, and his mother's sister, Mary the wife of Cleophas, and Mary Magdalene" (John 19:25). It is possible that John was listing four of the witnesses: (1) the mother of Jesus, Mary, (2) an unnamed sister of Jesus's mother, (3) Mary, the wife of Cleophas, and (4) Mary Magdalene. According to tradition, however, Mary, the wife of Cleophas, may have been a sister to Joseph, husband of Mary, the mother of Jesus.

THE WIFE OF CLEOPHAS MOURNS AT THE CRUCIFICTION OF CHRIST.

COLOSSIANS

The Colossians were inhabitants of the city of Colossae, a leading city in the Roman province of Asia (located in the western part of modern Turkey). Paul formulated his epistle to the Colossians on behalf of the community of Saints residing there. Among the noted Saints associated with Colossae were Epaphras (see Colossians 1:7–8; 4:12–13) and individuals of the household of Philemon (see Colossians 4:9, 17; Philemon 1:1–2, 10).

COMFORTER (SEE THE ENTRY FOR HOLY GHOST.)

CORINTHIANS

The Corinthians were inhabitants of Corinth, an important commercial city in the Roman province of Achaia in the southern part of Greece. Paul established a Christian community there (see Acts 18:1–18) and addressed his Corinthian epistles to the Saints with roots in that part of the realm. Among the noted Corinthian Saints were Aquila and Priscilla (see Acts 18:1–3).

CORNELIUS (Meaning: horn; related, perhaps, to the Latin word *cornu*.)

Cornelius, a centurion stationed at Caesarea, is thought to be the first of the Christian converts of Gentile stock to come into the Church directly, rather than through the avenue of conversion initially to the Jewish faith and full compliance with Jewish practices. Cornelius was "a devout man, and one that feared God with all his house, which gave much alms to the people, and prayed to God always" (Acts 10:2). He was guided to the fold of Christ by an angelic visitation:

> He saw in a vision evidently about the ninth hour of the day an angel of God coming in to him, and saying unto him, Cornelius.
>
> And when he looked on him, he was afraid, and said, What is it, Lord? And he said unto him, Thy prayers and thine alms are come up for a memorial before God.
>
> And now send men to Joppa, and call for *one* Simon, whose surname is Peter:
>
> He lodgeth with one Simon a tanner, whose house is by the sea side: he shall tell thee what thou oughtest to do. (Acts 10:3–6)

Cornelius then sent a delegation to Joppa the following day where Peter concurrently received a visionary witness of the remarkable development about to happen in the Church (see Acts 10:11–16).

At that very hour, the party from Cornelius arrived at the place where Peter was staying and declared unto him the reason for their petition. Peter then journeyed the next day to Caesarea where he was met by Cornelius, who "fell down at his feet, and worshipped him. But Peter took him up, saying, Stand up; I myself also am a man" (Acts 10:25–26). Soon thereafter, Peter unfolded his inspired message to the assembled crowd, beginning with the words: "Of a truth I perceive that God is no respecter of persons: But in every nation he that feareth him, and worketh righteousness, is accepted with him. The word which God sent unto the children of Israel, preaching peace by Jesus Christ: (he is Lord of all)" (Acts 10:34–36). During the delivery of Peter's witness, the Holy Ghost witnessed to the truth and Peter challenged all to be baptized (Acts 10:44–48).

Later, when Peter returned to Jerusalem for a conference, some of the disciples there raised the issue of the propriety of having discourse with the uncircumcised (i.e., Gentiles), and

PETER TEACHES CORNELIUS, WHO BECOMES THE FIRST GENTILE CONVERT TO CHRISTIANITY.

Peter, recounting his experiences, declared, "Forasmuch then as God gave them the like gift as he did unto us, who believed on the Lord Jesus Christ; what was I, that I could withstand God? When they heard these things, they held their peace, and glorified God, saying, Then hath God also to the Gentiles granted repentance unto life" (Acts 11:17–18). Thus, the experience involving Cornelius opened the gateway to the universal delivery of the gospel in keeping with the Abrahamic Covenant and according to the Savior's ultimate directive concerning the apostolic ministry: "Go ye therefore, and teach all nations, baptizing them in the name of the Father, and of the Son, and of the Holy Ghost: Teaching them to observe all things whatsoever I have commanded you: and, lo, I am with you alway, even unto the end of the world" (Matthew 28:19–20). (See also the entry for Proselytes.)

Council

The word *council* is used to indicate the group of Jewish chief priests, scribes, and elders (around seventy-one in number) belonging to the singularly powerful assembly of the Sanhedrin. The antagonism of the Sanhedrin toward Jesus Christ and His cause is pervasive in the New Testament, as in this example: "Then gathered the chief priests and the Pharisees a council, and said, What do we? for this man doeth many miracles. If we let him thus alone, all men will believe on him: and the Romans shall come and take away both our place and nation" (John 11:47–48). There are twenty-one other occurrences of the word *council* in the King James Version of the New Testament. Many of these apply to the Sanhedrin, as in the following reference to the actions of the Lord's Jewish adversaries: "Now the chief priests, and elders,

and all the council, sought false witness against Jesus, to put him to death" (Matthew 26:59). Other uses of the word *council* might apply to the Sanhedrin or to lesser tribunals in the land:

- in the Lord's comment during the Sermon on the Mount (see Matthew 5:21–22)
- in the Lord's instructions to His disciples (see Matthew 10:16–17)
- in this additional counsel (see Mark 13:9)

Not all associated with the "council" were vehemently anti-Christian—the Pharisee Nicodemus defended the Savior before his brethren (see John 7:50–51), and the prominent teacher Gamaliel was moderate and circumspect in his judgment (see Acts 5:33–40). Nevertheless, the Sanhedrin conspiracy resulted, ultimately, in the Crucifixion of the Savior and severe actions against His leading successors—Peter and John (see Acts 5), Paul (see Acts 23), and Stephen (resulting in his martyrdom, see Acts 6–7). The days of the Restoration in our time are replete with campaigns by the leading tribunals of government to defeat the cause of Zion—not Sanhedrin-like in their constituency but, nevertheless, equally viral in their determination to destroy the Church. It was at the hands of such circles of government that Joseph Smith and his brother Hyrum were martyred on June 27, 1844 (see D&C 135). (See entry for Sanhedrin.)

DAMARIS (MEANING: HEIFER.)

Damaris was an Athenian woman who was among those responding with belief to the discourse of Paul on Mars' Hill: "Howbeit certain men clave unto him, and believed: among the which was Dionysius the Areopagite, and a woman named Damaris, and others with them" (Acts 17:34).

DANIEL (MEANING: GOD IS MY JUDGE OR A JUDGE OF GOD.)

The Savior invoked the prophet Daniel's warning in His counsel concerning future events, including perilous times to be aware of (see Matthew 24:14–15; see also Mark 13:14). In his vision of the rise and fall of worldly empires leading up to the Second Coming, Daniel spoke of the destructive consequences of wicked designs (see Daniel 11:31; see also Daniel 12:11).

In the Joseph Smith Translation of Matthew (covering Matthew 23:39 and Matthew 24) contained in the Pearl of Great Price, Daniel's reference is included twice. The first of these Daniel references might well apply to the imminent destruction of Jerusalem by the Romans in AD 70 and the second to future events of dislocation and turmoil to come upon Jerusalem and upon the world in general just prior to the Second Coming.

DANIEL IS SPARED IN THE LION'S DEN.

DAVID (MEANING: BELOVED.)

David is mentioned fifty-eight times in the New Testament. He was the celebrated king of Judah and Israel who united the tribes as one great nation and ensured that the government was based upon righteous principles and the law of God. He is also one of the most tragic figures in the Old Testament because of his transgression with Bathsheba and Uriah, thus becoming the epitome of personal remorse and suffering over sin.

Among the memorable references to David in the New Testament are the following:

- **lineage of Christ** (see Matthew 1:17; Luke 3:31; 2 Timothy 2:8; Revelation 22:16)
- **annunciation** (see Luke 1:31–33; Romans 1:3)
- **Bethlehem** (see John 7:41–42)
- **the disciples censured for picking and eating grain on the Sabbath** (see Matthew 12:3-4; Mark 2:23-28; Luke 6:1-5; 1 Samuel 21:3-6)
- **adulation by the people as Christ rode into the city of Jerusalem** (see Matthew 21:8-9; Mark 11:7-10). The title *son of David* is applied to the Savior often in the New Testament
- **silencing the detractors with references to David's words from the Psalms** (see Matthew 22:41-46; Mark 12:35-37; Luke 20:39-44; Psalm 110:1)
- **Judas** (see Acts 1:15-16)
- **additional citations from the writings of David:** In Peter's sermon on the day of Pentecost, he said concerning Christ, "For

DAVID, KING OF ISRAEL, RECORDS HIS HISTORY AND WRITES HIS POETIC PSALMS.

33

David speaketh concerning him, I foresaw the Lord always before my face, for he is on my right hand, that I should not be moved" (Acts 2:25; see also Psalm 16:8); other writings include a prophecy concerning retribution against the Lord's anointed (see Acts 4:25; see also Psalm 2:1–2.); Paul concerning faith, grace, and works (see Acts 4:6; see also Psalm 32:1; 69:22; Romans 11:9); and Paul concerning heeding the word of the Lord today (see Hebrews 4:7; Psalm 95:7)

- **testimony of Paul** (see Acts 13:22–23)

DEMETRIUS (Meaning: follower of Demeter.)

1. Demetrius was a silversmith in Ephesus who instigated an uprising of his peers against Paul and the Christians for threatening their industry (see Acts 19:24–27).

DEMETRIUS INSTIGATES AN UPRISING AMONG HIS PEERS.

When the craftsmen and other citizens gathered in an assembly to consider the matter, there was confusion and rancor. Paul was counseled by his colleagues not to go into the assembly. The "townclerk" (Acts 19:35) prevailed upon the multitude to resolve any differences in a lawful manner, and the assembly was dismissed. Paul left subsequently for Macedonia.

2. Demetrius was a Christian commended by John: "Demetrius hath good report of all men, and of the truth itself: yea, and we also bear record; and ye know that our record is true" (3 John 1:12).

DEVIL (See the entry for Satan.)

DIANA

Diana, goddess of the hunt (and of fertility and nurture) in Roman mythology, was associated with Artemis in Greek mythology. The great temple of Diana (Artemis) in Ephesus was one of the main centers of worship for the goddess and one of the seven wonders of the ancient world. It was because of the Christian position in opposition to pagan worship that the silversmiths of Ephesus rose up in riot against Paul and his associates: "And when the townclerk had appeased the people, he said, Ye men of Ephesus, what man is there that knoweth not how that the city of the Ephesians is a worshipper of the great goddess Diana, and of the image which fell down from Jupiter?" (Acts 19:35).

DIDYMUS (Meaning: twin.)

Didymus is the Greek equivalent of Thomas (an Aramaic name). Didymus occurs three times in the New Testament (see John 11:16; 20:24; 21:2), all in connection with the Apostle Thomas.

DIONYSIUS THE AREOPAGITE

Dionysius the Areopagite was an Athenian man who was among those responding with belief to the discourse of Paul on Mars' Hill: "Howbeit certain men clave unto him, and believed: among the which was Dionysius the Areopagite, and a woman named Damaris, and others with them" (Acts 17:34). An Areopagite was a member of the Areopagus (see Acts 17:19), the chief council or legislative court of justice in Athens that met in the open on Mars' Hill. The word *Areopagus* derives from the Greek words *pagos* ("hill") and *Ares* (the god Mars), hence "Mars' Hill."

DIOTREPHES (MEANING: NOURISHED BY JOVE OR JUPITER.)

Diotrephes was a Christian condemned by John for his pride and lack of fellowship (see 3 John 1:9–11).

DISCIPLE (MEANING: ONE WHO LEARNS.)

The term *disciple* or *disciples* is used frequently in the New Testament, being applied at times to members of the Twelve (see Matthew 10:1; 11:1; 20:17; Luke 9:1) and at other times to followers of the Savior in general (see Luke 14:27). The word *disciple* is also applied to followers of John the Baptist (see Matthew 9:14; Mark 2:18) and to followers of the Pharisees (see Mark 2:18).

DORCAS (MEANING: GAZELLE.)

Dorcas (Greek form of the Aramaic name Tabitha) was a righteous Christian woman at Joppa restored to life by Peter (see Acts 9:36–42).

DRUSILLA (MEANING: WATERED BY THE DEW.)

Drusilla is mentioned only once in the New Testament, in connection with the hearing

Peter restores Dorcas to life.

conducted by her husband, Felix, for the purpose of examining Paul at Caesarea: "And after certain days [following the formal hearing], when Felix came with his wife Drusilla, which was a Jewess, he sent for Paul, and heard him concerning the faith in Christ" (Acts 24:24). Drusilla was the youngest daughter of Herod Agrippa I and sister to Bernice. Felix was the Roman procurator of Judea from AD 52 until AD 59–60.

Eber

Heber is listed among the descendants of Adam in the lineage leading down to Christ (see Luke 3:35). Heber is equivalent to Eber, the great-grandson of Shem, the son of Noah (see Genesis 10:21–25; 1 Chronicles 1:17–19, 25). Eber is regarded as the founding ancestor of the Hebrew people (see Genesis 11:14–17; Numbers 24:24).

El (Meaning: might or strength.)

The name El in Hebrew and related languages was an appellation for "divine being." Elohim (plural form) is a familiar application in LDS discourse in reference to the Father. Other applications used in the scriptures include names such as Bethel (meaning "house of God"), Michael (meaning "who is like God"), Daniel (meaning "a judge is God"), Elijah (meaning "Jehovah is God"), and Israel (meaning "to strive with God," "prevail with God," or the like).

Elder/Elders

The word *elder* or *elders* is used sixty-nine times in the New Testament—in the Gospels, mostly in terms of a traditional priesthood office mentioned in conjunction with the "scribes" and the "chief priests."

Beginning with Acts 11, the word *elders* is generally used in a positive sense with respect to the administration of the early Church (see Acts 11:29–30; 14:23; 15:2; James 5:14; 1 Peter 5:1).

The term *elders* is also used frequently in the Revelation of John as part of his vision of the unfolding of the design of the Almighty: "And round about the throne were four and twenty seats: and upon the seats I saw four and twenty elders sitting, clothed in white raiment; and they had on their heads crowns of gold" (Revelation 4:4; see also Revelation 4:10; 5:5–6, 8, 11, 14; 7:11, 13; 11:16; 14:3; 19:4).

El Elyon (Meaning: the most high God.)

El Elyon is the Hebrew expression for "deity," rendered as follows in the passage where it occurs for the first time in the Old Testament: "And Melchizedek king of Salem brought forth bread and wine: and he was the priest of the most high God" (Genesis 14:18; see also verses 19 and 22). The expression "the most high God" (or "the Most High") occurs rather frequently thereafter in all the standard works.

ELI (MEANING: MY GOD.)

The Savior used this term of address in His expression of suffering while on the cross: "And about the ninth hour Jesus cried with a loud voice, saying, Eli, Eli, lama sabachthani? that is to say, My God, my God, why hast thou forsaken me?" (Matthew 27:46; see also Mark 15:34 where the term is rendered *Eloi*).

ELIAKIM (MEANING: GOD RAISETH UP.)

Eliakim is listed in the genealogical lineage of the Savior (see Matthew 1:13; Luke 3:30). Others of that same name are mentioned in the Old Testament, including Eliakim, the master of the household of King Hezekiah (see 2 Kings 18-19; 2 Chronicles 2; Isaiah 36-37); Eliakim as the original name of Jehoiakim, the second son of Josiah, whom the Egyptians set up as king of Judah (see 2 Kings 23:34); and Eliakim, the priest during the time of Nehemiah who assisted in the dedicatory service for the rebuilt wall of Jerusalem (see Nehemiah 12:41).

ELIAS

The name Elias (the Greek form of Elijah) appears thirty times in the New Testament, though not at all in the King James Version of the Old Testament. Elias, as a name, has several applications in the New Testament.

1. Elias is the equivalent to Elijah. Examples include: (1) his appearance on the Mount of Transfiguration (see Matthew 17:1-3; see also Mark 9:2-4; JST Mark 9:3); (2) Elijah and the widow (see Luke 4:25-26; see also 1 Kings 17); and (3) Elijah with power to control the elements (see James 5:17-18).

2. *Elias* is a title for one who serves as a forerunner, such as John the Baptist, who, in the authority of the Aaronic Priesthood, prepared the way in "the spirit of Elias" (D&C 27:7) for the Savior in the meridian of time. Concerning John the Baptist, the scriptures read, "For all the prophets and the law prophesied until John. And if ye will receive it, this is Elias, which was for to come" (Matthew 11:13-14; see also Luke 1:17), and "he [John the Baptist] said, I am the voice of one crying in the wilderness, Make straight the way of the Lord, as said the prophet Esaias [i.e., Isaiah, see Isaiah 40:3]" (John 1:23).

Elias as a title can also refer to all the heavenly messengers collectively who came to restore keys and authorities in the dispensation of the fulness of times, leading up to the Second Coming.

3. *Elias* is a title for the Savior, who restores all power and keys for the operation of the kingdom of God (see JST John 1:28; the equivalent reference is John 1:27, which does not include the words "that prophet, even Elias").

4. Elias was a prophet. Modern revelation has illuminated the meaning of "Elias" in fuller measure as both an individual prophet and a title. Along with other heavenly ministrants coming to restore their several keys, Elias the individual, a prophet of God during the days of Abraham, appeared to Joseph Smith and

Oliver Cowdery in the Kirtland Temple on April 3, 1836, "and committed the dispensation of the gospel of Abraham, saying that in us and our seed all generations after us should be blessed" (D&C 110:12). Elijah (identified as Elias in the New Testament) also appeared on that occasion to restore the sealing keys for priesthood ordinances (see D&C 110:13–16). In the Doctrine and Covenants, the term *Elias* is used seven times in its various meanings (D&C 27:6–7; 76:100; 77:9, 14; 110:12; 138:45).

ELIEZER (MEANING: GOD IS HELP.)

Eliezer is listed in the genealogical lineage of the Savior (see Luke 3:29). Other individuals with that same name are also included in the Old Testament, including the man whom Abram (Abraham) identified as "steward of my house" (Genesis 15:2)—apparently the same steward who later acted as emissary in the quest to obtain a wife for Isaac as recorded in Genesis 24–25; Eliezer who was a son of Moses and Zipporah (see Exodus 18:4; see also 1 Chronicles 23:15, 17; 26: 25); Eliezer who was a prophet who rebuked Jehoshaphat, king of Judah, for his alliance with Ahaziah, wicked king of Israel (see 2 Chronicles 20:35–37); and several others (see 1 Chronicles 7:8; 15:24; 27:16; Ezra 8:16; 10:18, 23, 31).

ELIJAH (MEANING: JEHOVAH IS MY GOD.)

Elijah, identified as Elias in the New Testament, is referred to several times in that canon: as present on the Mount of Transfiguration (see Matthew 17:1–3; Mark 9:2–4), in connection with his blessing of the widow of Zarephath and her son (see Luke 4:25; 1 Kings 17), and in a reference by James concerning Elijah's power to control the elements (see James 5:17–18). Elijah

is a singularly imposing figure in a long line of extraordinary prophetic servants of the Lord. Israelites and non-Israelites of his day felt his compelling influence (see 1 Kings 17–2 Kings 2; 2 Chronicles 21:12–15). He was called forth again on the Mount of Transfiguration (see Matthew 17:1–11) and touches countless lives today through the restored keys of the sealing power of the priesthood placed in his charge (see D&C 110:13–16). The story of Elijah is a dramatic confirmation of the fact that the Lord's work is always founded on prophetic ministry. The prophet Elijah occupied a central position in the design of God as the one holding the "keys of the power of turning the hearts of the fathers to the children, and the hearts of the children to the fathers" (D&C 27:9). It was this prophet whom God sent on April 3, 1836, to the Kirtland Temple to restore these sacred keys to Joseph Smith as an essential priesthood power in the dispensation of the fulness of times (see D&C 110:14–16; see also Malachi 4:5–6; 3 Nephi 25:5).

The Prophet Joseph Smith articulated the indispensable nature of the powers and keys of sealing restored to him, as the agent of the Restoration, through the prophet Elijah: "The greatest responsibility in this world that God has laid upon us is to seek after our dead. The Apostle says, 'They without us cannot be made perfect;' (Hebrews 11:40) for it is necessary that the sealing power should be in our hands to seal our children and our dead for the fulness of the dispensation of times—a dispensation to meet the promises made by Jesus Christ before the foundation of the world for the salvation of man" (*TPJS*, 356).

Through Elijah, the sealing powers were restored, by which we typically understand the work of temples. But the mission of Elijah

accomplished more than that, as the Prophet Joseph Smith also emphasized:

> Elijah was the last prophet that held the keys of this priesthood, and who will, before the last dispensation, restore the authority and delive[r] the Keys of this priesthood in order that all the ordinances may be attended to in righteousness. . . . It is true that the Savior had authority and power to bestow this blessing but the Sons of Levi were too predjudi[ced]. . . . And I will send Elijah the Prophet before the great and terrible day of the Lord &c &c. Why send Elijah because he holds the Keys of the Authority to administer in all the ordinances of the priesthood and without the authority is given the ordinances could not be administered in righteousness. (*WJS*, 43)

ELISABETH (MEANING: MY GOD IS AN OATH OR MY GOD IS ABUNDANCE.)

Elisabeth was the mother of John the Baptist. Her lineage, character, and circumstances are set forth in Luke 1:5–7. While performing his annual priestly duties in the temple, Zacharias learned through an angelic visitation from Gabriel that a blessed event was forthcoming (see Luke 1:13–14). The same angel appeared

ELIZABETH WELCOMES HER COUSIN MARY TO HER HOME.

later to Mary (see Luke 1:36–37). When Mary then visited Elisabeth in celebration of the development, the following memorable event transpired:

> And it came to pass, that, when Elisabeth heard the salutation of Mary, the babe leaped in her womb; and Elisabeth was filled with the Holy Ghost:
>
> And she spake out with a loud voice, and said, Blessed *art* thou among women, and blessed is the fruit of thy womb.
>
> And whence is this to me, that the mother of my Lord should come to me?
>
> For, lo, as soon as the voice of thy salutation sounded in mine ears, the babe leaped in my womb for joy.
>
> And blessed is she that believed: for there shall be a performance of those things which were told her from the Lord. (Luke 1:41–45)

ELISEUS

Eliseus is the New Testament form of the name *Elisha* (meaning "God shall save" or "God of salvation"), as in this sole occurrence: "And many lepers were in Israel in the time of Eliseus the prophet; and none of them was cleansed, saving Naaman the Syrian" (Luke 4:27).

Elisha was the companion and student of Elijah for several years and ultimately his successor as prophet in the northern kingdom of Israel. His calling came by divine command unto Elijah concerning future positions of secular and spiritual leadership (see 1 Kings 19:16, 19, 21).

The story of Elisha is conveyed for the most part in 2 Kings. Key episodes in the life of Elisha include:

- **Elisha becomes prophet** (see 2 Kings 2).
- **Elisha performs mighty miracles:** He multiplies the oil for the widow and the bread for the multitude, raises a child from the dead, and heals a reluctant Naaman the Syrian of leprosy by having him wash

in the Jordan seven times (see 2 Kings 4–5; see also Luke 4:27 concerning the reference of the Savior to Eliseus).

- **Elisha is surrounded by the hosts of heaven:** Later Elisha counsels the king of Israel how to contend with the Syrian hosts; chariots of fire protect Elisha as the Syrians are blinded and defeated (see 2 Kings 6–7).

The ministry of Elisha lasted more than half a century, concurrent with the reigns of Jehoram, Jehu, Jehoahaz, and Joash. The prophet Elisha had a humble dependence upon the Lord, and he was able to perform the mighty miracles because of his spirit of service and devotion to the Lord's cause. These miracles exemplified Elisha's righteousness as well as the faith of the people for whom they were performed.

ELISHA (MEANING: GOD SHALL SAVE OR GOD OF SALVATION.)

The name *Elisha* does not occur in the New Testament; however, the equivalent name *Eliseus* is used on one occasion in reference to the miraculous healing of Naaman the Syrian by Elisha (see Luke 4:27; entry for Eliseus).

ELOI (SEE THE ENTRY FOR ELI.)

ELYMAS (SEE THE ENTRY FOR BAR-JESUS.)

EMMANUEL (MEANING: GOD WITH US.)

This title for the Son of God occurs only one time in the scriptures: "Behold, a virgin shall be with child, and shall bring forth a son, and they shall call his name Emmanuel, which being interpreted is, God with us" (Matthew 1:23). The equivalent term *Immanuel* occurs five times in the scriptures, as in the following: "Therefore the Lord himself shall give you a sign; Behold, a virgin shall conceive, and bear a son, and shall call his name Immanuel" (Isaiah 7:14; see also Isaiah 8:8; 2 Nephi 17:14; 18:8; D&C 128:22). (See the entry for Jesus Christ.)

ENOCH

The name Enoch occurs only three times in the New Testament: (1) in the genealogical lineage of Jesus Christ (see Luke 3:37); (2) in the discourse on faith given by Paul (see Hebrews 11:5–6); and (3) in a statement by Jude concerning Enoch's prophecy on the Second Coming (see Jude 1:14–15).

Enoch was the great high priest, seventh from Adam, who, along with his righteous city of Zion, was translated, as the Savior said, "into mine own

ENOCH AND HIS RIGHTEOUS PEOPLE ARE TAKEN INTO HEAVEN.

bosom" (D&C 38:4). From the biblical account we learn but few details of the life and ministry of Enoch (see Genesis 5:18–24; Luke 3:37; Hebrews 11:5; Jude 1:14); however, modern revelation provides a fuller vista of Enoch's extraordinary accomplishments (see Moses 6 and 7).

Enos (Meaning: man.)

Enos is mentioned only once in the New Testament (i.e., in the genealogical lineage of Jesus Christ): "Which was the son of Enos, which was the son of Seth, which was the son of Adam, which was the son of God" (Luke 3:38; see also Genesis 4:25–26; called "Enosh" in 1 Chronicles 1:1). The Old Testament gives scant information about the life of Enos beyond the fact that he had sons and daughters (including Cainan) and lived 905 years (see Genesis 5:6–11).

Epaphras (Meaning: lovely.)

Epaphras was a faithful member of the Church at Colossae, who instructed the Saints there in the principles of the gospel. He visited Paul during his confinement in Rome and elicited a tribute from the Apostle (see Colossians 1:7–10).

Paul characterized him as follows: "Epaphras, who is one of you, a servant of Christ, saluteth you, always labouring fervently for you in prayers, that ye may stand perfect and complete in all the will of God" (Colossians 4:12). Paul also called him "my fellowprisoner in Christ Jesus" (Philemon 1:23). Epaphras is a shortened version of the name Epaphroditus.

Epaphroditus (Meaning: lovely.)

Epaphroditus was a devout Christian who came from Philippi to visit Paul, was then imprisoned in Rome, and whom Paul sent back to the Philippians with his epistle, including a characterization of their coming emissary (see Philippians 2:25–30).

Epaphroditus had conveyed to Paul gifts from the Philippians, for which he gave sincere thanks: "But I have all, and abound: I am full, having received of Epaphroditus the things which were sent from you, an odour of a sweet smell, a sacrifice acceptable, wellpleasing to God. But my God shall supply all your need according to his riches in glory by Christ Jesus" (Philippians 4:18–19). Thus, we have from a few verses in the New Testament a memorable insight into the deeds of kindness that long-forgotten members of the Church performed in service to one another during the years when the early Christian Church was striving for vitality and continuity on the eve of the Great Apostasy destined to extinguish the fire of the divine cause until the time of the Restoration in our day. The contracted form of Epaphroditus is Epaphras (as in reference to another individual in Philemon 2:25 and 4:18).

Ephesians

The Ephesians were inhabitants of Ephesus, capital of the Roman province of Asia. Paul visited Ephesus at the end of his second missionary journey (see Acts 18:19–22) and subsequently made the city a significant base of operation during his third missionary journey, winning many converts for the Church among its inhabitants during his two-year stay. The growing influence of the Saints there resulted in an uprising instigated by the silversmiths, who were fearful that the profits from their manufacture of artifacts celebrating the goddess Diana (Artemis), whose chief temple was located in Ephesus, would be compromised (see Acts 19). Paul's epistle to the Ephesians contains his teachings concerning the Church. John the Revelator was also associated

Paul teaches the Ephesians.

with Ephesus and the Saints there: "I am Alpha and Omega, the first and the last: and, What thou seest, write in a book, and send it unto the seven churches which are in Asia; unto Ephesus, and unto Smyrna, and unto Pergamos, and unto Thyatira, and unto Sardis, and unto Philadelphia, and unto Laodicea" (Revelation 1:11).

EPICUREANS

The Epicureans are mentioned once in the New Testament in connection with the visit of Paul to Mars' Hill in Athens (see Acts 17:18). The Epicurean school of philosophy was named after Epicurus, the Greek philosopher (342–271 BC) who espoused the position that pleasure and freedom from fear and pain were central to a fulfilling life. Like the Sadducees, the Epicureans did not believe in an afterlife. Thus, Paul was mocked on Mars' Hill for preaching the doctrine of immortality and the resurrection (see Acts 17:32–33).

ERASTUS

1. Erastus is mentioned as one who "ministered unto" Paul at Ephesus and acted as his emissary (Acts 19:22; see also 2 Timothy 4:20).

2. Erastus was an influential citizen at Corinth, the "chamberlain [treasurer] of the city" (Romans 16:23), and a convert to the Church.

ESAIAS

1. The name Esaias, used twenty-one times in the King James Version of the New Testament, is the Greek form of the name Isaiah, whose words are often cited by the Lord and His disciples. (See the entry for Isaiah.)

2. Esaias was an ancient prophet, mentioned in latter-day scripture, who lived during the time of Abraham and was a key figure in the descent of the priesthood lineage: "And Gad [received the priesthood] under the hand of Esaias; And Esaias received it under the hand of God. Esaias also lived in the days of Abraham, and was blessed of him" (D&C 84:11–13; see also D&C 76:100).

ESAU (MEANING: HAIRY.)

Esau, son of Isaac and older twin brother of Jacob (see Genesis 25:24–28), is mentioned by name three times in the New Testament:

- in Paul's discussion concerning the doctrine of foreordination and its relation with faith and mercy (see Romans 9:12–13)
- in Paul's discourse on faith (see Hebrews 11:20).
- in Paul's exhortation concerning peace and holiness (see Hebrews 12:14–17)

ESAU AND JACOB REUNITE.

The story of how Esau sold his birthright to Jacob for "pottage" is well known (see Genesis 25: 29–34).

EUNICE (MEANING: GOOD VICTORY.)

Eunice, a Christian from Lystra (a city located in what is today Turkey), was the mother of Timothy, as the words of Paul confirm (see 2 Timothy 1:5). Paul recognized the devotion of Eunice to the spiritual education of her son: "And that from a child thou hast known the holy scriptures, which are able to make thee wise unto salvation through faith which is in Christ Jesus. All scripture is given by inspiration of God, and is profitable for doctrine, for reproof, for correction, for instruction in righteousness" (2 Timothy 3:15–16). Eunice was, therefore, worthy of her name, for she was victorious in imparting to Timothy his spiritual foundation.

In many ways, she was an echo of the nobility of the mothers of the sons of Helaman in the Book of Mormon—a century earlier in a distant land—which sons (like Timothy) had a grand spiritual heritage, being "taught by their mothers, that if they did not doubt, God would deliver them" (Alma 56:47).

EUNUCH (MEANING: BED-KEEPER.)

Eunuchs were a class of men who were castrated and were employed to watch over the harems of eastern rulers or occupy other positions of trust. The word *eunuch* or *eunuchs* occurs twenty-seven times in the scriptures and ten times in the New Testament—first in connection with the Savior's teachings on marriage, and second in reference to the experience of Philip in baptizing the Ethiopian eunuch.

When the Pharisees challenged the Savior in regard to the subject of adultery, He avoided stepping into their intended debate about leniency or strictness in regard to divorce and instead invoked the higher principle of divinely appointed marriage, beginning with Adam and Eve (see Matthew 19:4–6). Not giving up, the Pharisees then inquired about Moses allowing divorce in his day, and the Savior then pointed out: "Moses because of the hardness of your hearts suffered you to put away your wives: but from the beginning it was not so" (Matthew 19:8). His point was clear: the higher law of marriage, especially celestial marriage, called for righteousness, purity, honor, and absolute fidelity, with a commitment to an enduring eternal relationship. When his disciples subsequently wondered, given the exacting standards for marriage at the highest level of integrity, whether it would be better to avoid marriage altogether, the Savior assured them,

"All men cannot receive this saying, save they to whom it is given" (Matthew 19:11). He then extended His discussion to the issue of eunuchs, who, because of their condition, relinquished all attachment to the practice of marriage (see Matthew 19:12). He is likely suggesting that His hearers should "receive" in its fulness the higher doctrine of celestial marriage as the divine norm for relationships between the man and the woman. Without raising fault with the eunuchs, the Savior is surely guiding His listeners to understand that those choosing such a lifestyle were not subscribing to the norm, especially if they were acting in the spirit of some kind of fanatical religious zealotry. As He said earlier, concerning the higher law, "All men cannot receive this saying, save they to whom it is given" (Matthew 19:11).

A wonderful case of how a righteous eunuch came into the fold of Christ is the experience of Philip, one of the "seven men of honest report" (Acts 6:3) chosen for the ministry. The Spirit guided Philip to a place along a certain desert roadway: "And he arose and went: and, behold, a man of Ethiopia, an eunuch of great authority under Candace queen of the Ethiopians, who had the charge of all her treasure, and had come to Jerusalem for to worship" (Acts 8:27). The eunuch was sitting alone in his chariot, reading the following passage from Isaiah: "He was led as a sheep to the slaughter; and like a lamb dumb before his shearer, so opened he not his mouth: In his humiliation his judgment was taken away: and who shall declare his generation? for his life is taken from the earth" (Acts 8:32–33; see Isaiah 53:7-8). The eunuch inquired as to the meaning of this passage: "Then Philip opened his mouth, and began at the same scripture, and preached unto him Jesus. And as they went on their way, they came unto a certain water: and the eunuch said, See, here is water; what

doth hinder me to be baptized?" (Acts 8:35-36). Philip then baptized the man, who "went on his way rejoicing" (Acts 8:39).

EUTYCHUS (MEANING: FORTUNATE.)

Eutychus was a young man who experienced a tragic fall during the time that Paul was preaching to his listeners in the city of Troas, or Alexander Troas, located on the Aegean Sea at what is now the northern tip of Turkey's western coast: "And there sat in a window a certain young man named Eutychus, being fallen into a deep sleep: and as Paul was long preaching, he sunk down with sleep, and fell down from the third loft, and was taken up dead" (Acts 20:9). Paul responded directly: "And Paul went down, and fell on him, and embracing him said, Trouble not yourselves; for his life is in him. When he therefore was come up again, and had broken bread, and eaten, and talked a long while, even till break of day, so he departed. And they brought the young man alive, and were not a little comforted" (Acts 20: 10–12).

EVE (MEANING: THE MOTHER OF ALL LIVING.)

Eve, wife of Adam, is mentioned twice by name in the New Testament: once in the passage where Paul is likening the Church unto the spouse of Jesus (see 2 Corinthians 11:2–3) and a second time where Paul is explaining the different roles within the husband/wife partnership (see 1 Timothy 2:13).

From the latter-day vision of President Joseph F. Smith concerning the work of salvation in the spirit world, we have the most satisfying one-word attribute used to summarize the character and person of Eve—glorious (see D&C 138:38-39).

ADAM AND EVE WALK THROUGH THE GARDEN OF EDEN.

From the scriptural account, we can discern several subcategories for defining the word *glorious* used to describe Eve:

- **child of God:** Like Adam, Eve was created in the image of the Almighty (see Moses 6:9).
- **eternal motherhood:** Eve is the only child of God who has the eternal role to be the "mother of all living"—an appellation given to her by God and confirmed by Adam (see Moses 4:26; see also Genesis 3:20).

- **wisely discerning:** Eve had the capacity to weigh choices and act in ways to support the ultimate design of God for His children. When she was "beguiled" by Satan to partake of the forbidden fruit, she realized that the consequences of transgressing would be in the best interests of her children "as the mother of all living"—for they could not "live" in the eternal sense unless the plan of happiness were enacted, based on the agency of man. She, therefore, used her God-given agency in wisdom, for the Lord had extended that privilege, albeit with explicit consequences (see Moses 3:17). In careful consideration of what was at stake, Eve made the conscious decision to partake of the fruit (see Moses 4:6–13). As she later described her position with respect to this decision—having learned of the great plan of salvation from the Lord—Eve articulated her profound insight in the form of a glorious pronouncement (see Moses 5:11).

- **willing to sacrifice:** Through her conscious transgression, Eve took upon herself the agony and suffering attendant with bringing forth offspring (see Genesis 3:16; Moses 4:22).
- **industrious:** When the Lord expelled Adam and Eve from the Garden of Eden to till the earth, the couple initiated a partnership of productivity (see Moses 5:1). Thus, Eve was a laboring soul, just like her husband. They both worked toward the success of their commission as "our first parents" (1 Nephi 5:11).
- **prayerful:** Eve joined with her husband in fervent prayer, leading to the reception of further light and knowledge concerning God's love and compassion for them and the majesty of the plan of salvation and redemption (see Moses 5:4–10).
- **receptive and obedient:** "And Adam and Eve blessed the name of God, and they made all things known unto their sons and their daughters. . . . And Adam and Eve, his wife, ceased not to call upon God" (Moses 5:12, 16).
- **compassionate and concerned:** When her son Cain descended into the abyss of sin, Eve joined with her husband in the deepest sorrow (see Moses 5:27).

- **a great educator:** According to the record, Adam and Eve encouraged their offspring to keep a record of their experiences in mortality and, thus, to remember the covenants and promises and blessings of the Lord (see Moses 6:5–6).

Indeed, "our glorious Mother Eve" (D&C 138:39) was a child of God and the epitome of eternal motherhood—wisely discerning, willing to sacrifice, industrious, prayerful, receptive and obedient, compassionate with and concerned for her children, and a great educator. Such a glorious and noble personality is an abiding example for her posterity through all generations of time.

EZEKIAS

Ezekias is mentioned in the genealogical lineage leading to Jesus Christ (see Matthew 1:9–10). Ezekias is the Greek form of the name Hezekiah.

FATHER IN HEAVEN

The encompassing influence and divine leadership of our Father in Heaven is pervasive throughout the events of the New Testament chronicle, as it is in all dimensions and aspects of the human experience from the beginning of time. Our Father in Heaven—as presented in holy writ and confirmed to the devout and faithful through the Holy Ghost—is the Supreme Lord and God of all Creation, the Eternal Source of light and truth, the benevolent and ever-loving Father of our spirits (see Hebrews 12:9; 1 John 4:7–8), the Author of the glorious gospel plan of happiness (see Abraham 3:23, 27), the Exemplar of the pattern for all holiness and perfection, the merciful Grantor of agency unto His children, and the Benefactor of all mankind through the gift of His Only Begotten Son, whose atoning sacrifice empowers the process for achieving immortality and exaltation: "For God so loved the world, that he gave his only begotten Son, that whosoever believeth in him should not perish, but have everlasting life" (John 3:16). It is to our Father in Heaven that we pray, in the name of Jesus Christ, as directed by Jesus Christ Himself (see Matthew 6:9; 19:6–7; Luke 11:12; John 20:17; 2 Nephi 32:9; 3 Nephi 13:9; 18:19–23, 30; 19:6–7; 20:31; D&C 20:77, 79).

Our Father in Heaven has granted unto Jesus Christ the sacred commission to be His agent in governing and directing the unfolding of the divine gospel plan for the benefit of all humankind. The Savior declared during His intercessory prayer, "And this is life eternal, that they might know thee the only true God, and Jesus Christ, whom thou hast sent" (John 17:3). Later, the resurrected Savior admonished the Saints in ancient America, "Therefore I would that ye should be perfect even as I, or your Father who is in heaven is perfect" (3 Nephi 12:48; see also Matthew 5:48). In the latter days, He has assured the Saints concerning the harmony and oneness of the Godhead: "Which Father, Son, and Holy Ghost are one God, infinite and eternal, without end. Amen" (D&C 20:28).

The sacred unity of purpose reflected among the three members of the Godhead makes the term *God* or *Lord* in the scriptures often interchangeable in regard to the Father and the Son. But there are distinctions among the individual beings of the Godhead. Through the Prophet Joseph Smith was revealed this verity: "The Father has a body of flesh and bones as tangible as man's; the Son also; but the Holy Ghost has not a body of flesh and bones, but is a personage of Spirit. Were it not so, the Holy Ghost could not dwell in us" (D&C 130:22). Moreover, as Joseph Smith also confirmed, the Father has preeminence: "Everlasting covenant was made between three personages before the organization of this earth, and relates to their dispensation of things to men on the earth; these personages, according to Abraham's record, are called God the first, the Creator; God the second, the Redeemer; and God the third, the witness or Testator" (*TPJS*, 190). Paul declared, "But to us there is but one God, the Father, of

Heavenly Father presides at the Grand Council.

whom are all things, and we in him; and one Lord Jesus Christ, by whom are all things, and we by him" (1 Corinthians 8:6).

Because Jesus Christ is the divine Agent within the expanse of the Father's eternal dominion and infinite design, it is, for the most part, Jesus Christ who is the One revealed in the holy scriptures. On occasion, the Father makes His presence known, largely as a confirming witness to the mission of the Savior. At the baptism of the Savior, the Holy Ghost was manifested in the form of a dove, and the Father's voice was heard from heaven, saying, "This is my beloved Son, in whom I am well pleased" (Matthew 3:17). On the Mount of Transfiguration where Elias [Elijah] and Moses appeared to Peter, James, and John in the presence of the Savior, the same voice reverberated over the scene: "Behold, a bright cloud overshadowed them: and behold a voice out of the cloud, which said, This is my beloved Son, in whom I am well pleased; hear ye him" (Matthew 17:5). At the martyrdom of Stephen, we learn, "But he, being full of the Holy Ghost, looked up stedfastly into heaven, and saw the glory of God, and Jesus standing on the right hand of God, And said, Behold, I see the heavens opened, and the Son of man standing on the right hand of God" (Acts 7:55–56). As the risen Lord was about to appear before the assembled faithful at Bountiful in ancient America, the voice of the Father proclaimed the words of introduction: "Behold my Beloved Son, in whom I am well pleased, in whom I have glorified my name—hear ye him" (3 Nephi 11:7; see also 2 Nephi 31:11, 15). In our day, the boy Joseph Smith learned firsthand the individuality of the Father and the Son, as revealed in the First Vision: "When the light rested upon me I saw two Personages, whose brightness and glory

defy all description, standing above me in the air. One of them spake unto me, calling me by name and said, pointing to the other—This is My Beloved Son. Hear Him!" (JS–H 1:17).

In all of these instances, the Father is presented for what He is: an individual being of infinite glory who is the supreme God for us all. In all of these instances, as well, the divine commission of the Son is authenticated and validated. We pray to and worship the Father, always in the name of the Son.

Jehovah (Jesus Christ) is the Word presented as God in the Old Testament and confirmed as such in the New Testament account: "In the beginning was the Word, and the Word was with God, and the Word was God" (John 1:1). By the process of divine investiture, Jehovah speaks for the Father and as the Father. To Moses, Jehovah declared, as if officiating in the office of the Father, "I am the Beginning and the End, the Almighty God; by mine Only Begotten I created these things; yea, in the beginning I created the heaven, and the earth upon which thou standest" (Moses 2:1). He expressed the heavenly mission as follows: "For behold, this is my work and glory—to bring to pass the immortality and eternal life of man" (Moses 1:39). Within this context, Jehovah (Jesus Christ) is indeed the Father of the faithful in the sense that they are adopted into His fold and become His seed through obedience to the gospel plan: "And being made perfect, he became the author of eternal salvation unto all them that obey him" (Hebrews 5:9).

We can thank our Father in Heaven for His surpassing perfection; His mercy, goodness, mighty deeds, and wondrous works; His creative majesty and power; His greatness, holiness, and glory; His kindness in answering our prayers and keeping His covenants; and His loving-kindness,

PAUL TESTIFIES BEFORE FELIX.

righteous judgment, understanding, and ultimate victory in the battle for our souls. We can thank His Only Begotten Son (the Messiah) for the Atonement as consummated in the meridian of time and reported with wondrous elegance and surpassing inspiration in the pages of the New Testament. And we can strive with all our heart, might, mind, and strength to live worthy of the matchless blessings given by the Father, Son, and Holy Ghost.

FELIX (MEANING: HAPPY.)

Felix was the procurator of Judea to whom Paul was referred on a complaint by the Jewish authorities. Paul handled himself with dignity and persuasiveness (see Acts 24:14–16). Felix, "having more perfect knowledge of that way" (i.e., of the Christian doctrine and practice),

deferred giving judgment but detained Paul in protective custody (Acts 24:22). A few days later, Felix, in company of his wife Drusilla, "sent for Paul, and heard him concerning the faith in Christ. And as he reasoned of righteousness, temperance, and judgment to come, Felix trembled, and answered, "Go thy way for this time; when I have a convenient season, I will call for thee" (Acts 24:24–25). Paul, not producing any bribe as Felix might have hoped, was retained in confinement with some liberties of association with friends for a period of two years, while Felix himself was summoned to Rome to answer charges of mishandling his stewardship. The successor to Felix, Porcius Festus, found Paul still confined and took steps to bring him to trial in Jerusalem, causing Paul to appeal the case to Caesar.

FESTUS

Porcius Festus, succeeding Felix as procurator of Judea, brought Paul before the judgment seat at Caesarea, intending to arrange for his trial at Jerusalem. When Paul claimed the right of jurisdiction in Rome, Festus declared, "Hast thou appealed unto Cæsar? unto Cæsar shalt thou go" (Acts 25:12). Meanwhile, King Agrippa (Herod Agrippa II) and his sister Bernice arrived at Caesarea, and Paul was given a hearing before the king. After Paul had presented his case and borne witness to the truth, the following interchange occurred:

> And as he thus spake for himself, Festus said with a loud voice, Paul, thou art beside thyself; much learning doth make thee mad.
>
> But he said, I am not mad, most noble Festus; but speak forth the words of truth and soberness.
>
> For the king knoweth of these things, before whom also I speak freely: for I am persuaded that none of these things are hidden from him; for this thing was not done in a corner.
>
> King Agrippa, believest thou the prophets? I know that thou believest.
>
> Then Agrippa said unto Paul, Almost thou persuadest me to be a Christian. (Acts 26:24–28)

After conferring with his associates, Agrippa, convinced of Paul's innocence, said to Festus, "This man might have been set at liberty, if he had not appealed unto Cæsar" (Acts 26:32). Thereafter, arrangements were made to send Paul to Rome. Festus remained in office for two years before passing away.

FULLER/FULLERS

There is only one reference to *fuller* in the New Testament (in connection with the radiant appearance of the Savior while on the Mount of Transfiguration with Peter, James, and John) (see Matthew 17:3; Mark 9:3). The work of the fullers as a trade was to cleanse garments and render them white (see Jeremiah 2:22; Malachi 3:2). The so-called fuller's field (see 2 Kings 18:17; Isaiah 7:3; 36:2; 2 Nephi 17:3) was an area near the walls of Jerusalem where the fullers could carry on their trade.

GABRIEL (MEANING: MAN OF GOD.)

Gabriel was an angelic messenger who accomplished important priesthood errands for the Lord, including giving instructions to the prophet Daniel concerning the coming mission of the Messiah (see Daniel 9:20-27). When the mortal mission of the Messiah was about to unfold, it was the same Gabriel who appeared to Zacharias and informed him that his wife, Elisabeth, would give birth to a son, whose name was to be John and whose mission would be to prepare the way for the Savior:

> And thou shalt have joy and gladness; and many shall rejoice at his birth.
>
> For he shall be great in the sight of the Lord, and shall drink neither wine nor strong drink; and he shall be filled with the Holy Ghost, even from his mother's womb.
>
> And many of the children of Israel shall he turn to the Lord their God.

GABRIEL APPEARED TO MARY IN NAZARETH TO ANNOUNCE THAT SHE WOULD BE THE MOTHER OF CHRIST.

And he shall go before him in the spirit and power of Elias, to turn the hearts of the fathers to the children, and the disobedient to the wisdom of the just; to make ready a people prepared for the Lord.

And Zacharias said unto the angel, Whereby shall I know this? for I am an old man, and my wife well stricken in years.

And the angel answering said unto him, I am Gabriel, that stand in the presence of God; and am sent to speak unto thee, and to shew thee these glad tidings. (Luke 1:14–19)

Subsequently, Gabriel appeared to Mary in Nazareth and announced that she would bring forth a son, even Jesus, the anointed Son of God (see Luke 1:26–33).

Who is this Gabriel? From the Prophet Joseph Smith, we learn that he is none other than Noah, the ancient patriarch: "Then [the priesthood was given] to Noah, who is Gabriel: he stands next in authority to Adam in the Priesthood; he was called of God to this office, and was the father of all living in this day, and to him was given the dominion" (*TPJS*, 157; see also *HC* 3:385).

GADARENES

Inhabitants of the city of Gadara. (See the entry for Gergesenes.)

GAIUS

1. Gaius was a Roman emperor. (See the entry for Augustus, item 3.)

2. Gaius was a Christian of Macedonia who was with Paul in Ephesus during the uprising of the silversmiths: "And the whole city was filled with confusion: and having caught Gaius and Aristarchus, men of Macedonia, Paul's companions in travel, they rushed with one accord into the theatre" (see Acts 19:29).

3. Gaius of Derbe accompanied Paul into Asia and on to Jerusalem (see Acts 20:4).

4. Gaius of Corinth was a prominent Christian at whose home Paul was staying while he prepared the Epistle to the Romans: "Gaius mine host, and of the whole church, saluteth you" (Romans 16:23).

5. Gaius was a man of Corinth baptized by Paul (see 1 Corinthians 1:14). (Possibly the same as the individual in item 4.)

6. Gaius was a Christian in Asia Minor to whom the third epistle of John was addressed: "The elder unto the wellbeloved Gaius, whom I love in the truth" (3 John 1:1).

GALATIANS (THE GREEK NAME FOR GALLIA OR GAUL.)

The Galatians were residents of Galatia, the central region of Asia Minor. Paul visited Galatia on his second journey (see Acts 16:6) and also on his third journey (see Acts 18:23). The epistle of Paul to the Galatians emphasizes faith and spirituality as the core of the gospel, as contrasted with worship based on externalities.

GALLIO

Gallio was proconsul of the Roman province of Achaia, under emperor Claudius, at the time of Paul's visit at Corinth. When the Jews brought charges against Paul, claiming that he was persuading people to worship contrary to the provisions of the law, Gallio spoke out, even before Paul could defend himself, saying, "If it were a matter of wrong or wicked lewdness, O ye Jews, reason would that I should bear with you: But if it be a question of words and names, and of your law, look ye to it; for I will be no judge of such matters. And he drave them from the judgment seat" (Acts 18:14–16). When the Greek citizens then took Sosthenes, the chief ruler of the synagogue, "and beat him before the judgment seat" (Acts 18:17), Gallio looked the other way. Gallio was the elder brother of the philosopher Seneca. Paul was before Gallio, likely in the fall of AD 51 (see Acts 18:12).

GAMALIEL (Meaning: reward of God.)

Gamaliel was a Pharisee of great influence among the Jewish leaders and "a doctor of the law, had in reputation among all the people" (Acts 5:34). When Peter and John were arrested and imprisoned, an angel of the Lord delivered them and instructed them to go and preach in the temple "all the words of this life" (Acts 5:20). The high priest then located them and arranged for them to be delivered before the council (Sanhedrin) to answer charges. Peter then stood forth to bear witness of the truth (see Acts 5:29–32).

When the Jewish leaders were about to lay their hands on the Christians, Gamaliel stood forth to counsel moderation: "Ye men of Israel, take heed to yourselves what ye intend to do as touching these men. . . . Refrain from these men, and let them alone: for if this counsel or this work be of men, it will come to nought: But if it be of God, ye cannot overthrow it; lest haply ye

be found even to fight against God" (Acts 5:35, 38–39). Thereafter, the crowd beat the Apostles and, commanding them not to speak in the name of Jesus, let them go. "And they departed from the presence of the council, rejoicing that they were counted worthy to suffer shame for his name" (Acts 5:41). Paul himself was a student of Gamaliel (see Acts 22:3).

GENTILE/GENTILES (Meaning: nations.)

The word *gentiles* as used in the scriptures refers generally to those peoples who are not of the House of Israel. Gentiles can also refer to nations that do not yet have the gospel—even though there may be those of Israelite lineage among them (see Bible Dictionary, 679).

In the New Testament the word *Gentiles* or *Gentile* is used 101 times, largely in the context of the unfolding of the gospel message beyond those of Israelite heritage to encompass the entire world, as the charge of the Savior commanded: "Go ye therefore, and teach all nations, baptizing them in the name of the Father, and of the Son, and of the Holy Ghost: Teaching them to observe all things whatsoever I have commanded you: and, lo, I am with you alway, even unto the end of the world" (Matthew 28:19–20). Examples of this process include the baptism of the Ethiopian eunuch by Philip (see Acts 8), the baptism of the centurion Cornelius by Peter (see Acts 10–11), and the expansive missionary outreach of Paul, who called himself "the apostle of the Gentiles" (Romans 11:13).

GERGESENES

The Gergesenes were inhabitants of the village of Gergesa, close to the eastern shore of the Sea of Galilee. It was in that vicinity that Christ encountered two individuals possessed of evil spirits. The Savior cast the evil spirits into a herd of swine, which subsequently ran into the sea and perished (see Matthew 8:28–32).

Thereafter the keepers of the swine went and told all to the inhabitants of the city, who came forth to Jesus and bade Him—no doubt, out of fear—to leave their coastal area (see Matthew 8:33–34). In the account in Mark, the locale is given as "the country of the Gadarenes" (Mark 5:1; see also Luke 8:26)—meaning inhabitants of the city of Gadara, also located in that vicinity. Jesus is reported to have said to the man possessed of evil spirits (only one man, not two as in Matthew), "Go home to thy friends, and tell them how great things the Lord hath done for thee, and hath compassion on thee" (Mark 5;19; see also Luke 8:39).

GIDEON (MEANING: WARRIOR.)

Gideon is rendered Gedeon (the Greek form of the name) in the New Testament, occurring just once (in Paul's discourse of faith) (see Hebrews 11:32). Gideon was one of the leading figures represented in the book of Judges covering the turbulent period of time commencing with the death of Joshua (around 1477 BC) and extending to the birth of Samuel (around 1125 BC). The judgeship of Gideon commenced around 1263 BC. He was called to deliver Israel from bondage under the Midianites (see Judges 6:14). Gideon obeyed the command of the Lord to destroy the altar of Baal and the associated ceremonial grove (see Judges 6:28), thus earning the alternative name Jerubbaal (meaning "he that striveth against Baal") (see Judges 6:32; 7:1; 1 Samuel 12:11). He then prevailed over the forces of the Midianites by following the guidance of the Lord and applying an abundance of strategic know-

how to compensate for the smallness of his own army. Though triumphant, Gideon refused the kingship (see Judges 8:23). Gideon is remembered fondly as an exemplar of the victorious champion of right (see Isaiah 9:4; Hebrews 11:32).

GOD (SEE THE ENTRIES FOR FATHER IN HEAVEN, JESUS CHRIST, AND HOLY GHOST.)

GOD-FEARER (SEE THE ENTRY FOR PROSELYTES.)

GOG

The name Gog appears just once in the New Testament, in the prophecy concerning the final phase of earth's history at the end of the Millennium (see Revelation 20:6–9).

Gog was a ruler over the land and nation of Magog as cited in Ezekiel 38 and 39. Gog's predicted aggression against Israel and his ultimate defeat is emblematic of the final victory of the forces of God against evil—both at the time of the Second Coming and ultimately at the end of the millennial period in the so-called battle of Gog and Magog (see Revelation 20:7–9; see also D&C 88:110–116, concerning the final triumph of Michael and his forces against Satan and his minions).

GRECIANS/GREEKS

The inhabitants of Greece are identified as descendants of Javan in the Old Testament (see Genesis 10:1–2). The book of Daniel refers to the land "Grecia" (see Daniel 8:21; 10:20; 11:2) and the book of Zechariah to the land of "Greece" (see Zechariah 9:13). The New Testament refers only once to "Greece" (see Acts 20:2) but three times uses the word *Grecians* (i.e., Hellenists or Greek-speaking Jews): (1) "And in those days, when the

PAUL TEACHES THE PEOPLE OF ATHENS.

number of the disciples was multiplied, there arose a murmuring of the Grecians against the Hebrews, because their widows were neglected in the daily ministration" (Acts 6:1). In response to this event, the Apostles called "seven men of honest report, full of the Holy Ghost and wisdom" (Acts 6:3) to provide the needed service; (2) "And he [Paul] spake boldly in the name of the Lord Jesus, and disputed against the Grecians: but they went about to slay him. Which when the brethren knew, they brought him down to Cæsarea, and sent him forth to Tarsus" (Acts 9:29–30). Paul, recently converted, had challenged the Grecians (Jews of foreign heritage) and was now accepted by the disciples; (3) "And some of them [the followers of Christ] were men of Cyprus and Cyrene, which, when they were come to Antioch, spake unto the Grecians, preaching the Lord Jesus. And the hand of the Lord was with them:

and a great number believed, and turned unto the Lord" (Acts 11:20–21). Again, these Grecians were evidently Greek-speaking Jews of foreign descent now living in the Holy Land.

The word *Greeks* or *Greek* is used rather frequently in the New Testament and generally designates "Hellenes" (i.e., individuals of Greek descent), as in John 12:20 and Acts 14:1 (see Bible Dictionary, 697). The gospel was preached in Greek as soon as the missionary program extended beyond Palestine. "We know that Jesus spoke Aramaic and that the Gospels as we now have them were almost certainly composed originally in Greek" (*JCWNT*, 53).

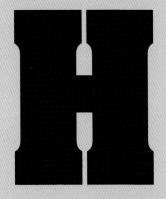

Heathen

The word *heathen* appears 142 times in the Old Testament and seven times in the New Testament (the plural form is not used in the scriptures)—in general as a way to distinguish the Lord's covenant people from the other nations of the earth. According to the commission of the Abrahamic Covenant (see Genesis 17:1-7; Abraham 2:8-11), the gospel is to be preached to all nations—including the heathen nations. The blessings of the priesthood are to be extended to all who will receive them in faith and devotion (see Galatians 3:7-9).

Heber (See the entry for Eber.)

Hebrews

Abraham was identified as a Hebrew (see Genesis 14:13; the first occurrence of the word in the Old Testament), as were Joseph in Egypt (see Genesis 39:14) and all of the Israelites during their sojourn in that country (Genesis 43:17; Exodus 1:15-19; 2:6-7, 11, 13). The Lord identified Himself as the God of the Hebrews when He called Moses into service (see Exodus 3:18; 5:3; 7:16; 9:1, 13; 10:3). Following the Exodus and the transition into the promised land, the covenant people were referred to as Hebrews, in contrast with the indigenous peoples (see 1 Samuel 4:6, 9; 13:3, 7, 19; 14:11, 21; 29:3). The word *Hebrew* may derive from an original word meaning "to cross" or "go beyond" (e.g., the other side of a river) or from a name such as Eber (or Heber), one of the ancestors of Abraham (see Genesis 10:21-25).

The word *Hebrews* occurs only three times in the New Testament: (1) "And in those days, when the number of the disciples was multiplied, there arose a murmuring of the Grecians against the Hebrews, because their widows were neglected in the daily ministration" (Acts 6:1); (2) in the words of Paul: "Are they Hebrews? so am I. Are they Israelites? so am I. Are they the seed of Abraham? so am I" (2 Corinthians 11:22); and (3) in Paul's self-characterization: "If any other man thinketh that he hath whereof he might trust in the flesh, I more: Circumcised the eighth day, of the stock of Israel, of the tribe of Benjamin, an

Hebrew of the Hebrews; as touching the law, a Pharisee" (Philippians 3:4–5). Except for the use of the word *Hebrew* in this last-cited reference, all uses of the word *Hebrew* (singular) in the New Testament (a total of eleven) refer to the Hebrew tongue, which was the language used in learned circles of legal and religious discourse among the Hebrew people, whereas Aramaic was the language of the common man.

HEROD

The Herodian family dynasty encompassed many individuals who figured into the New Testament chronicle, as outlined in the following chart:

Level One: Herod the Great (king from 37 BC to 4 BC; see Matthew 2:3)
  Level Two:
  • Aristobulus (by Herod's wife Mariamne I)
  • Herod Philip (by Mariamne II, daughter of Simon the high priest; see Matthew 14:3; Mark 6:17; Luke 3:19)
  • Herod Archelaus (by Herod's wife Malthace): ethnarch of Judea, Samaria, and Idumea, 4 BC to AD 6 (see Matthew 2:22)

• Herod Antipas (by Herod's wife Malthace): tetrarch of Galilee and Perea, 4 BC to AD 39 (see Matthew 14:1; Mark 6:14; Luke 9:7)
• Herod Philip (by Herod's wife Cleopatra): tetrarch of Ituraea and Trachonitis, 4 BC to AD 33–34 (see Luke 3:1)
  Level Three:
• Marcus Julius Agrippa I (also known as Herod Agrippa I; son of Aristobulus): tetrarch of Gaulanitis and Trachonitis (beginning AD 37), and Galilee and Perea (AD 39), and then king all of greater Judea (AD 41–44; see Acts 12:1–23)
• Herodias (sister of Marcus Julius Agrippa I): married to Herod Philip and later married Herod Antipas; her daughter was Salome (see Matthew 14:3; Mark 6:17)
  Level Four: (children of Marcus Julius Agrippa I, known as Herod Agrippa I)
• Bernice (mistress of the future emperor Titus; see Acts 25:13)
• Marcus Julius Agrippa II (also known as Herod Agrippa II): ruled region northeast of the Sea of Galilee from AD 55 until his death sometime before AD 93 (see Acts 25:13)
• Drusilla (wife of Antonius Felix, procurator of Judea, AD 52 to AD 59–60; see Acts 24:24)

The Herodian family were converts to the Jewish faith and aspired to establish and maintain a semi-independent realm, under the protection of Roman power (see also the genealogical chart in the Bible Dictionary, 701; also the Herodian Dynasty Chart in *JCWNT*, 38, 157).

HEROD AGRIPPA I

Also known as Marcus Julius Agrippa I, he was the son of Aristobulus and grandson of Herod the Great. During his tenure, Herod Agrippa I was tetrarch of Gaulanitis and Trachonitis (beginning AD 37), plus Galilee and Perea (AD 39), and then king of all greater Judea (AD 41–44). Following the Crucifixion of the Lord, Herod Agrippa I put James, brother of John, to death and would have eliminated Peter had an angel not intervened to liberate him (see Acts 12:1–10). His life of infamy was ended by the judgment of God: "And upon a set day Herod, arrayed in royal apparel, sat upon his throne, and made an oration unto them. And the people gave a shout, saying, It is the voice of a god, and not of a man. And immediately the angel of the Lord smote him, because he gave not God the glory: and he was eaten of worms, and gave up the ghost" (Acts 12:21–23).

HEROD ANTIPAS

Herod Antipas, son of king Herod the Great by his wife Malthace, was governor of Galilee and Perea during the entire period of the life of the Savior. He was identified as "Herod the tetrarch" in a number of passages of the New Testament (see Matthew 14:1; Luke 3:19; 9:7; Acts 13:1). His life was characterized by misdeeds and lack of honor. He was responsible for the beheading of John the Baptist (see Matthew 14:1–12). Later, when Pilate learned that Jesus belonged to the jurisdiction of Herod Antipas, he sent Him to be examined by Herod (see Luke 23:8–11)

HERODIANS

The Herodians constituted a Jewish political party sympathetic to the cause of Herodian family leadership. The famous dictum of the Savior about how to serve Caesar as well as God came in the context of an audience with the Herodians and the Pharisees: "Then saith he unto them, Render therefore unto Cæsar the things which are Cæsar's; and unto God the things that are God's" (Matthew 22:21; see also Mark 12:13).

Herodians are also mentioned in connection with the event where the Savior healed a man on the Sabbath: "And the Pharisees went forth, and straightway took counsel with the Herodians against him, how they might destroy him" (Mark 3:6).

HERODIAS

Herodias was the sister of Marcus Julius Agrippa I, also known as Herod Agrippa I. She married Herod Philip, her uncle and stepbrother of Herod Antipas, and then later left him to marry Herod Antipas, her step-uncle. John the Baptist censured Herod Antipas for this relationship (see Matthew 14:4), for which Herod then imprisoned him and later caused him to be beheaded at the request of the daughter of Herodias (see Matthew 14:10). In the account given in Mark, it is stated that it was Herodias herself who counseled her daughter to ask for the head of John the Baptist (see Mark 6:24). The daughter was Salome (not named in the New Testament account).

HIGH PRIEST

The office of high priest in the Melchizedek Priesthood has been a cardinal position in the governance of the kingdom of God from the beginning.

The New Testament contains fifty-five references to the title *high priest*—covering a wide span of events and relationships constituting a major contrast between two divergent applications of the term: one presenting the "high priest" as the defining essence of the leadership movement designed to thwart, repress, and destroy the work of the Savior, and the other presenting the "high priest"—even "the Apostle and High Priest of our profession, Christ Jesus" (Hebrews 3:1)—as the central exemplar of divine leadership. On the one hand, we see the retributive and scheming nature of the high priest Annas or the high priest Caiaphas (see the entries for those persons), and on the other hand we see the contrasting nature set forward by Paul, based on the life and example of Jesus:

> And no man taketh this honour unto himself, but he that is called of God, as was Aaron.
>
> So also Christ glorified not himself to be made an high priest; but he that said unto him, Thou art my Son, to day have I begotten thee.
>
> As he saith also in another place, Thou art a priest for ever after the order of Melchisedec.
>
> Who in the days of his flesh, when he had offered up prayers and supplications with strong crying and tears unto him that was able to save him from death, and was heard in that he feared;
>
> Though he were a Son, yet learned he obedience by the things which he suffered;
>
> And being made perfect, he became the author of eternal salvation unto all them that obey him; Called of God an high priest after the order of Melchisedec. (Hebrews 5:4–10)

The sacrificial service of the high priesthood through all generations was a prefigurement of the atoning work of the great High Priest, as Paul confirms (see Hebrews 9:11–12, 15).

When the Great Apostasy brought an end to the succession of divinely appointed priesthood offices and administrative systems restored by the Savior, the office of high priest was placed in reserve until "the times of refreshing" could come "from the presence of the Lord" (Acts 3:19) and until "the times of restitution of all things" (Acts 3:21) could be inaugurated with the advent of the dispensation of the fulness of times in our day.

Holy Ghost

The Holy Ghost is the third member of the Godhead. The presence of the Holy Ghost in the New Testament text is pervasive, the term *Holy Ghost* being used ninety times (including two instances with "gift of the Holy Ghost"), *Spirit of God* twelve times, *Spirit of the Lord* five times, *Holy Spirit* four times, *Comforter* four times, and *Spirit* (capitalized to indicate a member of the Godhead) dozens of times. Some of the key manifestations of the Holy Ghost in the New Testament include the following:

- the divine conception of Jesus (see Matthew 1:18; Luke 1:35)
- the promise of Gabriel concerning the coming of John the Baptist (see Luke 1:15, 31, 67)
- the ministry of John the Baptist as a forerunner to Jesus (see Matthew 3:11; Mark 1:8; Luke 3:16; John 1:33)
- the baptism of Jesus Christ (see Matthew 3:16; Mark 1:10; Luke 3:22; John 1:32; 1 Nephi 11:27; 2 Nephi 31:8; D&C 93:15)

- the Savior being led by the Holy Ghost into the wilderness (see Luke 4:1)
- The Savior's teachings about the sacredness of the witness of the Holy Ghost (see Matthew 12:31–32; also Mark 3:29; Luke 12:10)
- the Savior's promise of guidance to His disciples through the Holy Ghost (see Mark 13:11; also Luke 12:12)
- The Savior on the power of prayer (see Luke 11:13)
- the Savior's commission to the Twelve on missionary work (see Matthew 28:19–20)
- the Savior's teachings about the Holy Ghost (as a gift) to be given after His earthly mission was completed (see John 7:38–39)
- the resurrected Lord bestowing the Holy Ghost on His disciples (see John 20:19–23)
- the resurrected Lord, having spent forty days instructing them, now promising His disciples that they should soon act through the Holy Ghost to carry out their mission (see Acts 1:4–9; 11:15–16)
- the dispensing of the Holy Ghost on the Day of Pentecost (see Acts 2:1–4)
- Peter's discourse on the Day of Pentecost (see Acts 2:38–39)
- Peter's testimony before Annas, Caiaphas, and their associates (see Acts 4:8, 10–12, 31)
- the calling of the seven special ministers (see Acts 6:3)
- the martyrdom of Stephen (see Acts 7:55).
- the conversion of Paul (see Acts 9:17)
- growth of the Church (see Acts 9:31)
- Peter's manifestation that the gift of the Holy Ghost was available to all believers of any extraction (see Acts 10:44–47; 15:8)
- the calling of new leaders (see Acts 13:2–3)
- guidance by the Spirit (see Acts 8:29; 16:6)
- Paul teaching the correct mode of baptism (see Acts 19:6)
- Paul concerning the Holy Ghost as the agent of divine love (see Romans 5:5)
- Paul on the Spirit's influence to confirm our true identity (see Romans 8:14)
- Paul on the blessings of the Spirit (see 1 Corinthians 2:9–11; Isaiah 64:4)
- Paul on the sanctity of the body (see 1 Corinthians 6:19–20; 3:16)
- Paul on personal revelation (see 1 Corinthians 12:3)
- Paul on the Spirit as the agent of deliverance (see 2 Corinthians 3:17)
- Paul on the Holy Spirit of Promise (see Ephesians 1:13)
- Paul on the purifying influence of the Spirit through the covenant (see Hebrews 10:15–17; Jeremiah 31:31–33)
- Peter on the Holy Ghost as the inspiration for scripture (see 2 Peter 1:20–21)
- John on how to identify the Spirit (see 1 John 4:2)
- John on the three members of the Godhead (see 1 John 5:7)

From the Creation forward, the Holy Spirit, as God's agent of light and truth, is found at work through all the generations of time guiding, illuminating, warning, counseling, confirming, and blessing the lives of God's children—through both prophet-leaders and inspired laypersons within the kingdom.

So important is the role of the Holy Ghost that the only transgression that would place an individual outside the grasp of redemption from the second death (a separation from God) is to commit blasphemy against the Holy

Ghost: "Having denied the Holy Spirit after having received it, and having denied the Only Begotten Son of the Father, having crucified him unto themselves and put him to an open shame" (D&C 76:35; see also D&C 132:27). By way of contrast is the grand and glorious fulfillment of one's celestial destiny through honor and obedience, according to the views reflected in the inspired prayer of the Prophet Joseph Smith: "And that they may grow up in thee, and receive a fulness of the Holy Ghost, and be organized according to thy laws, and be prepared to obtain every needful thing" (D&C 109:15; see also 1 Nephi 10:17).

I

IMMANUEL (MEANING: GOD WITH US.)

The name Immanuel is equivalent to Emmanuel, the latter occurring only one time in the scriptures: "Behold, a virgin shall be with child, and shall bring forth a son, and they shall call his name Emmanuel, which being interpreted is, God with us" (Matthew 1:23). On the other hand, Immanuel does not occur in the New Testament but does occurs five times in other scriptural passages, as in the following: "Therefore the Lord himself shall give you a sign; Behold, a virgin shall conceive, and bear a son, and shall call his name Immanuel" (Isaiah 7:14; see also Isaiah 8:8; 2 Nephi 17:14; 18:8; D&C 128:22). (See the entry for Jesus Christ.)

ISAAC (MEANING: HE LAUGHETH.)

Isaac, son of Abraham, is mentioned twenty times in the New Testament, initially in the context of the genealogical lineage of the Savior (see Matthew 1:2; Luke 3:34) and often thereafter to revisit the theme of how the Lord identified Himself to Moses on the

ABRAHAM CONFERS THE BIRTHRIGHT TO ISAAC.

mount: "Moreover he said, I am the God of thy father, the God of Abraham, the God of Isaac, and the God of Jacob" (Exodus 3:6).

The New Testament cites this deific formula on several occasions (see Matthew 22:32; Mark 12:26; Luke 20:37; Acts 3:13; 7:32). Isaac is also mentioned a number of times to illustrate a point of doctrine: First, the Savior teaching about repentance (see Luke 13:28); second, Paul showing that Israel consists of the people of promise, but others outside of the seed of Israel can also have the blessings of the gospel on the basis of adoption through faith and obedience (see Romans 9:6–7; Galatians 4:28); third, Paul on the faith of Abraham and Isaac (see Hebrews 11:9–20); and fourth, James on the importance of both faith and works (see James 2:20–22).

ISAIAH (MEANING: THE LORD IS SALVATION.)

The prophet Isaiah, identified in the King James Version of the New Testament as Esaias—the Greek rendition of the name—is mentioned twenty-one times in that canon. Truly Isaiah was the consummate articulator of the coming atoning mission of the Savior, who, along with the gospel writers and stewards, cited the words of Isaiah with power in the following applications:

- prophecy about John the Baptist (see Isaiah 40:3; Matthew 3:3; Luke 3:4; John 1:23; the related passage in Mark 1:3 does not mention Esaias)
- prophecy about the coming of Christ to the land of inheritance of Zebulun and Naphtali (see Matthew 4:13–16; Isaiah 9:1–2)
- prophecy about the healing acts of the Savior (see Matthew 8:16–17; Isaiah 53:4)
- prophecy about the quiet and unpretentious acts of the Savior (see Matthew 12:15–21; Isaiah 42:1–3)

ISAIAH RECORDS PROPHECIES OF THE COMING MESSIAH.

- prophecy about the Savior speaking in parables: (see Matthew 13:13-17; Isaiah 29:10, 18; Jeremiah 5:21; the passage in Romans 11:10-12 invokes the same ancient prophecy without ascribing the words to Esaias).
- prophecy about the hardness of heart to prevail among future leaders in Israel, in this case the scribes and Pharisees (see Matthew 15: 6-9; Isaiah 29:13)
- prophecy about the coming of one anointed (i.e., the Messiah) to preach the gospel and bless the people (see Luke 4:16-21; Isaiah 61:1-2)
- prophecy about the Savior not being believed by the people (see Isaiah 29:10, 18; 53:1; John 12:37-41; Acts 28:23-28; Romans 10:15-17)
- prophecy about the atoning sacrifice of the Savior (see Acts 8:27-33)
- prophecy about the Lord saving a remnant of His people (Romans 9:25-29; Isaiah 10:20-23)

In his prophetic and inspired discourse, Isaiah captures with consummate skill the grand and sweeping contours of the Lord's plan for mankind. If blessings of peace and spiritual awakening are to be forthcoming unto Israel, then Israel must obey; the disobedient are to be scattered and chastened until they reform their ways. Nevertheless, in the Lord's due time, He will remember His promises to the faithful and reign as Lord and King in the midst of His children forever. Isaiah is unequalled in his ability to speak as if viewing a panoramic vista encompassing the entire range of the Lord's plan of salvation—from the premortal existence to the meridian of time to the millennial reign and the ultimate consummation of covenant blessings. Often Isaiah will span the entire range of man's existence in the space of a verse or two—always returning to the central theme of the Messiah, the Savior of mankind.

ISHMAEL (MEANING: GOD HEARETH.)

Ishmael, son of Abraham by Hagar, is not mentioned by name in the New Testament but is referred to by Paul in his discourse to the Galatians concerning becoming heirs of Christ through adoption (see Galatians 4:22-23). Speaking in terms of an allegory, Paul lets Ishmael represent the Mosaic law of limitation and outward ceremony while Isaac represents the higher law leading to spiritual liberation. These two positions are then said to constitute "two covenants" (Galatians 4:24)—or two different ways of viewing the pathway forward. Bruce R. McConkie has described this Pauline explication as follows:

> The first is the old covenant, the law of Moses, the law of carnal commandments, the preparatory gospel, the covenant God made with Israel, through Moses, to prepare them for the second. The second is the new covenant, the everlasting covenant, the fulness of the gospel, the covenant God offers to make with all men, through Christ, to prepare them for the fulness of his glory. The old covenant was the lesser law; the new is the higher law. Moses was the mediator of the old covenant, standing between God and his people, pleading

their cause, seeking to prepare them for the coming of their Messiah. Jesus is the mediator of the new covenant, standing between God and all men, pleading their cause, seeking to prepare them for that celestial inheritance reserved for the saints. (*DNTC*, 2:477)

Thus, Ishmael represents the old way of doing things (the way Paul's Jewish listeners, by tradition, had been practicing), and Isaac represents the new way that Christ has brought forward as the means for spiritual deliverance.

Through the magnificence of the plan of salvation and exaltation empowered through the Atonement, all the righteous, from whatever extraction, can become "joint-heirs with Christ; if so be that we suffer with him, that we may be also glorified together" (Romans 8:17).

ISHMAELITES (SEE ENTRY FOR ISHMAEL.)

ISRAEL (MEANING: ONE WHO PREVAILS WITH GOD OR LET GOD PREVAIL.)

During the time of his conflict with his twin brother, Esau, Jacob experienced an event in which he wrestled all night with a messenger from God who asked, "What is thy name? And he said, Jacob. And he said, Thy name shall be called no more Jacob, but Israel: for as a prince hast thou power with God and with men, and hast prevailed" (Genesis 32:27–28; see also Genesis 35:10; Hosea 12:1–5).

Thereafter, *Israel* was the name applied to Jacob and *Israel* or *Israelites* to his posterity: "All these are the twelve tribes of Israel: and this is it that their father spake unto them, and blessed them; every one according to his blessing he blessed them" (Genesis 49:28; see also Genesis 49:7, 16, 24; Exodus 3:13–16; 5:1; 19:5–6; 20:22; Deuteronomy 14:2; and frequently throughout the Old Testament, the New Testament, and the Book of Mormon). In due course, after the kingdom was separated into two, the northern part came to be designated Israel and the southern part Judah.

In a general sense, the term *Israel* is applied to all those who are true believers in Christ, as Paul explained, "Brethren, my heart's desire and prayer to God for Israel is, that they might be saved" (Romans 10:1; see also Romans 11:7; Galatians 6:16; Ephesians 2:12; 1 Peter 2:9). Similarly, the Doctrine and Covenants uses the term *Israel* to denote all of those belonging to the covenant people of God, literally or through adoption, according to their obedience to gospel principles.

The name *Israel* or *Israelites* occurs in the New Testament frequently (some seventy-seven times), often in connection with a phrase such as "people of Israel," "house of Israel," "children of Israel," "land of Israel," "God of Israel," "faith of Israel," and "King of Israel." Here are some examples from well-known passages:

- the unfolding of the character of John the Baptist (see Luke 1:80)
- Jesus, concerning the centurion who appealed unto him to heal his servant (see Matthew 8:10; see also Luke 7:9)
- Nathanael to Jesus (see John 1:49)
- Jesus to Nicodemus, who inquired about the meaning of being born again (see John 3:10)
- Jesus to the scribe who asked which of the commandments should be considered the primary one (see Mark 12:29–30)

- the scribes and elders mocking Jesus on the cross (see Matthew 27:42; Mark 15:32)
- the words of the two disciples on the way to Emmaus who, unbeknownst to them, were conversing with the resurrected Lord (see Luke 24:21)
- Peter, during his great sermon on the Day of Pentecost (see Acts 2:22)
- Paul, concerning the principle of adoption into the fold of Christ (see Romans 9:6)
- Paul, concerning the merciful invitation of the Lord to His often unresponsive people (see Romans 10:21)

ISRAELITES (SEE THE ENTRY FOR ISRAEL.)

Jacob (Meaning: supplanter.)

1. Jacob, the younger of the twin sons of Isaac and Rebekah, is mentioned fairly often in the New Testament, as in references concerning the lineage of the Savior (see Matthew 1:2; Luke 3:34; Acts 7:8); the annunciation of the coming of the Lord (see Luke 1:33); the trio of patriarchs Abraham, Isaac, and Jacob (see Matthew 8:11; Luke 13:28); references to the God of Abraham, Isaac, and Jacob (see Matthew 22:32; Mark 12:26; Luke 20:37; Acts 3:13; 7:32); the story of Jacob and Joseph (see Acts 7:12–15); the relationship of Jacob and Esau (see Romans 9:13); the reference to "the Deliverer" who "shall turn away ungodliness from Jacob" (Romans 11:26); the example of the faith of Jacob (see Hebrews 11:9, 20–21); and the conversation between the Savior and the Samaritan woman at Jacob's well concerning the living water (see John 4:11–13).

It was through Jacob and his seed that the covenant promises granted unto Abraham and Isaac were continued.

2. Jacob was the father of Joseph, husband of Mary, the mother of Jesus (see Matthew 1:15–16; Luke 3:23 also states that Heli is named as Joseph's father. Concerning these two differing genealogical lineages, see *JCWNT*, 111–113).

James

James is the anglicized form of the Hebrew name Jacob. The following individuals called James are included in the New Testament:

1. James, son of Zebedee and brother of John, received his call as one of the Twelve under the following circumstances:

> And Jesus, walking by the sea of Galilee, saw two brethren, Simon called Peter, and Andrew his brother, casting a net into the sea: for they were fishers.
>
> And he saith unto them, Follow me, and I will make you fishers of men.

And they straightway left *their* nets, and followed him.

And going on from thence, he saw other two brethren, James *the son* of Zebedee, and John his brother, in a ship with Zebedee their father, mending their nets; and he called them.

And they immediately left the ship and their father, and followed him. (Matthew 4:18-22; see also Mark 1:16-20; Luke 5:7-11)

When Jesus ordained His Apostles, He conferred special names on some: "And he ordained twelve, that they should be with him, and that he might send them forth to preach, And to have power to heal sicknesses, and to cast out devils: And Simon he surnamed Peter; And James the son of Zebedee, and John the brother of James; and he surnamed them Boanerges, which is, The sons of thunder" (Mark 3:14-17). James was one of the three Apostles who occupied a place of special leadership in the fold of the Savior, as confirmed by the following events:

- the restoring of life to the deceased twelve-year-old daughter of Jairus, one of the rulers of the synagogue (see Mark 5:37, 41; see also Luke 8:49-56)
- Transfiguration on the Mount (see Matthew 17:1-3; Mark 9:2-4; Luke 9:28-31)
- Garden of Gethsemane (see Matthew 26:36-38; see also Mark 14:32-34)

On one occasion, James and John approached the Savior with a special request: "Grant unto us that we may sit, one on thy right hand, and the

James writing an epistle.

other on thy left hand, in thy glory" (Mark 10:37). The Savior responded that such an honor was not His to give but, rather, would be reserved for those for whom it should be prepared. When the other ten Apostles were "displeased" with James and John on this occasion (see Mark 10:41), the Savior took the opportunity to teach a fundamental lesson about the kingdom of God: "Whosoever will be great among you, shall be your minister: And whosoever of you will be the chiefest, shall be servant of all. For even the Son of man came not to be ministered unto, but to minister, and to give his life a ransom for many" (Mark 10:43-45). Sometime later, on the mount of Olives, it was Peter, James, and John, in company with Andrew, who learned from the Savior that the temple complex would one day be destroyed and that they should take heed "lest any man deceive you:

For many shall come in my name, saying, I am Christ; and shall deceive many" (Mark 13:5-6). When the time drew nigh for the consummation of the Savior's atoning sacrifice, James and John were inclined to appeal to heaven for retributive force in the face of those who might reject Him or come against Him: "Lord, wilt thou that we command fire to come down from heaven, and consume them, even as Elias [Elijah] did [see 2 Kings 1:14]? But he turned, and rebuked them, and said, Ye know not what manner of spirit ye are of. For the Son of man is not come to destroy men's lives, but to save them" (Luke 9:54-56). The Savior would obediently go forward to consummate His anointed mission and do the will of the Father. As it turned out, James also gave his life when Herod Agrippa I killed him (see Acts 12:1-2), the only Apostle whose martyrdom is confirmed in the New Testament. (See the entry for Herod Agrippa I.)

James participated with Peter and John in the latter-day restoration of the Melchizedek Priesthood, most likely in late May 1829 (see D&C 27:12-13; 128:20)—following the restoration of the Aaronic Priesthood under the hands of John the Baptist on May 15, 1829 (see D&C 13).

2. James, son of Alphaeus, was also one of the Twelve (see Matthew 10:3; Mark 3:18; Luke 6:15; Acts 1:13).

3. James, known traditionally as "James the Just," was the brother of Jesus: "But other of the apostles saw I none, save James the Lord's brother" (Galatians 1:19; see also Jude 1:1). James also had other siblings, as the Lord's audience confirmed on one occasion: "Is not this the carpenter's son? is not his mother called Mary? and his brethren, James, and Joses, and Simon, and Judas? And his sisters, are they not all with

us? Whence then hath this man all these things?" (Matthew 13:55-56; see also Mark 6:3). James was an important leader in the early Church at Jerusalem, as confirmed by these references:

- When Peter was delivered from prison by an angel, he came to a gathering of friends who were astonished to see him (see Acts 12:17).
- James gave decisive leadership when the Apostles in Jerusalem were called together in a special council to resolve a dispute in Antioch concerning the Gentile converts and the Mosaic law of circumcision (see Acts 15:13-15, 19; 21:18; Galatians 2: 9-12).
- James was among those who witnessed the return of the resurrected Lord (see 1 Corinthians 15:5-8).

James evidently came into the fold later, following the Resurrection (see John 7:3-5; Acts 1:14). According to historical accounts, James was martyred around AD 62. He was, in all probability, the author of the Epistle of James, one of the earliest of the New Testament writings—predating the Gospels, which were written perhaps three decades following the Resurrection (*JCWNT*, 54, 272).

It was James's reference about prayer (see James 1:5-6) that prompted the boy Joseph Smith to go into the woods to pray in the spring of 1829, leading to the transcendent event of the First Vision and the dawning of the Restoration in our day.

4. James, known as "James the less," was among those who witnessed the Crucifixion: "There were also women looking on afar off: among whom was Mary Magdalene, and Mary the mother of James the less and of Joses, and Salome; (Who also, when he was in Galilee, followed him, and ministered unto him;) and many other women

which came up with him unto Jerusalem" (Mark 15:40-41; see also Matthew 27:55-56; Luke 24:10). Some think that James the less is identical with James in number two, above.

JANNES AND JAMBRES

Jannes (pronounced jan'-ees) and Jambres (pronounced jam-breez) were sorcerers or magicians who confronted Moses in Egypt and who were invoked by Paul as symbolic emblems of the corrupt and vile pretenders of the last days who would attempt to undermine gospel truths: "Now as Jannes and Jambres withstood Moses, so do these also resist the truth: men of corrupt minds, reprobate concerning the faith" (2 Timothy 3:8). The names Jannes and Jambres do not occur in the Old Testament itself.

JEHOVAH (MEANING: UNCHANGEABLE ONE.) (SEE ENTRY FOR JESUS CHRIST.)

JEREMIAH (SEE THE ENTRY FOR JEREMIAS OR JEREMY.)

JEREMIAS OR JEREMY

Jeremias and Jeremy are both names in the New Testament that refer to the prophet Jeremiah, as in these three references:

- **the inquiry of the Savior about His reputation in the land** (see Matthew 16:13-14)
- **when Herod slew all the children in the Bethlehem area two years old and under** (see Matthew 2:17-18; Jeremiah 31:15)
- **after the betrayal of the Lord by Judas** (see Matthew 27:6-10; these words are closely reminiscent of the prophecy in Zechariah

11:12-13; however, Jeremiah also uses symbolism related to the potter and the potter's jar and also speaks of fields—see Jeremiah 18:1-4; 19:1-13; 32:15, 25). This Jeremy is not to be confused with the Jeremy who was a priesthood leader mentioned twice in the Doctrine and Covenants in connection with the lineage of the priesthood prior to the time of Moses (see D&C 84:9-10). More details concerning the life and character of this ancient Jeremy are not known at this time

Historically, the Hebrew prophet Jeremiah (meaning "raised up by Jehovah") served during the days of Lehi and Daniel. The book of Jeremiah is one of the major prophetic books of the Old Testament, along with Isaiah, Lamentations (also written by Jeremiah), Ezekiel, and Daniel. Jeremiah prophesied during a forty-year period, from around 626 BC to 585 BC. His themes resound through the generations of time. He declares with power and authority the central governing principles of the gospel—that peace and happiness depend on obedience to and honoring the covenants of the Lord, including developing a personal and spiritual relationship with Him; that the consequences of sin are destruction and war, dislocation and scattering, misery and woe; that the Lord will chasten His people until they learn to be virtuous and righteous; and that He will eventually establish a new covenant with His faithful children and gather them in from the four quarters of the earth to be their King.

JESUS (MEANING: GOD IS HELP, JEHOVAH IS HELP, OR SAVIOR.)

1. Jesus is the Greek form for the Hebrew name Joshua or Jeshua, as used in the following reference

from the New Testament: "Which [tabernacle] also our fathers that came after brought in with Jesus into the possession of the Gentiles, whom God drave out before the face of our fathers, unto the days of David" (Acts 7:45; see also Hebrews 4:8).

Historically, Joshua, son of Nun, was the one chosen to assume the leadership of the House of Israel following the days of Moses (see Numbers 27:18-23; 34:17; Deuteronomy 1:38; 3:28; 31:3, 23; 34: 9).

Traditionally, the authorship of the book of Joshua is assigned to Joshua himself, with the exception of the concluding section (Joshua 24:29-33), which was added by another writer. The book of Joshua is the historical sequel to Deuteronomy, the last book of the Pentateuch (Genesis, Exodus, Leviticus, Numbers, and Deuteronomy—constituting the "law" in terms of Jewish tradition). The book of Joshua stands as the first of the "prophets" in this continuing tradition. The time span covered is from just after the passing (translation) of Moses until the death of Joshua (around 1427 BC). Probably the most well-known pronouncement of Joshua concerns the principle of agency: "Choose you this day whom ye will serve. . . . but as for me and my house, we will serve the Lord" (Joshua 24:15).

2. Jesus was a member of the Church mentioned by Paul (see Colossians 4:11).

3. Jesus was the name ordained for the Savior according to the direction given by the angel Gabriel (see Luke 1:30-31; 2:21; Matthew 1:21, 25).

JESUS CHRIST (JESUS MEANING: GOD IS HELP, JEHOVAH IS HELP, OR SAVIOR; CHRIST MEANING: THE ANOINTED OR MESSIAH.)

Jesus Christ, acting under the will of the Father, is the supreme divine personage in the New Testament as well as in all of holy writ. He is the atoning Savior of all of God's children and, "being made perfect, he became the author of eternal salvation unto all them that obey him" (Hebrew 5:9). His life as the mortal Messiah is well known, embracing the following main dimensions: birth and upbringing, baptism by John the Baptist, preparation for the ministry, calling and organizing the Twelve, performance of great miracles, teaching the people, interaction with his detractors and enemies, expansion of Church leadership and charge to His priesthood leaders, the Crucifixion, Resurrection, and final instruction to the Saints (for detailed references, see the Bible Dictionary under "Gospels— Harmony of the Gospels").

The Atonement of the Redeemer— established by the Father and embraced by the Son from before the foundation of the world— became an everlasting reality during His mortal

CHRIST BEING INVITED IN.

74

sojourn on earth in the meridian of time. The key manifestations of His eternal mission—from *Jehovah* ("Unchangeable One" and "First Born"), to *Messiah* or *Christ* ("Anointed"), to *Creator*, to *Emmanuel* ("God Among Us"), to *Jesus* ("Jehovah is Help" or "Savior"), and finally, to *King* ("King of the Jews" while on the cross [see Luke 23:38] and future millennial King)—were unfolded in glory and truth during His mortal ministry. Through His suffering in Gethsemane and on Golgotha, and through His triumph and resurrection, He accomplished the divine mission laid to His charge on behalf of mankind: "And behold, I am the light and the life of the world; and I have drunk out of that bitter cup which the Father hath given me, and have glorified the Father in taking upon me the sins of the world, in the which I have suffered the will of the Father in all things from the beginning" (3 Nephi 11:11).

The keys roles of the Lord—as Jehovah, Messiah/Christ, Creator, Emmanuel, Jesus/Savior, and King—are enunciated clearly in the Old Testament and Pearl of Great Price, just as they are confirmed and unfolded in the New Testament, Book of Mormon, and Doctrine and Covenants. Magnificent in scope and detail, inspiring in thematic content, and riveting in its anecdotal abundance, the Old Testament is the foundational scripture of the divine canon. Above all else in terms of mission and purpose, the Old Testament—supported by the books of Moses and Abraham from the Pearl of Great Price—constitutes a grand and glorious exposition of the character, qualities, and mission of the Messiah, even Jesus Christ, the Mediator of the sacred covenant with the Father. The thoughtful and prayerful reader cannot read these passages of scripture concerning the Savior without being touched spiritually with

JESUS IS THE CHRIST.

the profound significance of His love, the mercy of His longsuffering, and the majesty of His divine intercession on behalf of mankind.

Understanding the interrelated matrix of spiritual agendas that constitute the mission of the Lord serves as a kind of lens through which to view the unfolding panorama of God's dealings with His people during all the dispensations of time recorded in the Old Testament and the Pearl of Great Price. The overarching theme of these and all other scriptures of the sacred canon is the Lord Jesus Christ and His central role in the plan of salvation. As Nephi declared, "And now, behold, my beloved brethren, this is the way; and there is none other way nor name given under heaven whereby man can be saved in the kingdom of God. And now, behold, this is the doctrine of Christ, and the only and true doctrine of the Father, and of the Son, and of the Holy Ghost, which is one God, without end. Amen" (2 Nephi 31:21; see also Moses 6:51–52).

Let us consider briefly the various dimensions of the Lord's calling as depicted in the Old Testament and the Pearl of Great Price—for that is the foundation upon which the mortal ministry of Jesus Christ can be illuminated and understood:

1. Jehovah: In the King James Version of the Old Testament, the word LORD (with each letter capitalized) signifies that the original text upon which the translation into English was based contained at that point the name Jehovah, which means "Unchangeable One." Out of respect for Deity, Jewish readers did not speak aloud the name Jehovah (or any of its variants) but instead substituted a Hebrew word such as *Adonai*, meaning "Lord." The name Jehovah signifies everlasting, endless, and eternal God, a reflection of the supernal constancy of Deity, the Word of God: "The grass withereth, the flower fadeth: but the word of our God shall stand for ever" (Isaiah 40:8). In latter-day scripture, this everlasting state of being is confirmed: "Listen to the voice of the Lord your God, even Alpha and Omega, the beginning and the end, whose course is one eternal round, the same today as yesterday, and forever" (D&C 35:1; see also 2 Nephi 2:4; 27:23; 29:9; Alma 31:17; Mormon 9:9; Moroni 10:19; D&C 20:12; Hebrews 13:8).

It was under the auspices of this transcendent function of everlasting and unchanging God—the Eternal I Am—that Jehovah conversed with Moses on the mount (see Exodus 3:13-15).

The nature of Jehovah as an eternal, unchanging, and everlasting being derives from His relationship to and grounding in the Father, Elohim. Jehovah is in very deed the Son of God, even the First Born: "I will declare the decree: the LORD hath said unto me, Thou art my Son; this day have I begotten thee" (Psalm 2:7). Furthermore, "Also I will make him my firstborn, higher than the kings of the earth. My mercy will I keep for him for evermore, and my covenant shall stand fast with him. His seed also will I make to endure for ever, and his throne as the days of heaven" (Psalm 89:27-29). Isaiah confirmed the same truth: "Who hath wrought and done it, calling the generations from the beginning? I the LORD, the first, and with the last; I am he" (Isaiah 41:4; see also Isaiah 7:14-16; 9:6-7). In the New Testament, Book of Mormon, and the Doctrine and Covenants this defining position as the first as well as the last, applied to Jesus Christ, is embodied in the appellation "Alpha and Omega" (see Revelation 1:8).

The qualities of Jehovah are made clear from the scriptural account. Not only is Jehovah endless and eternal, but He also serves everlastingly as a member of the Godhead under the direction of the Father and in conjunction with the Holy Ghost. The qualities of the Son that radiate from this magnificent position of grace and truth include divinity, everlasting nature, and godliness. These are the same qualities of Jehovah to which His disciples are to aspire through obedience to His gospel plan of exaltation and by enduring in faith and honor to the end. What a glorious blessing it is to have a resplendent and perfected personage—even Jehovah—as our spiritual model and eternal guide: "Therefore, what manner of men ought ye to be? Verily I say unto you, even as I am" (3 Nephi 27:27).

2. Messiah/Christ: *Messiah* is an Aramaic word meaning "the Anointed." Aramaic belongs to the Semitic language group (which also includes Hebrew and Arabic) and became the official language of the Assyrian and, later, the Babylonian and Persian empires. For centuries, Aramaic was the dominant language in Jewish worship and daily life; Jesus himself spoke Aramaic.

The Greek equivalent of *Messiah* is "Christ." The word *Christ* does not appear in the King James Version of the Old Testament but does appear in the book of Moses from the Pearl of Great Price in four verses (Moses 6:52, 57; 7:50; 8:24). The title *Messiah* appears only twice in the Old Testament (in Daniel 9:25 and 9:26) and only once in the Pearl of Great Price (Moses 7:53). What is important about the terms *Messiah* and *Christ* is the underlying meaning of these titles, which is "the Anointed"—signifying that Jesus was divinely commissioned of the Father to carry out the work of redemption and Atonement on behalf of all mankind. He was foreordained to His supernal mission (see Abraham 3:27; Genesis 3:14-15; Job 19:25; 38:1-7; Isaiah 25:8-9). Jesus—as the Messiah and the Christ—is the authorized and empowered agent of the Father with the express calling to carry out the divine mission of saving and exalting mankind in keeping with the eternal principles of truth and spiritual deliverance (see Isaiah 61:1-3).

The Old Testament confirms the divine authority of Jesus in a variety of additional passages, including this memorable one from Isaiah: "For unto us a child is born, unto us a son is given: and the government shall be upon his shoulder: and his name shall be called Wonderful, Counsellor, The mighty God, The everlasting Father, The Prince of Peace. Of the increase of his government and peace there shall be no end, upon the throne of David, and upon his kingdom, to order it, and to establish it with judgment and with justice from henceforth even for ever" (Isaiah 9:6-7; see also Genesis 49:10; Isaiah 10:27; 11:1-9).

The qualities of the Messiah/Christ are reflected with clarity in the scriptures. To officiate in this singularly indispensable and lofty capacity as the Anointed One, Jesus must necessarily embody qualities such as being omnipotent, chosen, and mighty to effect change for good. We would expect the prophets of God throughout successive dispensations to have promised and foretold the work and ministry of Jesus in this respect. And such is the case, as the following Old Testament excerpts demonstrate (arranged, in general, according to the chronology of the prophetic utterances):

- **triumph over evil** (see Numbers 24:17).
- **enduring reign of the eternal Lawgiver** (see Genesis 49:10; JST Genesis 50:24; Ezekiel 21:27)
- **Omnipotent Shepherd** (see Genesis 49:24; Jeremiah 33:14-16)
- **symbolism of the sacrificial Lamb of God** (see Exodus 12:46; Psalm 34:20)
- **great prophet to arise** (see Deuteronomy 18:15, 18-19)
- **heavenly kingdom to prevail over earthly kingdoms** (see Psalm 2:6-12; Psalm 68:18)
- **the Son to be crucified** (see Psalm 22:1, 16, 18; 69:8-9, 20-21; Isaiah 50:5-9; 53:1-12; Zechariah 11:12; 13:6)
- **Everlasting Priest after the order of Melchizedek** (see Psalm 110:1-4; Micah 5:1-3)
- **Chief Cornerstone**—"The stone which the builders refused is become the head stone of the corner. This is the Lord's doing; it is marvellous in our eyes" (Psalm 118:22-23; see also Psalm 132:17; Isaiah 28:16)
- **virgin birth**—"Therefore the Lord himself shall give you a sign; Behold, a virgin shall conceive, and bear a son, and shall call his name Immanuel" (Isaiah 7:14)

- **Prince of Peace**—"For unto us a child is born, unto us a son is given: and the government shall be upon his shoulder: and his name shall be called Wonderful, Counsellor, The mighty God, The everlasting Father, The Prince of Peace" (Isaiah 9:6; see also Isaiah 11:1–5)
- **Glorious Sovereign** (see Isaiah 22:21–23)
- **victory over death** (see Isaiah 25:8–9)
- **glory of the Lord to be revealed** (see Isaiah 40:4–5)
- **means of liberation** (see Isaiah 42:1, 6–7; 55:1–4)
- **Redeemer** (see Isaiah 59:20; 61:1–3; Ezekiel 37:1–28; Hosea 13:4–14)
- **Atonement** (see Daniel 9:24–26)
- **Savior**—"Yet I am the Lord thy God from the land of Egypt, and thou shalt know no god but me: for there is no saviour beside me" (Hosea 13:4; see also Jonah 2:9)
- **Judge of Glory** (see Habakkuk 3:3–4, 18)
- **Builder of the Temple of the Lord**—"Thus speaketh the Lord of hosts, saying, Behold the man whose name is The Branch [i.e., the Messiah]; and he shall grow up out of his place, and he shall build the temple of the Lord: Even he shall build the temple of the Lord; and he shall bear the glory, and shall sit and rule upon his throne; and he shall be a priest upon his throne: and the counsel of peace shall be between them both" (Zechariah 6:12–13; see also Zechariah 3:8–9)
- **appearance in the latter-day temple**—"Behold, I will send my messenger, and he shall prepare the way before me: and the Lord, whom ye seek, shall suddenly come to his temple, even the messenger of the covenant, whom ye delight in: behold, he shall come, saith the Lord of hosts" (Malachi 3:1)

3. Creator: The Unchangeable and Anointed One served as the principal divine agent in laying the foundation of the world through the Creation itself. When God directed by His word that the Creation should proceed (see Moses 2–3; Genesis 1–2; Deuteronomy 4:32), it was through the Word of God (i.e., Jehovah, Messiah, Christ) that this divine process was initiated and completed: "By the word of the Lord were the heavens made; and all the host of them by the breath of his mouth" (Psalm 33:6); Thus, the Word of God was Creation incarnate. John the Apostle rendered this verity using the following celebrated language: "In the beginning was the Word, and the Word was with God, and the Word was God. The same was in the beginning with God. All things were made by him; and without him was not any thing made that was made. In him was life; and the life was the light of men. And the light shineth in darkness; and the darkness comprehended it not" (John 1:1–5).

What greater symbolic representation could there be of the office and function of the Creator and Life-giver than the image of being the "Light of the World"? "And God said, Let there be light: and there was light. And God saw the light, that it was good: and God divided the light from the darkness" (Genesis 1:3–4; see also Moses 2:3–4).

Many additional references from the Old Testament confirm and expand on the mission of the Word of God as Creator. For example, the Lord asked Job, in his adversity, "Where wast thou when I laid the foundations of the earth? declare, if thou hast understanding. Who hath laid the measures thereof, if thou knowest? or who hath stretched the line upon it? Whereupon are the foundations thereof fastened? or who laid the corner stone thereof; When the morning stars sang together, and all the sons of God shouted for

CHRIST CREATED THE HEAVENS AND EARTH AND ALL THINGS THAT IN THEM ARE.

joy?" (Job 38:4–7; see also Job 10:8–12; 26:12–13). Clearly, the one most capable of understanding our plight as mortals and rendering succor and solace concerning our privation and suffering is the Lord Himself, the Creator of heaven and earth: "And Hezekiah prayed before the Lord, and said, O Lord God of Israel, which dwellest between the cherubims, thou art the God, even thou alone, of all the kingdoms of the earth: thou hast made heaven and earth" (2 Kings 19:15).

The qualities of the Creator are unfolded in the sacred word. As Creator, Jehovah embodies specific qualities of office and character, including life-giving, creative, productive, and loyal agent of God. These are among the very qualities that go to define discipleship for the faithful who are committed to follow in the footsteps of the Savior by emulating His exemplary mode of living. Should we not also seek to sustain and nurture life, be creative and productive in wholesome and uplifting ways, and display loyalty and obedience to God in all our dealings?

Using these same qualities, the Son of God governed and governs the vital process of generating and preserving life itself—beginning with the Creation and continuing with the unfolding of the process of dynamic growth of all living things pertaining to this world and all other worlds: "And worlds without number have I created; and I also created them for mine own purpose; and by the Son I created them, which is mine Only Begotten" (Moses 1:33). The Gatekeeper of the eternal realm (2 Nephi 9:41) is also the Gatekeeper of life—the Curator of the principles and processes of enlivenment and growth for all creation. Jehovah oversees and administers the transition between the potential and the real, between the spiritual creation (as described in Moses 3:5) and the actual, emerging (natural) creation.

79

The predominant quality of Jesus Christ as Creator is One who completes and One who—through faith, obedience, power, and divine light—generates and sustains life unto salvation. What an extraordinary being is this Creator, even Jehovah the Messiah and Christ, to generate as the Word of God all the conditions and processes by which we, as sons and daughters of God, can enjoy mortal life and look forward with hope, faith, and covenant valor to the time when we shall inherit immortality and eternal life in the mansions of the Father and the Son. In that joyous hour, the faithful shall meet once again the very Creator of our being, look upon His face with rapture, and speak His name in love: "And he shall be called Jesus Christ, the Son of God, the Father of heaven and earth, the Creator of all things from the beginning" (Mosiah 3: 8; see also Moses 6:63; 7:56; Abraham 4:20).

4. Emmanuel (Immanuel): One of the greatest of all the miracles of the gospel is the condescension of the Father and the Son, that the great Jehovah—the Unchangeable One, the Anointed One (being Messiah and Christ), even the grand Creator of heaven and earth—should deem it to be His essential mission to do the will of the Father and come among mortals to bring to pass for all mankind the effectual conditions of faith, salvation, and redemption. In this capacity, His office and title are known as *Emmanuel* (also rendered *Immanuel*)—that is, "God Among Us." As the Only Begotten of the Father, He accepted His mortal mission to serve as the Messenger of the Covenant and experienced birth, grew to manhood, completed His ministry as the Good Shepherd, and suffered betrayal and death as the "author of eternal salvation" (Hebrews 5:9).

The chronicle of Emmanuel's mortal experience is woven through prophetic utterance into the fabric of the Old Testament. The Psalmist foresaw the work of the mortal Messiah: "The Lord is high above all nations, and his glory above the heavens. Who is like unto the Lord our God, who dwelleth on high, Who humbleth himself to behold the things that are in heaven, and in the earth!" (Psalm 113:4-6). Isaiah envisioned the infinite humility of the Son in submitting Himself willingly to His detractors: "The Lord God hath opened mine ear, and I was not rebellious, neither turned away back. I gave my back to the smiters, and my cheeks to them that plucked off the hair: I hid not my face from shame and spitting" (Isaiah 50:5-6). Continuing his inspired pronouncement, Isaiah articulates with consummate and unforgettable eloquence the pains of the Lord in doing the will of the Father upon the earth (see Isaiah 53:1-12).

The pathway of the Christ into mortality via the lineage of Abraham (the Davidic descent) is abundantly accounted for in the pages of the sacred record (see Psalm 89:3-4; see also 1 Samuel 16:1; 17:12; 2 Samuel 7:12-17; Psalm 132:11-18; Isaiah 9:6-7; 11:1-10: Jeremiah 23:5-6; 33:14-16; Zechariah 3:8-9; 6:10-15; 12:7-12).

Additional Old Testament references concerning the coming mortal mission of Jesus Christ include the following:

- great prophet to come (see Deuteronomy 18:18)
- child of God (see Isaiah 7:14; 9:6; Micah 5:2)
- victory over death (see Isaiah 25:8; 26:9)
- messenger of God (see Isaiah 40:8; 61:1; 1 Samuel 3:21)
- persecution by his detractors (see Psalm 22:15-18; 41:9; Zechariah 11:12-14)
- sufferings of the Master (see Zechariah 13:6)

The all-encompassing view of the condescension of the Only Begotten is that of the Good Shepherd who tends His flocks personally as "the shepherd, the stone of Israel" (Genesis 49:24). This role is memorably expressed in the 23rd Psalm—"The Lord is my shepherd; I shall not want" (verse 1)—but is also encapsulated in several other prophetic passages of great beauty and tenderness. Perhaps the most detailed view of the Good Shepherd Emmanuel is given in Ezekiel 34:11-19, including this statement: "I will feed them in a good pasture, and upon the high mountains of Israel shall their fold be: there shall they lie in a good fold, and in a fat pasture shall they feed upon the mountains of Israel" (Ezekiel 34:14).

The qualities of Emmanuel (Immanuel) are made specific in the scriptural record. The Good Shepherd, by nature of His divine calling and commission, radiates the qualities of being humble, patient, nurturing, personal, focused on the needs of the individual in loving kindness, and exhibiting the characteristics of the longsuffering, noble counselor. Are these not the very qualities that the followers of Christ should aspire to emulate if they are to fulfill the measure of their spiritual potential?

The scriptures illustrate abundantly the manner in which the Lord works one on one, in mercy and kindness, with His faithful servants. According to the Old Testament account, the Lord appeared in person to Abraham (see Genesis 12:7), Jacob (see Genesis 32:30), Moses (see Exodus 32:30-31; Numbers 12:6-8; Deuteronomy 5:24; 34:10), Isaiah (see Isaiah 6:1), Ezekiel (see Ezekiel 1:26-28), Amos (see Amos 9:1), and, no doubt, many other prophets.

5. Jesus: As already noted, the name Jesus is the Greek form of the name Joshua or Jeshua, meaning "God is Help" or "Jehovah is Help"

(i.e., "Savior"). The name implies the sacred office of Redeemer, Lamb of God, Bread of Life, the One who brings about the Atonement through the sacrificial Crucifixion, the One who ushers in the process of the Resurrection, the One who is therefore, in all respects, the Life of the World. In this capacity as Savior, the Son of God—even Jehovah, Messiah, Christ, Creator, Emmanuel—is the means for rescuing all mankind from the effects of the temporal death and enabling the faithful and obedient to escape the clutches of the second (or spiritual) death through compliance with the principles and ordinances of the gospel.

The Old Testament is a vibrant and compelling witness of the office of Savior and Redeemer as consummated in the Crucifixion and Resurrection of Jesus. The Psalmist anticipated the express words of the sacrificial Lamb of God—"My God, my God, why hast thou forsaken me?" (Psalm 22:1)—and discerned in prophetic vision the process of the Crucifixion—"The assembly of the wicked have inclosed me: they pierced my hands and my feet. I may tell all my bones: they look and stare upon me. They part my garments among them, and cast lots upon my vesture. But be not thou far from me, O Lord: O my strength, haste thee to help me" (Psalm 22:16-19). Isaiah foresaw in great detail the travail of the Lord on the cross (see Isaiah 53:5-12). Likewise, Zechariah was blessed to spiritually view the Crucifixion and Atonement from the perspective of the Savior (see Zechariah 12:10; 13:6; see also Daniel 9:26-27).

The redeeming death of the Savior secured the faith and hope of His followers in all ages (see Alma 34:15-16).

A number of Old Testament scriptures echo this principle:

- "But the righteous hath hope in his death" (Proverbs 14:32).
- "He will swallow up death in victory; and the Lord God will wipe away tears from off all faces; and the rebuke of his people shall he take away from off all the earth: for the Lord hath spoken it" (Isaiah 25:8).
- "He was oppressed, and he was afflicted, yet he opened not his mouth: he is brought as a lamb to the slaughter, and as a sheep before her shearers is dumb, so he openeth not his mouth. . . . And he made his grave with the wicked, and with the rich in his death; because he had done no violence, neither was any deceit in his mouth" (Isaiah 53:7, 9).
- "I will ransom them from the power of the grave; I will redeem them from death:

O death, I will be thy plagues; O grave, I will be thy destruction: repentance shall be hid from mine eyes" (Hosea 13:14; see also Jonah 1:17; Matthew 12:38–40; 16:4; Luke 11:29–30).

The concept of Jesus as the Lamb of God was made a regular part of the worship of ancient Israel through the ritual sacrifice of a lamb "without blemish" (Exodus 12:5)—one per household—during the Passover (see Exodus 12:13–14). Isaiah celebrated the symbolism of the Lamb of God with these words: "He is brought as a lamb to the slaughter, and as a sheep before her shearers is dumb, so he openeth not his mouth. . . . When thou shalt make his soul an offering for sin, he shall see his seed, he shall

JESUS IS THE RESURRECTED LORD.

prolong his days, and the pleasure of the Lord shall prosper in his hand" (Isaiah 53:7, 10).

The glorious Atonement and Resurrection of the Savior was the crowning triumph of His ministry.

Out of the shadowy abyss of divine suffering emerged triumphant the glory of the redemption and the Atonement. The Old Testament repeatedly celebrates this eternal victory: "For the life of the flesh is in the blood: and I have given it to you upon the altar to make an atonement for your souls: for it is the blood that maketh an atonement for the soul" (Leviticus 17:11; see also Leviticus 4:20–35; Job 19:25). Isaiah provides this prophetic comfort: "Fear not, thou worm Jacob, and ye men of Israel; I will help thee, saith the Lord, and thy redeemer, the Holy One of Israel" (Isaiah 41:14). And further, "He hath poured out his soul unto death: and he was numbered with the transgressors; and he bare the sin of many, and made intercession for the transgressors" (Isaiah 53:12).

Jesus the Atoning One is the singularly most potent prototype of the set of qualities that belong to "saviorhood": loving, obedient, redeeming, perfect, and spotless. He is so loving that He verily weeps when we fall short of our potential: "Wherefore, he suffereth for their sins; inasmuch as they will repent in the day that my Chosen shall return unto me, and until that day they shall be in torment; Wherefore, for this shall the heavens weep, yea, and all the workmanship of mine hands" (Moses 7:39–40). At the same time, He rejoices when we repent and follow in His footsteps: "For, behold, the Lord your Redeemer suffered death in the flesh; wherefore he suffered the pain of all men, that all men might repent and come unto him. And he hath risen again from the dead, that he might bring all men unto him, on conditions of

CHRIST WASHES THE APOSTLES' FEET.

repentance. And how great is his joy in the soul that repenteth!" (D&C 18:11–13).

Should we not, therefore, all strive to cultivate within ourselves these same qualities anticipated by the prophets of old and fulfilled in the mission of the Redeemer? Should we not ponder the patterns of saving grace reflected in the scriptures concerning the Savior and attempt to inculcate them into our daily lives with an attitude of thanksgiving and humble obedience?

6. King: Jehovah—the Unchangeable One and First Born of Elohim—was anointed in the premortal realm as Messiah and Christ to lay the foundation of the world through the Creation and serve as the Author of eternal salvation by coming to live among mortals in obedience to the will of the Father, for the purpose of completing His atoning mission as Jesus ("Jehovah is Help" or "Savior"), thus becoming the Redeemer unto all the world. In the final chapter of the history of this world, Jesus Christ will return in glory as King, Judge, Law-Giver, Mediator, Advocate, and Prince of Peace to usher in the millennial reign and take His place as the Covenant Father of all the righteous and redeemed.

The millennial reign of the Lord is predicted with prophetic certainty throughout the ancient record and described as having the following characteristics:

- everlasting (see Psalm 89:2-4; 132:10-11)
- theocratic in governance (see Isaiah 9:6-7; see also Isaiah 1:1-9)
- merciful (see Isaiah 16:5; 40:9-11)
- righteous (see Jeremiah 23:5-6; Zephaniah 3:15)
- all-consuming (see Daniel 2:44; 7:13-14; Zechariah 14:1-9)
- joyful (see Zechariah 2:10-13)
- glorious (see Psalm 24:10; see also Exodus 33:18-23; 40:34-35; Isaiah 6:3; 40:5; Ezekiel 1:26-28; Zechariah 2:5)

The ushering in of the millennial reign is a time of universal judgment, as scriptural records confirm (see Genesis 18:25; Deuteronomy 32:36; Judges 11:27; 1 Samuel 2:10). "And he shall judge the world in righteousness, he shall minister judgment to the people in uprightness" (Psalm 9:8; see also Psalm 7:8-11; 50:6; 58:11; 72:2-19; 82:8; 94:2; 96:1-13; Ecclesiastes 3:17; 12:14; Isaiah 2:4; 3:14;5:16; 11:3-4; 33:22; 51:5; Jeremiah 23:2-8; Daniel 7:13-14; Joel 3:12). All

the prophets down through the ages have spoken of the final judgment and the responsibility of man—according to his God-given agency and stewardship—to account for his every thought and deed (see 3 Nephi 27:16-17).

The qualities of the King unfold in power from the sacred canon. As presented in the scriptural account of the millennial reign, the Great Jehovah will consummate the final judgment and disposition of mankind by being just, merciful, righteous, full of grace, holy, and glorious. These are the qualities of His royal office (see Alma 34:15-16). Is it not incumbent upon all followers of Christ to emulate His example by aspiring to the same qualities He displays in perfected form—being just, merciful, righteous, full of grace, holy, and glorious? Surely our joy and peace in this world and the world to come will depend on the degree to which we can cultivate these qualities within our character, together with all others that pertain to the mission of the Lord as our eternal exemplar.

The overarching reach of divine influence in the lives of God's children traces a pattern of magnanimous grace and love on the part of the Lord. From Creator, to Jehovah ("Unchangeable One" and "First Born"), to Messiah or Christ ("Anointed"), to Emmanuel ("God Among Us"), to Jesus ("Jehovah is Help" or "Savior"), and, finally, to King, we can trace the agenda by means of which He sustains and perfects His immortal suzerainty as our Master and Redeemer, having glorified the Father through uncompromising obedience. By using the portrait of the Savior unfolded to our view in the ancient canon of scripture and expanded and augmented through modern-day revelation, we can bring to our study of the gospel a guiding lens through which we can discern the truth of God's design for our spiritual growth and perfection. In the final analysis, we perceive in His divine career many titles and offices, but He is only one Lord, many qualities but only one unified manifestation of divine love, and many influences and interactions with mankind but only one cause—"to bring to pass the immortality and eternal life of man" (Moses 1:39).

7. The Mortal Messiah: The key dimensions of the Redeemer's mission, outlined above, are clearly manifest in His mortal ministry as depicted in the New Testament. What are the main milestones of the Savior's magnificent mission on earth as the Only Begotten of the Father and the Redeemer of mankind?

CHRIST IS THE MORTAL MESSIAH.

- **annunciation** (see Luke 1:26–28, 30–33)
- **birth** (see Luke 2:10–14)
- **visit to the temple** (see Luke 2:27–32)
- **visit by the wise men** (see Matthew 2:1–2, 11)
- **youth** (see Luke 2:52)
- **baptism by John the Baptist** (see Matthew 3:16–17; see also Mark 1:9; 10:38; Luke 3:21; John 1:32; 1 Nephi 10:9; 2 Nephi 1:5; 11:27; 31:5)
- **being tempted by the devil in the wilderness** (see Matthew 4:10–11)
- **miracles** (see Matthew 4:23–24). Jesus performed countless miracles of healing: the woman who touched his garment (see Matthew 9:20–22; Mark 5:25–34; Luke 8:43–48), the man with palsy (Luke 5:18–26), ten men with leprosy (see Luke 17:11–19), the man blind from birth (see John 9:1–38), and many others. He also performed many miracles in the context of nature, such as calming the storm (see Matthew 8:23–27; Mark 4:35–41; Luke 8:22–25), turning water

into wine (see John 2:1–11), feeding the 5,000 with two fish and five loaves of bread (see Matthew 14:13–21; Mark 6:35–44; Luke 9:10–17; John 6:5–14), and walking on water (see Matthew 14:22–33; Mark 6:45–51; John 6:15–21). Moreover, Jesus raised individuals from the dead: Jairus's daughter (see Matthew 9:18–19, 23–26; Mark 5:21–24, 35–43; Luke 8:40–42, 49–56), the widow's son at Nain (see Luke 7:11–18), and Lazarus (see John 11:1–44).

- **calling of the Twelve** (see Matthew 10:1–2; see also Luke 6:13–16; 9:1–2; Mark 3:14; 6:7)
- **keys of the kingdom** (see Matthew 16:18–19)
- **Mount of Transfiguration** (see Matthew 17:1–3)
- **teachings—Sermon on the Mount** (see Matthew 5–7)
- **parables:** The rich treasure trove of parables used by Jesus—including the sower (see

Matthew 13:3-9; Mark 4:3-9; Luke 8:5-8), the lost sheep (see Matthew 18:12-14; Luke 15:3-7), the good Samaritan (see Luke 10:30-37), the prodigal son (see Luke 15:11-32), the ten virgins (see Matthew 25:1-13), and the talents (see Matthew 25:14-30)—contains both practical wisdom eternal truth to bless lives, enrich relationships, and enhance spirituality

- **Nicodemus and rebirth** (see John 3:3-5)
- **at the well** (see John 4:13-14)
- **Institution of the sacrament** (see Matthew 26:26-29; see also John 6:48-58)
- **intercessory prayer** (see John 17:19-22)
- **Gethsemane** (see Matthew 26:39-45; Mark 14:32-41)
- **before Pilate** (see Matthew 27:26; Mark 15:1-14; Luke 23:1-26; John 18:28-40)
- **Golgotha** (see John 19:26-30; Matthew 27:33-50; Mark 15:16-37)
- **Resurrection** (see Matthew 28:5-6; Mark 16:6-7)
- **final teachings** (see Matthew 28:19-20; Mark 16:15-18; John 21:15-17)
- **Ascension** (see Mark 16:19; Luke 24:51)

The Lord's disciples and associates testified of His mission:

- John the Baptist (see John 1:29)
- Peter (see Acts 3:19-21; 4:10-12; 2 Peter 1:16-19)
- John (see John 1:1-5; 19:11-13, 15-16)
- Stephen (see Acts 7:55-56)
- Paul (see Hebrews 5:8-10)

Beside the Old Testament and the New Testament, the Book of Mormon is verily "Another Testament of Jesus Christ"—a sacred witness that He lives and acts for the "immortality and eternal life of man" (Moses 1:39). The reader can follow the Savior's footprints throughout the pages of this unique chronicle. He is identified variously as the "Holy One of Israel" (2 Nephi 25:29), "the rock" (Helaman 5:12), the "Well Beloved" (Helaman 5:47), "the God of the land" (Ether 2:12), "the God of Israel, and the God of the whole earth" (3 Nephi 11:14), and various other appellations. Prophetic utterances about the divine nature of His being and His redeeming mission abound. He was seen of many prophets—including Nephi and Jacob (2 Nephi 11:2-3), the brother of Jared (Ether 3:13), and Moroni (Ether 12:39)—and, in His resurrected state, by thousands in the area of Bountiful (see 3 Nephi). He defined plainly the nature of His gospel as the divine plan of deliverance and exaltation, based on faith, repentance, baptism, receiving the gift of the Holy Ghost, and enduring to the end (see 3 Nephi 11:32-41; 27:13.27). He established His Church among the people and authorized His chosen servants to administer the saving teachings and ordinances of the gospel to lift and edify all those who come unto Him with a broken heart and contrite spirit (see 3 Nephi 12:19).

The most compelling and magnificent section of the Book of Mormon is the account of the visit of Jesus Christ to His "other sheep" (3 Nephi 15:21) on the American continent following His Crucifixion and Resurrection. From His visit, we derive priceless lessons on how to render operational the principles of charity in our own missions in mortality by becoming a living witness of His divine power, sharing with others the fundamentals of the gospel; enhancing for others (as He did) the gifts of peace, light, love, and life; encouraging everyone to take on the divine nature and increase spirituality, promoting scripture study and prayer, joining together often in sacramental worship, and learning to endure faithfully to the end.

The voice of the Savior is also heard throughout the pages of the Doctrine and Covenants, as in this exemplary witness:

> I am Alpha and Omega, Christ the Lord; yea, even I am he, the beginning and the end, the Redeemer of the world.
>
> I, having accomplished and finished the will of him whose I am, even the Father, concerning me—having done this that I might subdue all things unto myself—
>
> Retaining all power, even to the destroying of Satan and his works at the end of the world, and the last great day of judgment, which I shall pass upon the inhabitants thereof, judging every man according to his works and the deeds which he hath done.
>
> And surely every man must repent or suffer, for I, God, am endless. . . .
>
> Learn of me, and listen to my words; walk in the meekness of my Spirit, and you shall have peace in me.
>
> I am Jesus Christ; I came by the will of the Father, and I do his will. (D&C 19:1–4, 23–24; see also Moses 6:51–52; 2 Nephi 31:21; Mosiah 3:17)

JEW/JEWS

The term *Jew* or *Jews* occurs frequently in the New Testament. In the most specific sense, *Jews* refers to people of the lineage of Judah, son of Jacob. The earliest usage of the term *Jews* in the Old Testament occurs in this passage: "At that time Rezin king of Syria recovered Elath to Syria, and drave the Jews from Elath: and the Syrians came to Elath, and dwelt there unto this day" (2 Kings 16:6; around 740 BC). In a broader sense, the term can be applied to those who over the generations were citizens of Jerusalem, even though they were not of Jewish lineage (as in 2 Nephi 30:4). Thus, Lehi was part of the Jewish community in his day—although he was by lineage from the tribe of Joseph through Manasseh, son of Joseph (see Alma 10:3), while Ishmael and his posterity derived from the tribe of Ephraim, son of Joseph (see *JD* 23:184–185). The Doctrine and Covenants contains nineteen references to *Jews* and three to the word *Jew*—most of the references applying to the specific meaning of the term (i.e., of the lineage of Judah). In one poignant reference, the Lord gives utterance to the state of mind of the Jews at the time of the Second Coming when they realize that the millennial Lord is indeed the same Jesus Christ whom their leaders had crucified (D&C 45:51–53).

JOANNA (MEANING: WHOM JEHOVAH HAS GRACIOUSLY GIVEN.)

1. Joanna, son of Rhesa, is mentioned in the genealogical lineage of Jesus Christ (see Luke 3:27).

2. Joanna was among those who followed Christ and supported Him: "And certain women, which

had been healed of evil spirits and infirmities, Mary called Magdalene, out of whom went seven devils, And Joanna the wife of Chuza Herod's steward, and Susanna, and many others, which ministered unto him of their substance" (Luke 8:2–3). Joanna was also among the women who discovered the empty tomb and reported this event: "It was Mary Magdalene, and Joanna, and Mary the mother of James, and other women that were with them, which told these things unto the apostles" (Luke 24:10).

JOB (MEANING: PERSECUTED.)

Job, exemplar of patience and undeviating devotion to the Lord, is mentioned only one time in the New Testament, in a passage from James (see James 5:10–11).

There are few treatises or narratives that plumb the potential of man, his interrelationships with others, and his integrity of heart with more depth or illumination than the book of Job. The book of Job provides a poetic drama of unsurpassed intensity and meaning concerning the human condition, focusing on the misery and lowliness of man in comparison with the majesty and supremacy of God, the trials of life as a test of man's integrity and loyalty to his Creator (and not necessarily as evidence of unrighteousness), and the divine spark of testimony within man that God lives, guiding man toward a better state based on his obedience, patience, and willingness to endure to the end. The story of Job reminds us to ask ourselves if we, too, are true to our God and to His commandments. Working toward a more complete understanding of our purpose in the design of God, we can repent of our sins, embracing the gospel with valor and devotion, lifted by the assurance that we will be blessed according to the grace of God, after all we can do (see 2 Nephi 25:23).

JOEL

The prophet Joel is mentioned specifically only one time in the New Testament, in Peter's discourse given on the Day of Pentecost in Jerusalem when the power of the Holy Ghost was made manifest among many of those assembled who experienced the gift of tongues (see Acts 2:14–21).

Historically speaking, Joel, a prophet of Judah, was one of the twelve prophets of the Old Testament with shorter books. The time span of his writings is unknown—it could be as early as the ninth century or as late as the return from the Babylonian captivity following the decree of liberation of the Jewish people issued by Cyrus in 537 BC. Joel uses an occasion of dire famine and suffering to reflect on the perennial famine of truth among the unrighteous down through

JOB PRAISES GOD.

88

the generations of time. Such a famine would be relieved through the eventual restoration of the Lord's kingdom on earth—a day when vision and prophesy would again be made manifest among the faithful and penitent and the Lord would reign supreme.

JOHN

John, son of Zebedee and brother of James, was one of the Lord's Twelve Apostles in the meridian of time (see Matthew 4:21-22; Luke 5:1-11). When Jesus ordained His Apostles, He conferred special names on some: "And he ordained twelve, that they should be with him, and that he might send them forth to preach, And to have power to heal sicknesses, and to cast out devils: And Simon he surnamed Peter; And James the son of Zebedee, and John the brother of James; and he surnamed them Boanerges, which is, The sons of thunder" (Mark 3:14-17). John was one of the three Apostles, along with Peter and James, who occupied a place of special leadership in the fold of the Savior, as confirmed by the following events:

- the restoring of life to the deceased twelve-year-old daughter of Jairus, one of the rulers of the synagogue (see Mark 5:37, 41; Luke 8:49-56)
- Transfiguration on the Mount (see Matthew 17:1-3; Mark 9:2-4; Luke 9:28-31)
- Garden of Gethsemane (see Matthew 26:36-38; see also Mark 14:32-34)

John had a disposition of considerable energy and boldness (see Mark 10:37, 41-45; 13:5-6; Luke 9:54-56; see also the entry for James–item 1). He is mentioned in the Gospel of John (the anonymous author of which was most likely

JOHN SAW A MIGHTY ANGEL.

this same John) as follows: first, as a disciple (see John 13:23); second, at the Crucifixion (see John 19:26-27); and third, concerning Mary Magdalene and the discovery of the empty tomb (see John 20:2; 21:7, 20). John was ultimately exiled to the isle of Patmos, where he recorded the magnificent words of the book of Revelation (see Revelation 1:9).

The Gospel of John follows a declared purpose: "And many other signs truly did Jesus in the presence of his disciples, which are not written in this book: But these are written, that ye might believe that Jesus is the Christ, the Son of God; and that believing ye might have life through his name" (John 20:30-31). Unlike the synoptic Gospels of Matthew, Mark, and Luke—which present the narrative of Christ's life in similar fashion, as with "the same eye"—John presents a unique and profoundly moving unfolding of the thoughts and doctrines presented by the Savior at critical milestones in His ministry, always with the purpose of lifting one's perspective to the eternal level of understanding.

JOHN MARK (SEE THE ENTRY FOR MARK.)

JOHN THE BAPTIST

John the Baptist is one of the pivotal figures in the New Testament—and in the design of the Almighty for the blessing of mankind in general. John came into a family of senior years, one where the wife, Elisabeth, had not been favored with any children. Her husband, Zacharias, was a priest in the temple where, at the time of his annual service, he was astounded when the angel Gabriel appeared unto him (see Luke 1:12-17).

It was the same angelic messenger who subsequently announced to Mary in Nazareth the coming forth of her child, Jesus Christ, saying also, "And, behold, thy cousin Elisabeth, she hath also conceived a son in her old age: and this is the sixth month with her, who was called barren. For with God nothing shall be impossible" (Luke 1:36-37). We know from modern revelation how John was prepared in the early phase of his mortality to carry on the work of the Aaronic Priesthood (see D&C 84:26-28).

The work of John as the forerunner of Jesus Christ had been predicted several centuries before by both Malachi (see Malachi 3:1) and Nephi (see 1 Nephi 10:7-10). In fulfillment of these prophecies, John prepared himself and served the Lord faithfully:

- He accepted and unfolded his ministry as spokesperson for the way of truth (see Mark 1:4-8).
- John was then called upon to baptize the Son of God in an event of such importance that the presence of the Father and the Holy Ghost were also made manifest (see Matthew 3:13-17; see also Mark 1:9-11; Luke 3:21-22).
- The witness of John the Baptist that Jesus was indeed the Son of God came to him by revelation and was confirmed by the sign of the dove (see John 1:29-34).

John also prepared the way for some of the Savior's chosen disciples who were in his (John's) circle of followers. Andrew, brother of Peter, heard John say of Jesus, "Behold the Lamb of God!" (John 1:36), and followed Jesus (see John 1:29-42). Others may have followed in their footsteps (see Matthew 11:2-6; Luke 7:19-23; Acts 1:21-22). John the Baptist continued his service for a period of time after Jesus had commenced His own ministry (see John 3:23-24). It was during this final period of John's mission that he gave a magnificent testimony of the Savior (see John 3:25-36).

John was ultimately imprisoned by Herod Antipas and eventually beheaded in consequence of an evil conspiracy fomented by a woman named Herodias. Herodias was the sister of Marcus Julius Agrippa I, also known as Herod Agrippa I. She married Herod Philip, her uncle and stepbrother of Herod Antipas, and later left him to marry Herod Antipas, her step-uncle. John the Baptist censured Herod Antipas for this relationship, saying, "It is not lawful for thee to have her" (Matthew 14:4; see also Luke 3:19-20), bringing about his imprisonment and death (see Matthew 14:10). In the account given

JOHN THE BAPTIST TEACHES THE PEOPLE OF THE COMING CHRIST.

in Mark, it is stated that it was Herodias herself who counseled her daughter to ask for the head of John the Baptist (see Mark 6:24). The daughter was Salome (not named in the New Testament account).

The Savior has left us with a noble witness about John the Baptist: "He was a burning and a shining light: and ye were willing for a season to rejoice in his light" (John 5:35). While John was still imprisoned, the Savior said to the multitude:

> What went ye out into the wilderness for to see? A reed shaken with the wind?
>
> But what went ye out for to see? A man clothed in soft raiment? Behold, they which are gorgeously apparelled, and live delicately, are in kings' courts.

But what went ye out for to see? A prophet? Yea, I say unto you, and much more than a prophet.

This is he, of whom it is written, Behold, I send my messenger before thy face, which shall prepare thy way before thee.

For I say unto you, Among those that are born of women there is not a greater prophet than John the Baptist. (Luke 7:24–28)

From the Joseph Smith Translation of Mark 9:3, we learn that John the Baptist was present on the Mount of Transfiguration when Elias (Elijah) and Moses appeared in the presence of the Savior and His three disciples, Peter, James, and John—thus confirming the importance of John the Baptist among the circle of those holding essential priesthood keys.

It is instructive that baptism in this dispensation was inaugurated under the direction of John the Baptist, following his restoration of the Aaronic Priesthood and its keys.

JOHN THE BELOVED (SEE THE ENTRY FOR JOHN.)

JOHN THE REVELATOR (SEE THE ENTRY FOR JOHN.)

JONA OR JONAS

Jona (also called Jonas) was the father of Peter (see John 1:42; John 21:15–17).

JONAH (MEANING: DOVE.)

The memory of Jonah the prophet was invoked by the Savior when His inquiring detractors asked Him for a sign: "But he answered and said unto them, An evil and adulterous generation seeketh after a sign; and there shall no sign be given to it, but the sign of the prophet Jonas [Jonah]: For as Jonas was three days and three nights in the whale's belly; so shall the Son of man be three days and three nights in the heart of the earth" (Matthew 12:39–40; see also Matthew 16:4). By this the Savior was giving symbolic notice of His coming sacrificial Atonement and subsequent Resurrection. Luke gives this report: "And when the people were gathered thick together, he began to say, This is an evil generation: they seek a sign; and there shall no sign be given it, but the sign of Jonas the prophet. For as Jonas was a sign unto the Ninevites, so shall also the Son of man be to this generation" (Luke 11:29–30).

Historically, Jonah lived during the reign of Jeroboam, king of Israel from around 790 BC to around 749 BC (see 2 Kings 14:25). The book of Jonah was written by an unknown later writer describing episodes from the prophet's life. The writer uses Jonah's experiences to confirm the Lord's universal love for His children of all nationalities and origins—even the population of the Assyrian capital city. Just as Jonah had to learn the magnanimous nature of the Lord's charity and loving kindness, we, too, as followers of Christ are enjoined to practice obedience, tolerance, and brotherly kindness in sharing the gospel with everyone.

The key themes, events, personalities, and passages in the book of Jonah include:

- Jonah is called of the Lord to preach repentance to Nineveh, the great Assyrian capital city; Jonah abrogates his prophetic station by fleeing on a ship bound for Tarshish; the Lord sends a fierce storm, and the crew casts Jonah into the sea for fear of being lost; and Jonah is swallowed by a whale.
- Repenting of his wrongs, Jonah prays for deliverance and is rescued by the Lord.
- Jonah fulfills his prophetic office in Nineveh and the people, responding to his call, repent, causing the Lord to withhold the judgment decreed for the wicked.
- Having been the voice of warning, Jonah is displeased with the action of the Lord in sparing Nineveh out of mercy; the Lord prepares a gourd to shelter the vexed Jonah; and though Jonah is pleased with the gourd, the Lord destroys it the next day as a lesson to Jonah.

The story of Jonah is among the most well known in the Old Testament, in part because of his extraordinary undersea experience. But there are also multiple lessons of a spiritual nature to be learned from this account: the reality of obedience, the power of repentance, the gentleness of the Lord in teaching eternal lessons, and the mercy of the Lord in sparing the city of Nineveh when the citizens turned to Him. Through the eyes of Jonah, we have the opportunity to understand the Lord's love in extending His invitation to all, for all have a chance to repent and embrace the saving truths of the gospel.

JOSEPH (MEANING: GOD WILL ADD or GOD WILL INCREASE.)

1. Joseph, son of Jacob (Israel), is mentioned by Stephen in his recounting of Israelite history (Acts 7:9–15).

JONAH REPENTS OF HIS WRONG CHOICES, AND THE LORD SAVES HIM FROM THE WHALE.

Paul also includes brief mention of Joseph in connection with the principle of faith: "By faith Jacob, when he was a dying, blessed both the sons of Joseph; and worshipped, leaning upon the top of his staff. By faith Joseph, when he died, made mention of the departing of the children of Israel; and gave commandment concerning his bones" (Hebrews 11:21–22; see also the references to Joseph in John 4:5 and Revelation 7:8).

In the historical context, Joseph was the son of Jacob and Rachel (see Genesis 30:22–24) and holder of the birthright in Israel (1 Chronicles 5:1–2; the full story is given in Genesis 37–50). His dealings with his errant brothers, whom their father, Jacob, sent to gather provisions in Egypt during the time of acute famine, attest to Joseph's nature as one of compassion, mercy, and forgiveness—Christlike qualities in supreme measure (see Genesis 42–45). The lineage of Joseph largely accomplishes the fulfillment of the commission of the Abrahamic Covenant to carry the gospel and the blessings of the priesthood to the four quarters of the earth (see Abraham 2:9–11).

2. Joseph was the husband of the virgin Mary. His genealogical descent was traced in the Gospel of Matthew from the time of Abraham (see Matthew 1:1–16) to the final phase: "And Eliud begat Eleazar; and Eleazar begat Matthan; and Matthan begat Jacob; And Jacob begat Joseph the husband of Mary, of whom was born Jesus, who is called Christ"

(Matthew 1:15-16). The lineage of Joseph given in the Gospel of Luke traces the descent from Adam to Christ (see Luke 3:23-38), with Joseph's father identified as Heli (see Luke 3:23; see also *JCWNT*, 111-113). His relationship with Mary was engendered by divine decree (see Matthew 1:18-25).

The portrait of Mary and the babe in the stable at Bethlehem is not complete without the presence of the protective Joseph (see Luke 2:4-16). When the parents presented the infant before the Lord in Jerusalem in keeping with Mosaic practice, the devout Simeon uttered prophetic words in the temple about the mission of the child: "And Joseph and his mother marvelled at those things which were spoken of him" (Luke 2:33). The Lord later inspired Joseph to take flight into Egypt to preserve the child Jesus from the murderous decree of Herod (see Matthew 2:13) and then subsequently inspired him to return to Israel when Herod had passed away (see Matthew 2:19-23). When Jesus was twelve years old, his parents brought Him with them to Jerusalem for the annual feast of the Passover. Upon their return home, they assumed the lad was in the company—not realizing that He had remained behind to discourse with the elders in the temple. When they finally located Him, Mary and Joseph began to get just an inkling as parents that His appointed mission had already taken root within His heart (see Luke 2:48-52).

At Nazareth, Joseph supported his family by plying a trade rendered as "carpenter" in the King James Version of the New Testament (see Matthew 13:55; Mark 6:3). He was an honorable and righteous person, who most likely passed away prior to the Crucifixion—hence the logic of the Lord, from the cross, committing His mother Mary into the hands of John for care and keeping.

3. Joseph (i.e., Joseph of Arimathaea) was the gracious man who stepped forward after the time of the Crucifixion to take charge of the body of the Lord, prepare it, and commit it to a sepulchre (see Matthew 27:57-60). In the account Luke gives, Joseph is characterized as "a counsellor; and he was a good man, and a just: (The same had not consented to the counsel and deed of them;) he was of Arimathæa, a city of the Jews: who also himself waited for the kingdom of God" (Luke 27:50-51). In Mark's account, Joseph is deemed an "honourable counsellor, which also waited for the kingdom of God" (Mark 15:43). John calls him "a disciple of Jesus" (John 19:38). The word *counsellor* implies a member of the leading Jewish council or Sanhedrin—thus, Joseph was a person of considerable influence.

4. Joseph was one of two candidates deemed worthy to fill the office of apostleship after the betrayal and demise of Judas: "And they appointed two, Joseph called Barsabas, who was surnamed Justus, and Matthias. And they

JOSEPH INTERPRETS THE DREAMS OF FELLOW JAILMATES.

94

JOSEPH IS TOLD THAT HE IS TO WED MARY AND TO CARE FOR HER AND HER CHILD.

prayed, and said, Thou, Lord, which knowest the hearts of all men, shew whether of these two thou hast chosen, That he may take part of this ministry and apostleship, from which Judas by transgression fell, that he might go to his own place. And they gave forth their lots; and the lot fell upon Matthias; and he was numbered with the eleven apostles" (Acts 1: 23–26).

JOSES

1. Joses was one of the brothers of Jesus Christ, as confirmed by those from the Lord's home area (see Matthew 13:55; see also Matthew 27:56; Mark 6:3; 15:40, 47).
2. Joses was a Church leader with the surname of Barnabas. (See the entry for Barnabas.)

JOSHUA (SEE THE ENTRY FOR JESUS.)

JUDA (JUDAH) (MEANING: PRAISE.)

1. Juda is the rendering of the name Judah, in most cases in the New Testament, as in the reference to Juda, son of Jacob in the genealogy of Jesus Christ (see Luke 3:33). Paul reminds us of this heritage: "For it is evident that our Lord sprang out of Juda" (Hebrews 7:14; see also Revelation 5:5). The spelling of the name as *Judah* occurs only once in the New Testament, where Paul is teaching about the new covenant offered by the Lord: "Behold, the days come, saith the Lord, when I will make a new covenant with the house of Israel and with the house of Judah" (Hebrews 8:8).

Judah, fourth son of Jacob and Leah (see Genesis 29:35; 37:26–27; 43:3, 8; 44:16), was a principal figure in the perpetuity of the Abrahamic lineage as it extended down to Jesus Christ. Words from the final blessing of Jacob (Israel) upon the head of Judah bespeak the leadership role that this son was to fill (see Genesis 49:8–10).

Judah was the one who stepped forward among the sons of Jacob to advance an alternative to slaying their brother Joseph (see Genesis 37:26–27). It was Judah who assumed the role of protector and guarantor of Benjamin when Jacob was persuaded to allow his youngest son to return to the Egyptian court where Joseph was in charge (see Genesis 43:8). When Joseph received the birthright by virtue of the moral laxity of Reuben, Judah, nevertheless, maintained a vital role: "For Judah prevailed above his brethren, and of him came the chief ruler; but the birthright was Joseph's" (1 Chronicles 5:2).

Moses pronounced the following blessing upon the posterity of Judah: "And this is the blessing of Judah: and he said, Hear, Lord, the voice of Judah, and bring him unto his people: let his hands be sufficient for him; and be thou an help to him from his enemies" (Deuteronomy 33:7). In keeping with this spirit, the tribe of Judah assumed a continual position of leadership in Canaan, just as Ephraim would do over the generations.

2. Juda is the name of other later individuals mentioned in the lineage of Christ (see Luke 3:26, 27).

3. Juda is one of the brothers of the Savior (see Mark 6:3).

JUDAH (See the entry for Juda.)

JUDAS

1. Judas Iscariot (meaning, "belonging to the community of Kerioth"—see Joshua 15:25) was of the tribe of Judah and the only one of the Twelve who was not a Galilean. His calling as an Apostle is recorded in Matthew 10:4 and Luke 6:16. His conspiracy with the Jewish leaders against Christ is given in this passage: "Then one of the twelve, called Judas Iscariot, went unto the chief priests, And said unto them, What will ye give me, and I will deliver him unto you? And they covenanted with him for thirty pieces of silver. And from that time he sought opportunity to betray him" (Matthew 26:14–16; see also Mark 14:10; Luke 22:3–6). When some of the followers of Jesus were showing doubts, Peter confirmed his own testimony: "And we believe and are sure that thou art that Christ, the Son of the living God. Jesus answered them, Have not I chosen you twelve, and one of you is a devil? He spake of Judas Iscariot the son of Simon: for he it was that should betray him, being one of the twelve" (John 6:69–71). When His hour had finally come and Jesus was washing the feet of the disciples, Judas's evil deed was imminent: "The devil having now put into the

JUDAH EXPLAINS THE LOSS OF THEIR BROTHER JOSEPH TO THEIR FATHER, JACOB.

heart of Judas Iscariot, Simon's son, to betray him" (John 13:2). The chilling dialogue took place:

I speak not of you all: I know whom I have chosen: but that the scripture may be fulfilled, He that eateth bread with me hath lifted up his heel against me.

Now I tell you before it come, that, when it is come to pass, ye may believe that I am he.

Verily, verily, I say unto you, He that receiveth whomsoever I send receiveth me; and he that receiveth me receiveth him that sent me.

When Jesus had thus said, he was troubled in spirit, and testified, and said, Verily, verily, I say unto you, that one of you shall betray me.

Then the disciples looked one on another, doubting of whom he spake.

Now there was leaning on Jesus' bosom one of his disciples, whom Jesus loved.

Simon Peter therefore beckoned to him, that he should ask who it should be of whom he spake.

He then lying on Jesus' breast saith unto him, Lord, who is it?

Jesus answered, He it is, to whom I shall give a sop, when I have dipped it. And when he had dipped the sop, he gave it to Judas Iscariot, the son of Simon.

And after the sop Satan entered into him. Then said Jesus unto him, That thou doest, do quickly. (John 13:18–27)

Following the Crucifixion, the fate of Judas is recorded in the Gospel of Matthew: "And he cast down the pieces of silver in the temple, and departed, and went and hanged himself" (Matthew 27:5; see also the prophecy in Zechariah 11:12–13). Luke gives the following account in Acts: "Now this man purchased a field with the reward of iniquity; and falling headlong, he burst asunder in the midst, and all his bowels gushed out" (Acts 1:18). This inconsistency is resolved in the Joseph Smith Translation: "And he cast down the pieces of silver in the temple, and departed, and went, and hanged himself on a tree. And straightway he fell down, and his bowels gushed out, and he died" (JST Matthew 27:6).

2. Judas is a brother of the Lord ("And his brethren, James, and Joses, and Simon, and Judas"—Matthew 13:55; see also Mark 6:3 where the name is given as Juda) and the writer of the Epistle of Jude.

3. Judas (designated as "not Iscariot"—see John 14:22) was the brother of James and one of the Twelve called of the Lord: "And when it was day, he called unto him his disciples: and of them he chose twelve, whom also he named apostles; Simon, (whom he also named Peter,) and Andrew his brother, James and John, Philip and Bartholomew, Matthew and Thomas, James the son of Alphæus, and Simon called Zelotes, And Judas the brother of James, and Judas Iscariot, which also was the traitor" (Luke 6:13–16; see also Acts 1:13). According to the Bible Dictionary (see 719), this Judas was probably identical with the individual named Lebbaeus or Thaddaeus in the listing of the Twelve in the Gospel of Matthew (see Matthew 10:2–4; Mark 3:18).

JUDAS BETRAYS CHRIST.

When the Savior taught His disciples the principle "If ye love me, keep my commandments" (John 14:15), a remarkable dialogue resulted between Judas and Jesus (see John 14:22–27).

4. Judas, a native of Galilee, was the leader of a revolt against Roman rule, as described by Gamaliel, the Pharisee (see Acts 5:37).

5. Judas, surnamed Barsabas, was a prominent member of the Church in Jerusalem who assisted the Twelve in resolving a dispute with members of the Church in Antioch concerning the practice of circumcision (see Acts 15:22, 27). The productive service of Judas and Silas in Antioch was described as follows: "And Judas and Silas, being prophets also themselves, exhorted the brethren with many words, and confirmed them. And after they had tarried there a space,

they were let go in peace from the brethren unto the apostles" (Acts 15:32–33).

6. Judas was a man in Damascus who provided lodging to Paul after the latter's conversion (see Acts 9:11).

JUDE

Jude is the author of the Epistle of Jude. Also known as Judas or Juda, he was a brother of James and a brother of the Lord (see Matthew 13:55 and Mark 6:3). The opening line of his epistle reads, "Jude, the servant of Jesus Christ, and brother of James, to them that are sanctified by God the Father, and preserved in Jesus Christ, and called" (Jude 1:1). Jude exhorts the Saints to avoid apostate practices and keep holy the ordinances of the Church (see Jude 1:20–21). The Epistle of Jude has many similarities with 2 Peter. (See the entry for Judas–item 2.)

JULIUS

Julius was a centurion who treated Paul with kindness on his journey to Rome: "And when it was determined that we should sail into Italy, they delivered Paul and certain other prisoners unto one named Julius, a centurion of Augustus's band. And entering into a ship of Adramyttium, we launched, meaning to sail by the coasts of Asia; one Aristarchus, a Macedonian of Thessalonica, being with us. And the next day we touched at Sidon. And Julius courteously entreated Paul, and gave him liberty to go unto his friends to refresh himself" (Acts 27:1–3). (See the entry for Centurion, item 6.)

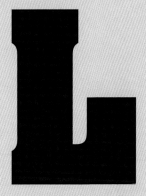

LAMB OF GOD

The title *Lamb of God*, meaning the Only Begotten Son who gave His life in the atoning sacrifice, is mentioned twice in the New Testament, both in the words of John the Baptist (John 1:29-30, 35-37).

CHRIST IS THE LAMB OF GOD.

Of Christ, Peter said, "But with the precious blood of Christ, as of a lamb without blemish and without spot: Who verily was foreordained before the foundation of the world, but was manifest in these last times for you" (1 Peter 1:19-20).

LAZARUS (MEANING: HELPED OF GOD.)

1. Lazarus was the brother of Martha and Mary who was raised from the dead by the Savior. The circumstances are touching (see John 11:19-29). Jesus was troubled by the anguish of Lazarus's sisters, Mary and Martha, as the text confirms:

> Jesus wept.
>
> Then said the Jews, Behold how he loved him!
>
> And some of them said, Could not this man, which opened the eyes of the blind, have caused that even this man should not have died?
>
> Jesus therefore again groaning in himself cometh to the grave.

It was a cave, and a stone lay upon it.

Jesus said, Take ye away the stone. Martha, the sister of him that was dead, saith unto him, Lord, by this time he stinketh: for he hath been dead four days.

Jesus saith unto her, Said I not unto thee, that, if thou wouldest believe, thou shouldest see the glory of God?

Then they took away the stone from the place where the dead was laid. And Jesus lifted up his eyes, and said, Father, I thank thee that thou hast heard me.

And I knew that thou hearest me always: but because of the people which stand by I said it, that they may believe that thou hast sent me.

And when he thus had spoken, he cried with a loud voice, Lazarus, come forth.

And he that was dead came forth, bound hand and foot with graveclothes: and his face was bound about with a napkin. Jesus saith unto them, Loose him, and let him go.

Then many of the Jews which came to Mary, and had seen the things which Jesus did, believed on him. (John 11:35–45)

Thus, the followers of the Christ celebrated life, while the Pharisees, evil in their disposition and jealous of the miracle of the Master, conspired in the background to thwart His

THE LORD COMMANDS LAZARUS TO RISE.

ministry and also put an end to the life of the restored Lazarus (see John 12:10).

2. Lazarus is the central figure of the Savior's parable of the rich man and the beggar and the one figure in any of the parables of Jesus given a personal name (see Luke 16:19–26). The parable reflects with compelling effectiveness the state of affairs awaiting mortals in the next life—based on their choices in mortality. Alma states the doctrine plainly in his counsel to Corianton, his then wayward son (see Alma 40:11–14).

In his vision of the work of salvation that the Savior organized in the spirit realm between the time of His Crucifixion and Resurrection, Joseph F. Smith also confirms the doctrine reflected in the parable about Lazarus, describing the joy and gladness of the righteous spirits, who "were assembled awaiting the advent of the Son of God into the spirit world, to declare their redemption from the bands of death" (D&C 138:16). When the Savior appeared to them, he preached the gospel to the righteous spirits (see D&C 138:19), and a miraculous program was launched to begin the quest across the great gulf separating those in paradise from those in darkness (see D&C 138:29-31). Thus, the postmeridian program of work for the dead was inaugurated and, through the blessing of the Restoration, unfolded in the latter-days through the power and keys of the priesthood once again restored for the salvation and exaltation of the faithful and obedient.

LEVI (MEANING: JOINED OR ADHERED TO.)

1. Levi was the third son of Jacob by Leah (see Genesis 29:34; 35:23). The motivation for naming him thus was explained as follows: "And she conceived again, and bare a son; and said, Now this time will my husband be joined unto

CHRIST CALLS LEVI (MATTHEW) TO THE TWELVE.

me, because I have born him three sons: therefore was his name called Levi" (Genesis 29:34)—the inference relating to Leah's self-consciousness about Jacob's favoring her sister, Rachel, though Rachel had not been able to bear children. Paul refers to Levi in his discourse concerning the higher priesthood and the principle of tithes (see Hebrews 7:5-9).

Levi is also mentioned in the book of Revelation (see Revelation 7:7). The blessing pronounced by Moses on the tribe of Levi (of which he and Aaron were members) included the promise of priestly assignments: "They shall teach Jacob thy judgments, and Israel thy law: they shall put incense before thee, and whole burnt sacrifice upon thine altar. Bless, Lord, his substance, and accept the work of his hands" (Deuteronomy 33:10-11). These words reflect the perpetual assignment given to the sons of Levi to provide service in support of the work of the priesthood on behalf of the House of Israel under the direction of Aaron and his sons (see Numbers 3, 4, 8).

2. Levi was the son of Melchi mentioned in the genealogical lineage of the Savior (see Luke 3:24).

3. Levi was the son of Simeon also mentioned in the genealogical lineage of the Savior (see Luke 3:29).

4. Levi, also called Matthew, was one of the Twelve called by Jesus (see Mark 2:14-17; Luke 5:27-32). (See the entry for Matthew.)

LEVITES

The Levites were descendants of Levi and, thus, stewards over various functions of leadership associated with the Aaronic Priesthood. The Levites are mentioned only once in the New Testament, concerning the ministry of John the Baptist (see John 1:19). (See the entry on Levi, item 1.)

LIBERTINES (Meaning: freedmen.)

The Libertines, as a group, are mentioned once in the New Testament as being among those opposing Stephen: "Then there arose certain of the synagogue, which is called the synagogue of the Libertines, and Cyrenians, and Alexandrians, and of them of Cilicia and of Asia, disputing with Stephen. And they were not able to resist the wisdom and the spirit by which he spake" (Acts 6: 9-10). The designation "freedmen" seems to indicate that the Libertines were descendants of Jewish captives taken to Rome after the defeat of Jerusalem by Pompey and then subsequently emancipated and allowed to return to their homeland.

LINUS

Linus, mentioned once in the New Testament, was a member of the Church at Rome and a friend of Paul and Timothy: "Do thy diligence to come before winter. Eubulus greeteth thee, and Pudens, and Linus, and Claudia, and all the brethren" (2 Timothy 4:21).

LOT (Meaning: a covering.)

Lot was Abraham's nephew who accompanied him to Canaan. In teaching His disciples about the Second Coming, the Lord used a reference to Lot (see Luke 17:28-33). Historically speaking, Lot, son of Haran (Abraham's brother), joined with the family entourage leaving Ur of the Chaldees for their journey to the land of Canaan (see Genesis 11:27, 31; 12:4-5; 13:1, 5; Abraham 2:4-5, 14-15). The estate of Abraham and the estate of Lot were so abundant that a separation of the two family groups was necessitated in order to find terrain of sufficient size for both. When Abraham granted Lot a choice of where he would reside, Lot favored the verdant plains, so "Abram dwelled in the land of Canaan, and Lot dwelled in the cities of the plain, and pitched his tent toward Sodom" (Genesis 13:12). That location exposed Lot to the battle that rocked the area in due time. Chedorlaomer, king of Elam, in league with three princes of Babylon, defeated the kings of Sodom, Gomorrah, and several other cities in that area who had revolted from their agreement to be subservient to Chedorlaomer (see Genesis 14:1-10). In the battle among these kings, the victors "took all the goods of Sodom and Gomorrah, and all their victuals, and went their way. And they took Lot, Abram's brother's son, who dwelt in

Lot flees the destruction of Sodom and Gomorrah.

103

Sodom, and his goods, and departed" (Genesis 14:11–12). Learning of this abduction, Abraham went out with 318 of his own men and routed the forces of Chedorlaomer. "And he brought back all the goods, and also brought again his brother Lot, and his goods, and the women also, and the people" (Genesis 14:16).

But Lot and his family were not altogether liberated from danger, for they dwelt by choice in a wicked city. Thus, messengers were sent to warn Lot to remove his family from the midst of evil, lest they should be present when the impending destruction from heaven should take place (see Genesis 19). When Lot seemed to resist, the messengers took forceful action: "And while he lingered, the men laid hold upon his hand, and upon the hand of his wife, and upon the hand of his two daughters; the Lord being merciful unto him: and they brought him forth, and set him without the city. And it came to pass, when they had brought them forth abroad, that he said, Escape for thy life; look not behind thee, neither stay thou in all the plain; escape to the mountain, lest thou be consumed" (Genesis 19:16–17). The escape was just in time (see Genesis 19:24–29; Luke 17:28–29; 2 Peter 2:7–8).

As it turned out, Lot's two sons, Moab and Ammon, became the ancestors of the Moabites and Ammonites (see Genesis 19:37–38; Deuteronomy 2:9, 19).

We can look back on the experience of Lot and remember to avoid following his example when he "pitched his tent toward Sodom" (Genesis 13:12). We are counseled well to focus our view on eternal things rather than on the enticements of the world. We can also remember to avoid the experience of Lot's wife when she disobeyed the counsel of the messengers of God by looking back: "Remember Lot's wife," said the Savior, when warning the people to prepare for the Second Coming by letting go of all earthly things in that hour and focusing on things of heaven (Luke 17:32). At the same time, we can garner from the story of Lot the mercy and compassion of the Lord in taking steps to save Lot and his family from the fiery destruction of Sodom and Gomorrah.

LOT'S WIFE (SEE THE ENTRY FOR LOT.)

LUCIFER (MEANING: THE SHINING ONE, LIGHT BRINGER, OR SON OF THE MORNING.) (SEE THE ENTRY FOR SATAN.)

LUKE

Luke is the author of the Gospel bearing his name as well as the Acts of the Apostles, the latter concerned chiefly with the growth of the Church in Gentile areas. He is mentioned only three times in the New Testament:

- "Luke, the beloved physician, and Demas, greet you" (Colossians 4:14).
- "Only Luke is with me. Take Mark, and bring him with thee: for he is profitable to me for the ministry" (2 Timothy 4:11).
- "There salute thee Epaphras, my fellowprisoner in Christ Jesus; Marcus, Aristarchus, Demas, Lucas, my fellowlabourers" (Philemon 1:23–24).

The Joseph Smith Translation of Luke 1:1 contains the author's self-designation: "I am a messenger of Jesus Christ." Luke had medical training and accompanied Paul on missionary activities, having joined him at Troas (see Acts 16:8): "And a vision appeared to Paul in the night; There stood a man of Macedonia, and prayed him, saying, Come over into Macedonia, and help us. And after he had seen the vision, immediately we endeavoured to go into Macedonia, assuredly gathering that the Lord had called us for to preach the gospel unto them" (see Acts 16:9–10). The use of the first person plural form ("we"), beginning with this passage in Acts, indicates that Luke was indeed a fellow traveler with Paul at that point and on a number of occasions beyond. Luke apparently spent several years at Philippi (see Acts 20:6). He was with Paul during the latter's second confinement at Rome (see 2 Timothy 4:11).

His purpose in writing the elegant Gospel of Luke is set forth at the beginning of that text (see Luke 1:1–3). Though Luke was himself not an eyewitness of the happenings associated with the ministry of the Lord, he was able to bring together a memorable and precious account from the witnesses of others.

MAGDALENE (SEE THE ENTRY FOR MARY, ITEM 2.)

MAGI (SEE THE ENTRY FOR WISE MEN OF THE EAST.)

MAGOG (MEANING: COVERING.)

Magog was one of the sons of Japheth, son of Noah (see Genesis 10:2; 1 Chronicles 1:5). The term *Magog* is also used in reference to a nation (see Ezekiel 38:2; 39:6), specifically in the context of the battle of Gog and Magog that will represent the triumph of the forces of heaven over the forces of evil in the final days—initiated at the time of the Second Coming and consummated in the closing battle against Satan and his forces at the end of the millennial period (see Ezekiel 38:16; 39:6-7; see also Revelation 20:8).

MALACHI (MEANING: MY MESSENGER.)

Malachi was the last of the Old Testament prophets. The book of Malachi, one of the twelve shorter prophetic books of the Old Testament, was written around 430 BC. Its central purpose was to call the people and their priests to repentance for gross shortcomings and remind them to prepare for the Second Coming and the judgments of the Lord. The main themes and references are as follows:

- The Lord reproves the people for their unrighteous offerings, and the name of the Lord is to be honored among the Gentile nations but, regretfully, not among His own chosen people.
- Priests are called to repentance for their unholy service, and the people are reproved for marrying outside of the House of Israel.
- The Lord's messenger is to prepare the way of the Second Coming of the Messiah.
- At the Second Coming the wicked are to be consumed in a judgment of fire, and Elijah is to return before that dreadful day.

Malachi was the grand prophet of transition—transition from the Old Testament to the New Testament and from those to the Book of

Mormon. With the fulfillment of the words of Malachi as given unto him by the Lord (see 3 Nephi 24:1), the grand sealing powers of the sacred temples were once again activated upon the earth. All those who were gathered forth from the peoples of the earth through the confirming message of the Book of Mormon could, therefore, receive the sublime blessings of the holy temples of God and continue their journey heavenward toward eternal life and exaltation.

MARK

Following the martyrdom of James at the hands of Herod Agrippa I (see Acts 12:1–2), Peter was incarcerated and then liberated by an angel of the Lord, whereupon he desired to join with the Saints once again in Jerusalem: "And when he had considered the thing, he came to the house of Mary the mother of John, whose surname was Mark; where many were gathered together praying" (Acts 12:12). This is the first mention of Mark (also with the name John, as indicated) in the New Testament.

Subsequently, Mark journeyed with Paul and Barnabas on their missionary journey (see Acts 12:35; 13:5), but then at Perga declined to continue with them and returned instead to Jerusalem (see Acts 13:13). He later accompanied Barnabas to Cyprus after Paul was disinclined to include John in the entourage because John had not remained with them earlier: "And Barnabas determined to take with them John, whose surname was Mark. But Paul thought not good to take him with them, who departed from them from Pamphylia, and went not with them to the work. And the contention was so sharp between them, that they departed asunder one from the other: and so Barnabas took Mark, and sailed unto Cyprus; And Paul chose Silas, and

departed, being recommended by the brethren unto the grace of God" (Acts 15:37–40).

The record shows that Mark was with Paul at Rome, suggesting that their earlier disagreement had been reconciled: "Aristarchus my fellowprisoner saluteth you, and Marcus, sister's son to Barnabas, (touching whom ye received commandments: if he come unto you, receive him;)" (Colossians 4:10); and "There salute thee Epaphras, my fellowprisoner in Christ Jesus; Marcus, Aristarchus, Demas, Lucas, my fellowlabourers" (Philemon 1:24). Mark was also with Peter: "The church that is at Babylon [probably Rome], elected together with you, saluteth you; and so doth Marcus my son" (1 Peter 5:13). Finally, the record also indicates that Mark spent some time with Timothy at Ephesus, as Paul confirms: "Only Luke is with me. Take Mark, and bring him with thee: for he is profitable to me for the ministry" (2 Timothy 4:11).

Mark imbues his Gospel narrative with a deep sense of awe and appreciation for the supernal Atonement of Jesus Christ—that the life of the Lamb of God from beginning to end was one of divine sacrifice accomplished for the salvation of mankind. Mark, too young to have associated directly with the Lord in His ministry, is thought to have depended on his mentor Peter for much of the detail of the descriptive account of Christ's ministry presented in the Gospel of Mark, which appears to predate the other three Gospel accounts (certainly Matthew and Luke), having been written possibly in the late 60s BC (see JCWNT, 80, 83).

MARTHA (MEANING: LADY.)

Martha, her sister Mary, and her brother Lazarus were beloved of the Savior (see John 11:5). Martha had received the Savior into her home when He was passing through the village of Bethany where she and her siblings lived: "And she had a sister called Mary, which also sat at Jesus's feet and heard his word. But Martha was cumbered about much serving, and came to him, and said, Lord, dost thou not care that my sister hath left me to serve alone? bid her therefore that she help me" (Luke 10:39–40). The Savior, aware of the worshipful demeanor of Mary at His feet, used the occasion to teach Martha a lesson in a tender way: "And Jesus answered and said unto her, Martha, Martha, thou art careful and troubled about many things: But one thing is needful: and Mary hath chosen that good part, which shall not be taken away from her" (Luke 10:41–42).

The relationship between this family and the Lord was deepened when Lazarus was stricken with a life-threatening illness. After the sisters had sent for Jesus, Jesus told His disciples, "This sickness is not unto death, but for the glory of God, that the Son of God might be glorified thereby. . . . Our friend Lazarus sleepeth; but I go, that I may awake him out of sleep" (John 11:4, 11)—meaning that a miracle was about to be performed.

Having arrived at the outskirts of the village, He was greeted by Martha, who was direct in her words of welcome: "Lord, if thou hadst been here, my brother had not died. But I know, that even now, whatsoever thou wilt ask of God, God will give it thee" (John 11:21–22). Jesus was likewise direct in His response: "Thy brother shall rise again" (John 11:23). Martha then took the long view, saying, "I know that he shall rise again in the resurrection at the last day" (John 11:24),

MARTHA QUESTIONS HER SISTER MARY'S MOTIVES.

whereupon Jesus uttered words of profound significance: "I am the resurrection, and the life: he that believeth in me, though he were dead, yet shall he live: And whosoever liveth and believeth in me shall never die. Believest thou this? She saith unto him, Yea, Lord: I believe that thou art the Christ, the Son of God, which should come into the world" (John 11:25-27).

At that point, Martha arranged for Mary to come out and meet the Lord (see John 11:32-36).

The bereaved then went to the burial place, a cave with a stone at the entrance. When the Savior directed that the stone be removed, Martha demurred, concerned about the condition of the body, now lifeless for four days. But the Savior replied, "Said I not unto thee, that, if thou wouldest believe, thou shouldest see the glory of God?" (John 11:40). After the stone was removed, Jesus cried to the Father and then restored Lazarus to life (see John 11:41-44).

Sometime later, at the time of the Passover, Jesus returned to visit the family, at which time Martha was seemingly content to serve the meal while her sister Mary again anointed: "There they made him a supper; and Martha served: but Lazarus was one of them that sat at the table with him. Then took Mary a pound of ointment of spikenard, very costly, and anointed the feet of Jesus, and wiped his feet with her hair: and the house was filled with the odour of the ointment" (John 12:2-3). Thus, the family was again united, both among themselves, as well as in the fold of the Savior.

Mary

1. Mary was the mother of Jesus Christ. No other woman in all of history has or will have as great and singular an honor as Mary who brought the Savior into the world. She was a native of Nazareth and of the tribe of Judah through the lineage of David (see Luke 3:23-33). Before her wedding to Joseph was consummated, the angel Gabriel announced to her the divinely appointed mission to which she was called (see Luke 1:28-33).

When Mary inquired how she should bring forth the heavenly child, the angel stated, "The Holy Ghost shall come upon thee, and the power of the Highest shall overshadow thee: therefore also that holy thing which shall be born of thee shall be called the Son of God" (Luke 1:35). The angel having also informed her that her cousin Elisabeth was at that time expecting a child, Mary

MARY IS THE MOTHER OF GOD.

journeyed the long distance to see Elisabeth, who greeted her with words of confirmation and encouragement (see Luke 1:42–45). Then Mary pronounced the celebrated expression of her exultation (see Luke 1:46–55).

When Mary returned to Nazareth, her future husband, Joseph, was directed by the angel in a dream to proceed with the marriage plans (see Matthew 1:20–23).

Close to the time of giving birth, Mary accompanied her husband to Bethlehem in compliance with the order of Caesar Augustus to have all citizens participate in a census—and thus unfolded the supernal event of the Savior's birth in the lowly stable, announced by the hosts of heaven, welcomed by shepherds and the believers, and blessed by the hand of the Father (see Luke 2:1–10; Micah 5:2). Mary and Joseph then brought their young baby to Jerusalem to satisfy the requirements of the Mosaic order in the temple, where both Simeon and Anna proclaimed the verity of the divine birth as a blessing of salvation and redemption for mankind (see Luke 2:22–38).

When the wise men from the East came later to seek the child, Mary was present (see Matthew 2:11). Thereafter came the flight to Egypt to escape the murderous plot by Herod the Great against all children two years old or younger in Bethlehem and its vicinity and the return to Nazareth after the king had died (see Matthew 2).

From that point on, Mary and her husband continued their parental duties in such a manner that "the child grew, and waxed strong in spirit, filled with wisdom: and the grace of God was upon him" (Luke 2:40). When he was twelve years of age, Mary and Joseph took him to Jerusalem for the annual celebration of the Feast of the Passover. But when they began the return journey with their entourage of relatives and friends, thinking the boy was in the company, they discovered, to their surprise, after being a day on the road, that he was not to be found. Returning anxiously, they learned after three days of searching that he had stayed back to interact with the doctors in the temple, amazing them with his "understanding and answers" (Luke 2:47). "And he said unto them, How is it that ye sought me? wist ye not that I must be about my Father's business? And they understood not the saying which he spake unto them. And he went down with them, and came to Nazareth, and was subject unto them: but his mother kept all these sayings in her heart. And Jesus increased in wisdom and stature, and in favour with God and man" (Luke 2:49–52).

Subsequent to that event, we encounter Mary only occasionally in the remainder of the record:

- She was at the wedding in Cana where Jesus began his sequence of miracles (see John 2:11).
- Mary was present again sometime later in Capernaum (see Matthew 12:46–50).
- Mary was at the foot of the cross when Jesus gave His loving directive for the nurture and care of His mother (see John 19:25–27).
- Mary is present with the disciples in the upper room following the Ascension: (see Acts 1:14).

2. Mary Magdalene was from Magdala, a community located on the western shore of the Sea of Galilee. We first learn of her during the account of the Lord's ministry among the various towns in that area: "And it came to pass afterward [after forgiving the woman who had anointed His feet], that he went throughout every city and village, preaching and shewing the glad

Mary Magdalene sees the resurrected Christ.

tidings of the kingdom of God: and the twelve were with him, And certain women, which had been healed of evil spirits and infirmities, Mary called Magdalene, out of whom went seven devils, And Joanna the wife of Chuza Herod's steward, and Susanna, and many others, which ministered unto him of their substance" (Luke 8:1–3). Mary Magdalene was among the group of women who followed after the Lord on His final journey into Jerusalem and were present at the Crucifixion (see Matthew 27:55–56).

After Joseph of Arimathea had removed the body of the Lord and placed it in the sepulcher, the women provided caring services: "And the women also, which came with him from Galilee, followed after, and beheld the sepulchre, and how his body was laid. And they returned, and prepared spices and ointments; and rested the sabbath day according to the commandment" (Luke 23:55–56; see also Mark 15:47). Then, as the Sabbath was completed, the miracle became

evident (see Matthew 28:1–8; the account in Mark 16:1 makes clear that the "other Mary" mentioned in this account was Mary, the mother of James, and that a woman named Salome was also present; see also Luke 24:10; John 20:1).

Responding to the report of the women, Peter and John rushed to the sepulchre to confirm the news, returning afterward to their own place of abode. However, Mary Magdalene remained behind and became the first witness to the Resurrection of the Lord:

> But Mary stood without at the sepulchre weeping: and as she wept, she stooped down, and looked into the sepulchre,
>
> And seeth two angels in white sitting, the one at the head, and the other at the feet, where the body of Jesus had lain.
>
> And they say unto her, Woman, why weepest thou? She saith unto them, Because they have taken away my Lord, and I know not where they have laid him.
>
> And when she had thus said, she turned herself back, and saw Jesus standing, and knew not that it was Jesus.
>
> Jesus saith unto her, Woman, why weepest thou? whom seekest thou? She, supposing him to be the gardener, saith unto him, Sir, if thou have borne him hence, tell me where thou hast laid him, and I will take him away.
>
> Jesus saith unto her, Mary. She turned herself, and saith unto him, Rabboni; which is to say, Master.

Jesus saith unto her, Touch me not [JST John 20:17 reads, "Hold me not"]; for I am not yet ascended to my Father: but go to my brethren, and say unto them, I ascend unto my Father, and your Father; and to my God, and your God.

Mary Magdalene came and told the disciples that she had seen the Lord, and that he had spoken these things unto her. (John 20:11–18; see also Mark 16:9, naming her as the first to see the risen Lord.)

3. Mary was the sister of Martha and Lazarus, the man whom the Savior raised from the dead. Of this family, it was said, "Now Jesus loved Martha, and her sister, and Lazarus" (John 11:5). Martha had received the Savior into her home when He was passing through the village of Bethany where she and her siblings lived: "And she had a sister called Mary, which also sat at Jesus's feet, and heard his word. But Martha was cumbered about much serving, and came to him, and said, Lord, dost thou not care that my sister hath left me to serve alone? bid her therefore that she help me" (Luke 10:39–40). The Savior responded with tenderness and understanding: "And Jesus answered and said unto her, Martha, Martha, thou art careful and troubled about many things: But one thing is needful: and Mary hath chosen that good part, which shall not be taken away from her" (Luke 10:41–42). Sometime later, the sisters sent for the Savior

Mary sits at the feet of Jesus as he teaches her.

when their brother Lazarus contracted a serious illness. Before the Savior could arrive, Lazarus passed away, leaving his sisters in deep mourning. Observing the weeping Mary and her friends, Jesus "groaned in the spirit, and was troubled, And said, Where have ye laid him? They said unto him, Lord, come and see. Jesus wept. Then said the Jews, Behold how he loved him!" (John 11:33–36). Jesus then went to the burial place and, to the joy of all, restored Lazarus to life once more (see John 11:41–44). At the time of Passover, Jesus returned to visit with the family: "There they made him a supper; and Martha served: but Lazarus was one of them that sat at the table with him. Then took Mary a pound of ointment of spikenard, very costly, and anointed the feet of Jesus, and wiped his feet with her hair: and the house was filled with the odour of the ointment" (John 12:2–3; see also the references in Mark 14:3 and Matthew 26:6, which indicate that the gathering was at the home of Simon the leper). This action caused Judas Iscariot to ask of the Savior, "Why was not this ointment sold for three hundred pence, and given to the poor? This he said, not that he cared for the poor; but because he was a thief, and had the bag, and bare what was put therein" (John 12:5–6). To this the Lord replied, "Let her alone: against the day of my burying hath she kept this. For the poor always ye have with you; but me ye have not always" (John 12:7–8). Mary seems to have had the premonition that the Savior would in the future be sacrificed as the Lamb of God.

4. Mary, the mother of James and Joses, was among the women of Galilee who were present at the Crucifixion: "And many women were there beholding afar off, which followed Jesus from Galilee, ministering unto him: Among which was Mary Magdalene, and Mary the mother of James and Joses, and the mother of Zebedee's children" (Matthew 27:55-56); "There were also women looking on afar off: among whom was Mary Magdalene, and Mary the mother of James the less and of Joses, and Salome; (Who also, when he was in Galilee, followed him, and ministered unto him;) and many other women which came up with him unto Jerusalem" (Mark 15:40-41). As Joseph of Arimathea placed the body of Jesus in the tomb, this Mary, along with Mary Magdalene, witnessed the event: "And Mary Magdalene and Mary the mother of Joses beheld where he was laid" (Mark 15:47). The account in Matthew gives this report in regard to the same event: "And there was Mary Magdalene, and the other Mary, sitting over against the sepulchre" (Matthew 27:61), the inference being that "the other Mary" was Mary, the mother of Joses.

This Mary also accompanied Mary Magdalene at the end of the Sabbath in order to visit the tomb (see Matthew 18:1; Mark 16:1-2). The account in Luke gives the following introductory detail: "Now upon the first day of the week, very early in the morning, they came unto the sepulchre, bringing the spices which they had prepared, and certain others with them" (Luke 24:10). The scriptures then go on to identify the women, following their discovery of the empty tomb, as follows: "It was Mary Magdalene, and Joanna, and Mary the mother of James, and other women that were with them, which told these things unto the apostles" (Luke 24:10).

A question remains concerning the relationship between this Mary and Mary the mother of Jesus. The siblings of the Savior are identified in Mark 6:3 by His contemporaries as follows: "Is not this the carpenter, the son of Mary, the brother of James, and Joses, and of

Juda, and Simon? and are not his sisters here with us?" If the James and Joses mentioned in the expression "Mary the mother of James and Joses" (Matthew 27:56) are the same as the James and Joses in this passage from Mark 6:3, then Mary, the mother of James and Joses, would be identical with Mary the mother of Jesus.

5. Mary, wife of Cleophas, is mentioned by name in only one passage of the New Testament: "Now there stood by the cross of Jesus his mother, and his mother's sister, Mary the wife of Cleophas, and Mary Magdalene" (John 19:25). If "Mary the wife of Cleophas" is an appositive (extended alternative identification) of "his mother's sister," then the implication is that Mary had a sister who was also named Mary (i.e., Mary the wife of Cleophas). On the other hand, if "his mother's sister" is in sequence with "Mary the wife of Cleophas" (i.e., not the same person), then an unnamed sister of the mother of Jesus was present at the Crucifixion, along with the other three Marys. According to a later historical tradition, Mary, the wife of Cleophas, was a sister of Joseph, the Lord's earthly father, hence an aunt to Jesus.

6. Mary was the mother of John Mark, author of the Gospel of Mark: "And when he [Peter, following his deliverance from prison by an angel] had considered the thing, he came to the house of Mary the mother of John, whose surname was Mark; where many were gathered together praying" (Acts 12:12). Apparently, this Mary was a person of means whose home served as a place of gathering for the Saints.

7. Mary was a Christian at Rome who showed kindness to Paul: "Greet Mary, who bestowed much labour on us" (Romans 16:6).

MARY MAGDALENE (SEE THE ENTRY FOR MARY, ITEM 2.)

MATTHEW (MEANING: GIFT OF GOD.)

Matthew was an Apostle of the Lord Jesus Christ and the author of the Gospel of Matthew. He is identified as Matthew in only three verses of the New Testament:

- his calling by the Lord (see Matthew 9:9)
- in the listing of the Twelve in the Gospel of Matthew (see Matthew 10:2-4)
- in the listing of the Twelve in the Gospel of Luke (see Luke 6:13-16)

In the account of Matthew's calling by the Lord given in Mark, the name of Levi is used instead: "And as he passed by, he saw Levi the son of Alphæus sitting at the receipt of custom, and said unto him, Follow me. And he arose and followed him" (Mark 2:14). Note the wording in Luke: "And after these things he went forth, and saw a publican, named Levi, sitting at the receipt of custom: and he said unto him, Follow me. And he left all, rose up, and followed him. And Levi made him a great feast in his own house: and there was a great company of publicans and of others that sat down with them" (Luke 5:27-29). The scribes and Pharisees murmured at this action, saying, "Why do ye eat and drink with publicans and sinners?" (Luke 5:20). The response of the Lord is memorable: "And Jesus answering said unto them, They that are whole need not a physician; but they that are sick. I came not to call the righteous, but sinners to repentance" (Luke 5:31-32).

Matthew, originally a tax collector in Capernaum, prepared his gospel account to confirm for his Jewish audience—so inclined to turn a blind eye to the prophetic ministry of the Savior—that Christ was indeed the foretold Messiah, not only for the house of Israel but also for the Gentile believers. The account ends with the charge of the Lord to carry the gospel message "to all nations" (Matthew 28:19–20). It is thought that the Gospel of Matthew was developed largely in keeping with the patterns of the Gospel of Mark, written earlier (see *JCWNT*, 66–67).

MATTHIAS (MEANING: GIFT OF JEHOVAH.)

Matthias was the disciple chosen to fill the place of Judas in the Twelve: "And they appointed two, Joseph called Barsabas, who was surnamed Justus, and Matthias. And they prayed, and said, Thou, Lord, which knowest the hearts of all men, shew whether of these two thou hast chosen, That he may take part of this ministry and apostleship, from which Judas by transgression fell, that he might go to his own place. And they gave forth their lots; and the lot fell upon Matthias; and he was numbered with the eleven apostles" (Acts 1:23–26). Both of the candidates for the apostleship were long-standing followers of Christ, according to the statement leading up to the selection: "Wherefore of these men which have companied with us all the time that the Lord Jesus went in and out among us, Beginning from the baptism of John, unto that same day that he was taken up from us, must one be ordained to be a witness with us of his resurrection" (Acts 1:21–22). Nothing more of Matthias is known from the record.

MELCHIZEDEK (MEANING: KING OF RIGHTEOUSNESS.)

Melchizedek was a great prophet and leader who lived at the time of Abraham, around two millennia before the coming of Christ.

Paul mentions him several times in the New Testament (with the spelling *Melchisedec*) in connection with the priesthood of the Lord (see Hebrews 5:5–6, 9–10; 6:20).

Paul gives the following portrait of Melchizedek: "For this Melchisedec, king of Salem, priest of the most high God, who met Abraham returning from the slaughter of the kings, and blessed him; To whom also Abraham gave a tenth part of all; first being by interpretation King of righteousness, and after that also King of Salem, which is, King of peace. . . . Now consider how great this man was, unto whom even the patriarch Abraham gave the tenth of the spoils" (Hebrews 7:1–2, 4). Though Melchizedek was great and though the Levitical priesthood after the time of Moses had the commission to service the tithes of Israel over the generations, there would arise, declared

MELCHIZEDEK TEACHES THE GOSPEL.

Paul, an even greater priest of an order higher than the priesthood of Aaron (the Levitical order)—Jesus Christ:

> For that after the similitude of Melchisedec there ariseth another priest,
>
> Who is made, not after the law of a carnal commandment, but after the power of an endless life.
>
> For he testifieth, Thou art a priest for ever after the order of Melchisedec. . . .
>
> For the law [of Moses] made nothing perfect, but the bringing in of a better hope did; by the which we draw nigh unto God. . . .
>
> By so much was Jesus made a surety of a better testament. (Hebrews 7:15–17, 19, 22)

Paul invokes the greatness of Melchizedek as a type and shadow of the supremacy of the Son of God, reminding his audience that the Aaronic/Levitical order instituted at the time of Moses to serve the needs of the people when they were unwilling to embrace the fulness of God's offering of truth unto them had been augmented by a new and glorious manifestation of priesthood blessings through the ministry of the Messiah, of whom God declared, "Thou art a priest for ever after the order of Melchisedec" (Hebrews 7:21).

Were it not for modern-day revelation, we would enjoy only a narrow glimpse into the life of this distinguished and noble prophet. The story of Melchizedek is the story of peace, for it represents the transformation of a wayward society through the redemptive power of spiritual principles, such as faith, repentance, and committed righteousness. When Melchizedek assumed the office of prophet/leader, Salem (later called Jerusalem) was under a veil of spiritual darkness and rebellion, "yea, they had all gone astray" (Alma 13:17). But Melchizedek was well prepared for his mission: "Now Melchizedek was a man of faith, who wrought righteousness; and when a child he feared God, and stopped the mouths of lions, and quenched the violence of fire. And thus, having been approved of God, he was ordained an high priest after the order of the covenant which God made with Enoch" (JST Genesis 14:26). What Melchizedek accomplished was nothing short of a miracle, for his influence on the people had the astounding effect of bringing them all back into the fold (see Alma 13:18–19).

So great was Melchizedek's office and stature that he was also placed in charge of the abundance of the Lord's kingdom: "And he lifted up his voice, and he blessed Abram, being the high priest, and the keeper of the storehouse of God; Him whom God had appointed to receive tithes for the poor. Wherefore, Abram paid unto him tithes of all that he had, of all the riches which he possessed, which God had given him more than that which he had need" (JST Genesis 14:36–39). Through the portrait of Melchizedek augmented by modern revelation, we can understand much better the magnificence of the holy priesthood, its eternal nature, its relationship to the atoning mission of the Son of God, the sacred role of covenants in our eternal progression, and how we, too, can become the sons and daughters of God through the power of the priesthood and the blessings of the gospel.

Melchizedek is the prototype of the person who engenders and promotes peace. He is verily a type of the Master Himself, the divine Prince of Peace. Peace of mind and heart should be one of our main goals as we seek happiness here and in the hereafter.

What made Melchizedek so great? Why was he so honored to have the Lord's priesthood named after him? The answer is that he "exercised mighty faith" (Alma 13:18), magnified his holy office in the priesthood, and preached repentance. Preaching repentance is the commission given of God to all His holy prophets since the world began, and it will continue to be so until the end. The eternal message of the gospel of Jesus Christ is to have mighty faith unto repentance, that all might come unto Christ. That is the message that all of the great prophets have given—including Melchizedek. Melchizedek's success in bringing his people to repentance is reflected in the outcomes of his labors. His people became a holy people like unto the people of Enoch, for that is what Melchizedek sought: "And his people wrought righteousness, and obtained heaven, and sought for the city of Enoch which God had before taken, separating it from the earth, having reserved it unto the latter days, or the end of the world. . . . And this Melchizedek, having thus established righteousness, was called the king of heaven by his people, or, in other words, the King of peace" (JST Genesis 14:34, 36).

As we come to appreciate the great role Melchizedek played—even unto the ordaining of our forefather Abraham, through whose lineage we are blessed (see D&C 84:14)—we can understand how our daily lives are affected for good by the contribution and example of that ancient prophet after whom the higher priesthood is named. Melchizedek helped to prepare Abraham for his mission, and through Abraham and his seed, all the nations of the earth shall be blessed. Melchizedek was of the order of the priesthood that opened up the blessings of eternal life, as the Prophet Joseph Smith confirmed: "The King of Shiloam (Salem) had power and authority over that of Abraham, holding the key and the power of endless life" (*TPJS*, 322). It is our joy to bring to others the gospel of Jesus Christ through the blessings of the Abrahamic Covenant so that they, like the people of Melchizedek, might enjoy peace through righteousness and the blessings of covenant principles and ordinances.

MERCURIUS

Mercurius was a Roman god equivalent to the Greek god Hermes. When Paul and Barnabas were preaching in the city of Lystra in Lycaonia, a Roman province in Asia Minor (located in today's southcentral Turkey), they encountered a crippled man: "The same heard Paul speak: who stedfastly beholding him, and perceiving that he had faith to be healed, Said with a loud voice, Stand upright on thy feet. And he leaped and walked. And when the people saw what Paul had done, they lifted up their voices, saying in the speech of Lycaonia, The gods are come down to us in the likeness of men. And they called Barnabas, Jupiter; and Paul, Mercurius, because he was the chief speaker" (Acts 14:9–12). Paul then used the occasion to correct the false perceptions of the crowd, which wanted to make sacrifices unto the visitors:

> Sirs, why do ye these things? We also are men of like passions with you, and preach unto you that ye should turn from these vanities unto the living God, which made heaven, and earth,

and the sea, and all things that are therein:

Who in times past suffered all nations to walk in their own ways.

Nevertheless he left not himself without witness, in that he did good, and gave us rain from heaven, and fruitful seasons, filling our hearts with food and gladness. (Acts 14:15–17)

Thereafter, certain Jews came forward and persuaded the people to stone Paul, who was injured but not in the least dissuaded from continuing to preach the gospel of Jesus Christ in that area of the country (see Acts 14:19–28).

MESSIAH

Messiah is the Aramaic name equivalent to *Christ* (from the Greek). Messiah occurs only twice in the Old Testament (Daniel 9:25–26) and twice in the New Testament (as "Messias"):

- in the announcement by Andrew to his brother Simon Peter (see John 1:41)
- in the words of the Samaritan woman at the well (see John 4:25–26)

While the Doctrine and Covenants has only three references to the Messiah, the Book of Mormon contains many references to the Messiah. In chapter ten of 1 Nephi, the Messiah is referred to no fewer than eight times by Nephi in quoting the testimony of his father, Lehi, concerning Jesus Christ. Here is one example: "Yea, even six hundred years from the time that my father left Jerusalem, a prophet would the Lord God raise up among the Jews—

even a Messiah, or, in other words, a Savior of the world" (1 Nephi 10:4). Another celebrated passage, in which Lehi is teaching his son Jacob about the miracle of the Atonement of the Lord, reads as follows: "Wherefore, how great the importance to make these things known unto the inhabitants of the earth, that they may know that there is no flesh that can dwell in the presence of God, save it be through the merits, and mercy, and grace of the Holy Messiah, who layeth down his life according to the flesh, and taketh it again by the power of the Spirit, that he may bring to pass the resurrection of the dead, being the first that should rise" (2 Nephi 2:8).

In another remarkable prophetic passage concerning the Savior, Nephi uses the name Messiah five separate times in a single verse in reference to the Jewish people one day coming

CHRIST PRAYING

to believe in the mission of the Redeemer (see 2 Nephi 25:18).

There is one glorious reference to Messiah in the Pearl of Great Price, conveying the words of the Lord before Enoch: "And the Lord said: Blessed is he through whose seed Messiah shall come; for he saith—I am Messiah, the King of Zion, the Rock of Heaven, which is broad as eternity; whoso cometh in at the gate and climbeth up by me shall never fall; wherefore, blessed are they of whom I have spoken, for they shall come forth with songs of everlasting joy" (Moses 7:53). (See also the entry for Jesus Christ.)

METHUSELAH (MEANING: MAN OF THE DART OR JAVELIN.)

Methuselah, son of Enoch, was the longest surviving of the ancient patriarchs (see Genesis 5:21–27; 1 Chronicles 1:3; Moses 6:25; 8:2–7). Methuselah, written as *Mathusala*, is mentioned one time in the New Testament (in Luke's genealogical lineage of Jesus Christ): "Mathusala, which was the son of Enoch, which was the son of Jared, which was the son of Maleleel, which was the son of Cainan, Which was the son of Enos, which was the son of Seth, which was the son of Adam, which was the son of God" (Luke 3:37–38).

MICHAEL (MEANING: WHO IS LIKE GOD.)

Michael, the prince and archangel, is mentioned only twice in the New Testament (see Jude 1:9; Revelation 12:7). In the New Testament reference to Michael in Jude 1:9, we read, "Yet Michael the archangel, when contending with the devil he disputed about the body of Moses, durst not bring against him a railing accusation,

but said, The Lord rebuke thee." Michael clearly left to God the ultimate judgment against the devil, while standing firm concerning the status of Moses, translated at the end of his mortal ministry. According to Bruce R. McConkie, "It appears, then, that Satan—ever anxious to thwart the purposes of God—'disputed about the body of Moses,' meaning that he sought the mortal death of Israel's lawgiver so that he would not have a tangible body in which to come—along with Elijah, who also was taken up without tasting death—to confer the keys of the priesthood upon Peter, James, and John" (*DNTC*, 3:424). Michael was no stranger to the tactics of the devil, as John the Revelator confirmed regarding the role played by Michael in the premortal existence: "And there was war in heaven: Michael and his angels fought against the dragon; and the dragon fought and his angels, And prevailed not; neither was their place found any more in heaven" (Revelation 12:7–8).

He is mentioned three times in the Old Testament, in the grand vision revealed to Daniel concerning the events of the last days where Michael will defend and deliver the faithful (see Daniel 10:13, 21; 12:1).

More than this is not revealed about Michael in the Bible; however, modern-day scripture provides a more complete understanding of his role in the designs of heaven. In latter-day revelation, Adam is described as follows: "And the Lord appeared unto them [the ancient patriarchs], and they rose up and blessed Adam, and called him Michael, the prince, the archangel" (D&C 107:54; see also D&C 128:21). The premortal Michael is, therefore, the same individual as the mortal Adam, destined to play an essential role in the unfolding of Heavenly Father's plan for the salvation and exaltation of His children.

"Michael, mine archangel" (D&C 29:26) will have the assignment to accomplish the final defeat of Satan and his hosts at the end of the millennial period (see D&C 88:112–115)–just as he defeated Lucifer (Satan) and his followers in the premortal realm (see Revelation 12:7–8).

On the occasion of the assembly at Adam-ondi-Ahman, where Adam, three years prior to his death, rendered his final blessing unto his posterity, the Lord appeared and said unto Adam, "I have set thee to be at the head; a multitude of nations shall come of thee, and thou art a prince over them forever" (D&C 107:55). The title of *prince* in this context opens the view to the extraordinary authority and responsibility conferred upon Adam (Michael) by the Lord: "Who hath appointed Michael your prince, and established his feet, and set him upon high, and given unto him the keys of salvation under the counsel and direction of the Holy One, who is without beginning of days or end of life" (D&C 78:16).

Adam–Michael, first father, father of all, prince of all, archangel, head of a multitude of nations–is a figure of supernal importance in the work and glory of God, beginning in the premortal realm, continuing throughout mortality, and extending into the eternities. Joseph Smith confirmed that Adam (Michael) "is the father of the human family, and presides over the spirits of all men" (*TPJS*, 157). Daniel was given a vision of the future gathering involving Adam, "the Ancient of days," in his capacity as one holding the keys of salvation (Daniel 7:9–14, 22). This consummating assembly is also spoken of in the Doctrine and Covenants (see D&C 27:5–13; 120) and marks the defining moment in time when Adam will receive from those holding priesthood stewardships and keys an accounting of those keys over which he (Adam) presides, prior to conveying them back

to Jesus Christ, the millennial King. Adam's presence is also manifested in connection with the Prophet Joseph Smith's remarkable vision of the celestial world of glory (see D&C 137:5) and in President Joseph F. Smith's vision of the work of salvation inaugurated by the Savior in the spiritual realm (see D&C 138:38, 40). (See also the entry for Adam.)

MOSES

Moses, the great prophet of liberation and the law for the Israelite people, is mentioned frequently in the New Testament—eighty times, to be specific. Moses serves at the great transitional frontier of history and doctrine between the old and the new testaments or covenants, being both the type and shadow of the new and glorious prophet heralded and manifested in the person of the Messiah and King as well as the iconic figure constituting the essence of tradition for the Jewish rabbis and leaders. It was in the shadow of Moses that these leaders crouched in the vain attempt to secure and preserve their power and influence threatened by the advent of the Christian era.

Concerning the latter dimension of the Mosaic tradition, the Savior frequently shed light on the contrast between benighted misinterpretation and practice of the law by his Jewish detractors and the dawning of a higher order of truth and spirituality manifested in the gospel of Jesus Christ–or the new covenant revealed through the ministry of the Only Begotten. Consider these examples:

- the hypocrisy of the traditionalists (see Matthew 23:1–3, 11–12)
- the setting aside of the word of God (see Mark 7:9–13)

- blindness to the scriptures (see John 5:39, 46-47)
- insisting on a sign (see John 6:30-35)
- lack of forgiveness (see John 8:5-11)
- murderous intent disguised as propriety (see John 7:19)
- placing a priority on external practice rather than on internal values and truth, as in the plot against Stephen (see Acts 6:14)
- reluctance to recognize the higher order of the gospel, as in the case of certain Christian people at Antioch (see Acts 15:1)

With regard to the transition from the law of Moses—given to the children of Israel as a preparatory framework of development and growth—to the higher law of the Lord, Paul said, "Wherefore the law was our schoolmaster to bring us unto Christ, that we might be justified by faith. But after that faith is come, we are no longer under a schoolmaster. For ye are all the children of God by faith in Christ Jesus" (Galatians 3:24-26). The New Testament references to Moses frequently echo this transition, as in the following passages:

- **The witness of John the Baptist:** "John bare witness of him, and cried, saying, This was he of whom I spake, He that cometh after me is preferred before me: for he was before me. And of his fulness have all we received, and grace for grace. For the law was given by Moses, but grace and truth came by Jesus Christ" (John 1:15-17).
- **The witness of Philip:** "Philip findeth Nathanael, and saith unto him, We have found him, of whom Moses in the law, and the prophets, did write, Jesus of Nazareth, the son of Joseph. And Nathanael said unto him, Can there any good thing come out of Nazareth? Philip saith unto him, Come and see" (John 1:45-46).
- **The Savior to Nicodemus:** "And as Moses lifted up the serpent in the wilderness, even so must the Son of man be lifted up: That whosoever believeth in him should not perish, but have eternal life" (John 3:14-15).
- **The resurrected Lord to His disciples:** "And he said unto them, These are the words which I spake unto you, while I was yet with you, that all things must be fulfilled, which were written in the law of Moses, and in the prophets, and in the psalms, concerning me" (Luke 24:44).
- **The witness of Peter after the healing of the lame man:** "For Moses truly said unto the fathers, A prophet shall the Lord your God raise up unto you of your brethren, like unto me; him shall ye hear in all

Moses receives the Ten Commandments from the Lord.

things whatsoever he shall say unto you" (Acts 3:22).

- **The witness of Stephen prior to his martyrdom:** "This is that Moses, which said unto the children of Israel, A prophet shall the Lord your God raise up unto you of your brethren, like unto me; him shall ye hear" (Acts 7:37).

Moses himself had a presence in the meridian of time on the Mount of Transfiguration, when he appeared under the direction of the Savior to transact sacred priesthood assignments (see Matthew 17:1–5; see also Mark 9:2–8; Luke 9:28–36). Moreover, during His mortal ministry, the Savior taught about the righteous role of Moses in the gospel plan of happiness, as in these two examples:

- the parable of the beggar Lazarus (see Luke 16:29–31)
- the discourse of the risen Lord to the two disciples on the road to Emmaus (see Luke 24:27)

From time to time, the Apostle Paul invoked the memory of Moses in teaching the principles of the higher law of salvation and atonement, as in these examples:

- justification and forgiveness through the Atonement (see Acts 13:38–39)
- on the transparent gospel of hope and liberty (see 2 Corinthians 3:12–18)
- on the faithfulness of Moses and supremacy of the Lord (see Hebrews 3:1–6)

The final mention of Moses in the New Testament comes in reference to a future day when the Saints of God will sing a song of jubilation: "And they sing the song of Moses the servant of God, and the song of the Lamb, saying, Great and marvellous are thy works, Lord God Almighty; just and true are thy ways, thou King of saints" (Revelation 15:3).

From the perspective of Israelite history, Moses is a personage of singularly imposing stature. The meaning of his name is disputed, with alternatives such as "drawn or pulled out (of the water)" or "son, has provided." Thus, for example, the word *Rameses* (title of the Pharaohs), based on the Egyptian word *moses* (meaning "son" or "has provided") signifies "Ra (the sun god) has provided a son." In any case, Moses was the prophet of God who prefigured Christ's redeeming mission by liberating the Israelites from Egyptian bondage, sustaining them in their journeys, serving as the agent for the revelation of the Ten Commandments, establishing the presence of the Tabernacle among the people, and providing leadership to guide them through the wilderness—even to the gateway of the promised land, where deliverance awaited many of them. These five missions—liberation, sustenance, revelation of the Lord's commandments, the establishment of the Tabernacle, and homeward guidance—define the grand commission of the prophet Moses.

In addition to what we learn about Moses in the Old Testament, modern scripture sheds further light on the mission and person of Moses. It was Moses who appeared to Joseph Smith and Oliver Cowdery in the Kirtland Temple on April 3, 1836, to restore the keys of "the gathering of Israel from the four parts of the earth, and the leading of the ten tribes from the land of the north" (D&C 110:11). In all, Moses is mentioned twenty-seven times throughout the Doctrine and Covenants. Some of the key passages depict Moses as an exemplar of one who receives and acts on the spirit of revelation (see

MOSES PARTS THE RED SEA.

D&C 8:3), as the prototype for the ministry of Joseph Smith (i.e., the only one appointed to receive commandments and revelations for God's people as the chosen prophet; see D&C 28:2), as a key figure in the lineage of the priesthood (see D&C 84:6; 133:54–55; 136:37), as one given the mission to sanctify his people "that they might behold the face of God" (see D&C 84:23), as the forebear of those "sons of Moses" who shall serve with devotion in the temples of God and fulfill the commission of the Abrahamic Covenant (see D&C 84:31–34), as the prototype of the president of the high priesthood who is to "preside over the whole church, and to be like unto Moses" (D&C 107:91), as the one who restored the keys of the gathering of Israel in the latter days (see D&C 110:11), as the one who built the Tabernacle of

the Lord as an ancient model of the temple (see D&C 124:38), as one of the "great and mighty ones" assembled in the "vast congregation of the righteous" perceived in vision by Joseph F. Smith (see D&C 138:38), plus many passages concerning the law of Moses. Additionally, Moses is mentioned in the current headings/summaries of sections 74, 84, and 110.

Additionally, Moses is mentioned by name some seventy-five times in the Book of Mormon. His remarkable qualities and accomplishments are celebrated throughout the pages of this sacred scripture: the dividing of the Red Sea (see 1 Nephi 4:2; 17:26; Helaman 8:11), his authoring the five initial books of the Bible (see 1 Nephi 5:11; 19:23), smiting the rock to obtain water for the Israelites (see 1 Nephi 17:29), deliverance of Israel from

Egypt (see 2 Nephi 3:10), his radiant countenance while on the mount (see Mosiah 13:5), his prophecies of the coming of the Messiah (see Mosiah 13:33), his references to the Son of God (see Alma 33:19), the lifting of the brazen serpent as a type of the Savior (see Helaman 8:14), and many other references. Of major significance as a theme in the Book of Mormon is the fulfillment of the law of Moses through the ministry and Atonement of the Savior. The resurrected Lord declared to the Saints in Bountiful:

> Behold, I say unto you that the law is fulfilled that was given unto Moses.
>
> Behold, I am he that gave the law, and I am he who covenanted with my people Israel; therefore, the law in me is fulfilled, for I have come to fulfil the law; therefore it hath an end.
>
> Behold, I do not destroy the prophets, for as many as have not been fulfilled in me, verily I say unto you, shall all be fulfilled.
>
> And because I said unto you that old things have passed away, I do not destroy that which hath been spoken concerning things which are to come.
>
> For behold, the covenant which I have made with my people is not all fulfilled; but the law which was given unto Moses hath an end in me. (3 Nephi 15:4–8; see also 3 Nephi 20:23; Ether 12:11)

From the very beginning of the Book of Mormon, the transcendence of the Atonement as

the key to salvation and exaltation is emphasized, the law of Moses being a preparatory protocol pointing to the Savior and His redeeming mission (see 2 Nephi 2:5–8).

The book of Moses in the Pearl of Great Price is a masterful refinement and augmentation of the biblical account as revealed through the Prophet Joseph Smith. It is from chapter one of Moses, concerning the supernal experience of Moses upon the mount where he met God and received his divine commission, that we have the priceless verity about the purpose of God: "For behold, this is my work and my glory—to bring to pass the immortality and eternal life of man" (Moses 1:39). Upon the completion of his years in the wilderness, Moses did not die in the literal sense (as implied in Deuteronomy 34:5–7) but was translated, enabling him to complete his mission of conveying essential priesthood keys on the Mount of Transfiguration in the meridian of time (see Matthew 17:3; Alma 45:19) and then, as a resurrected being, during the Restoration in the latter days (see D&C 110:11; 133:54–55).

Naaman (Meaning: pleasantness.)

Naaman was a nobleman in the royal court of Syria: "Now Naaman, captain of the host of the king of Syria, was a great man with his master, and honourable, because by him the Lord had given deliverance unto Syria: he was also a mighty man in valour, but he was a leper" (2 Kings 5:1). In speaking in the synagogue in His native Nazareth one day, Jesus referred to an incident in Naaman's life when he was cured of leprosy by Elisha the prophet (see Luke 4:27).

The historical background for Jesus' reference is as follows: Naaman's wife had a maid who had been captured from among the Israelites by the Syrians. This young girl was concerned about Naaman's disease and said to her mistress, "Would God my lord were with the prophet that is in Samaria! for he would recover him of his leprosy" (2 Kings 5:3). When the prophet Elisha heard that Ben-hadad II, the Syrian king, had sent a letter of request to Joram, king of Israel, on behalf of Naaman, Elisha, knowing of the hesitancy of the king of Israel concerning the matter, declared, "Let him come now to me, and

he shall know that there is a prophet in Israel" (2 Kings 5:8). So Naaman and his company came before the house of Elisha, seeking a blessing:

> And Elisha sent a messenger
> unto him, saying, Go and wash

NAAMAN WASHES IN THE JORDAN AND IS HEALED.

in Jordan seven times, and thy flesh shall come again to thee, and thou shalt be clean.

But Naaman was wroth, and went away, and said, Behold, I thought, He will surely come out to me, and stand, and call on the name of the LORD his God, and strike his hand over the place, and recover the leper.

Are not Abana and Pharpar, rivers of Damascus, better than all the waters of Israel? may I not wash in them, and be clean? So he turned and went away in a rage.

And his servants came near, and spake unto him, and said, My father, if the prophet had bid thee do some great thing, wouldest thou not have done it? how much rather then, when he saith to thee, Wash, and be clean?

Then went he down, and dipped himself seven times in Jordan, according to the saying of the man of God: and his flesh came again like unto the flesh of a little child, and he was clean. (2 Kings 5:10–14)

Returning whole unto the house of Elisha, Naaman declared, "Behold, now I know that there is no God in all the earth, but in Israel: now therefore, I pray thee, take a blessing of thy servant" (2 Kings 5:15). But Elisha refused compensation for his services, and Naaman departed in peace. Why did Jesus refer to this incident when speaking to the people in His native area of Nazareth? Because they were incredulous at His claim that He was the fulfillment of ancient prophecy—and they said, "Is not this Joseph's son?" (Luke 4:22). Jesus included in his response these words: "And many lepers were in Israel in the time of Eliseus [Elisha] the prophet; and none of them was cleansed, saving Naaman the Syrian" (Luke 4:27). The Savior's listeners in Nazareth were incensed at this reference, since Naaman was a Syrian and not of the house of Israel and since the Savior implied that Naaman had more faith and a higher degree of obedience than could be found among the Israelites. Certainly the point was well taken by Jesus in regard to the skeptical and distrusting leaders among the Jewish contemporaries in the area where Jesus grew up. Hence His declaration—even before the Naaman reference: "Verily I say unto you, No prophet is accepted in his own country" (Luke 4:24).

NACHOR (SEE THE ENTRY FOR NAHOR.)

NAHOR

Nahor was the father of Terah, who was the father of Abram, later named Abraham (see Genesis 11:24; 1 Chronicles 1:26). In the Gospel of Luke, the name is rendered *Nachor* in the presentation of the genealogical lineage of the Savior: "Which was the son of Jacob, which was the son of Isaac, which was the son of Abraham, which was the son of Thara, which was the son of Nachor" (Luke 3:34).

NAPHTALI (MEANING: WRESTLINGS.)

Naphtali was the fifth son of Jacob (Israel) by Bilhah, Rachel's handmaid (see Genesis 30:8; 35:25; 46:24; Exodus 1:4). For a segment from the blessing later pronounced upon Naphtali and his posterity by Jacob, see Genesis 49:21 (see also Moses's blessing upon this tribe given in Deuteronomy 33:23; Joshua 19:32–39). One celebrated member of the tribe was Barak, who responded to the commission of Deborah, judge of Israel, to wage the triumphant battle against the encroaching Canaanites under command of Sisera (see Judges 4–5). Naphtali is referred to in two instances in the New Testament, in reference to the "land of Nephthalim" (Matthew 4:15; see also verse 13) and "the tribe of Nepthalim" (Revelation 7:6).

NATHAN (MEANING: HE HAS GIVEN.)

Nathan was a son of David and Bathsheba (see 2 Samuel 5:14; 1 Chronicles 3:5; 14:4; Zechariah 12:12). He is mentioned in the genealogical lineage of the Savior given by Luke (see Luke 3:31).

NATHANAEL (MEANING: GOD HAS GIVEN.)

Nathanael was an associate of Philip during the ministry of the Savior: "Jesus saw Nathanael coming to him, and saith of him, Behold an Israelite indeed, in whom is no guile! Nathanael saith unto him, Whence knowest thou me? Jesus answered and said unto him, Before that Philip called thee, when thou wast under the fig tree, I saw thee. Nathanael answered and saith unto him, Rabbi, thou art the Son of God; thou art the King of Israel" (John 1:47–49). Nathanael was also among those favored to see the risen Lord (see John 21:2). Nathanael is customarily thought to be the same as Bartholomew, one of the original Twelve Apostles: in Matthew 10:3, Mark 3:18, and Luke 6:14 there is a paring of Philip and Bartholomew, with no mention of Nathanael (see also Acts 1:13); whereas John refers only to Philip and Nathanael, but never Bartholomew. In section 41 of the Doctrine and Covenants, Edward Partridge is commended by the Lord: "His heart is pure before me, for he is like unto Nathanael of old, in whom there is no guile" (D&C 41:11).

NAZARENE (MEANING: BELONGING TO NAZARETH.)

Nazareth was a small community located to the west of the Sea of Galilee, about midway between the southern tip of that sea and the shores of the Mediterranean Sea. Nazareth was the home of Joseph and the place of upbringing of the son given to him and to Mary for nurture and care. It was to Nazareth that Joseph brought his wife and the young child after their return from the flight to Egypt to escape the murderous campaign of Herod: "And he [Joseph] came and dwelt in a city called Nazareth: that it might be fulfilled which was spoken by the prophets, He shall be called a Nazarene" (Matthew 2:23). The scriptural source of that ancient prophecy is not identified, but the news of Nazareth was also known to the prophets of ancient America: "And it came to pass that I [Nephi] looked and beheld the great city of Jerusalem, and also other cities. And I beheld the city of Nazareth; and in the city of Nazareth I beheld a virgin, and she was exceedingly fair and white" (1 Nephi 11:13). Jesus grew up in Nazareth—hence the phrase "Jesus of Nazareth" that occurs frequently in the New Testament. It was also in Nazareth that the "Nazarene" Jesus Christ announced the commencement of His ministry (see Luke 4:16–21).

Nazareth and the Nazarenes were anathema to the conspiring enemies of the Church that Jesus founded. Ananias the high priest, through his spokesperson Tertullus, alleged before Felix the seditious intent of Paul in promoting the cause of the Savior: "For we have found this man a pestilent fellow, and a mover of sedition among all the Jews throughout the world, and a ringleader of the sect of the Nazarenes" (Acts 24:5). Yet, it was the cause of the Nazarenes and the atoning mission of Jesus of Nazareth that would open the gateway for salvation and exaltation for all of mankind.

NAZARITE/NAZIRITE (MEANING: ONE SEPARATED UNTO THE LORD OR A CONSECRATED MAN; FROM THE HEBREW WORD *NAZIR*, MEANING CONSECRATED OR SEPARATED.)

The term *Nazarite* (or *Nazirite*) does not occur in the New Testament, but it occurs a dozen times in the Old Testament in singular or plural form. An individual under the vow of a Nazarite would abstain from strong drink, avoid cutting the hair from the head, and avoid any contact with persons deceased (see Numbers 6). The Nazarite vow could be for life, as in the case of Samson (see Judges 13:5, 7; 16:17) or Samuel (see 1 Samuel 1:11), or for only a shorter, defined period of time (see Amos 2:11–12). John the Baptist appears to have conformed with the pattern of a Nazarite: "For he shall be great in the sight of the Lord, and shall drink neither wine nor strong drink; and he shall be filled with the Holy Ghost, even from his mother's womb" (Luke 1:15). Paul also might have taken Nazaritic vows for a defined period of time (see Acts 18:18; 21:23–26). The term *Nazarite* (or *Nazirite*) is not to be confused with the term *Nazarene*, having to do with the geographical name.

NICODEMUS

We learn in the Gospel of John, "There was a man of the Pharisees, named Nicodemus, a ruler of the Jews" (John 3:1). Nicodemus, a member of the Sanhedrin, the leading Jewish council, came in secret to Jesus during the night hour to learn more of His teachings, saying, "Rabbi, we know that thou art a teacher come from God: for no man can do these miracles that thou doest, except God be with him" (John 3:2). Jesus took the opportunity to teach Nicodemus the fundamental doctrine of the gospel:

> Jesus answered and said unto him, Verily, verily, I say unto thee, Except a man be born again, he cannot see the kingdom of God.
>
> Nicodemus saith unto him, How can a man be born when he is old? can he enter the second time into his mother's womb, and be born?
>
> Jesus answered, Verily, verily, I say unto thee, Except a man be born of water and of the Spirit, he cannot enter into the kingdom of God.
>
> That which is born of the flesh is flesh; and that which is born of the Spirit is spirit.
>
> Marvel not that I said unto thee, Ye must be born again.
>
> The wind bloweth where it listeth, and thou hearest the sound thereof, but canst not tell whence it cometh, and whither it goeth: so is every one that is born of the Spirit. (John 3:3–8)

Nicodemus, wondering and confused, asked, "How can these things be?" (John 3:9). The Savior uttered words that have become an echoing ensign of divine truth across the centuries:

And no man hath ascended up to heaven, but he that came down from heaven, even the Son of man which is in heaven.

And as Moses lifted up the serpent in the wilderness, even so must the Son of man be lifted up:

That whosoever believeth in him should not perish, but have eternal life.

For God so loved the world, that he gave his only begotten Son, that whosoever believeth in him should not perish, but have everlasting life.

For God sent not his Son into the world to condemn the world; but that the world through him might be saved. (John 3:13-17)

Nicodemus was unquestionably touched with the verity of Christ's doctrine, for he later defended the Savior to his Pharisee associates who were intent on destroying the Christian cause (see John 7:50-53). Nicodemus later honored the crucified Lord: "And after this Joseph of Arimathæa, being a disciple of Jesus, but secretly for fear of the Jews, besought Pilate that he might take away the body of Jesus: and Pilate gave him leave. He came therefore, and took the body of Jesus. And there came also Nicodemus, which at the first came to Jesus by night, and brought a mixture of myrrh and aloes, about an hundred pound weight" (John 19:38-39).

NICOLAITANS

In his vision of the seven congregations of the Church during his day, John the Revelator received counsel concerning the walk of life being followed by the Saints of Ephesus, Smyrna, Pergamos, Thyatira, Sardis, Philadelphia, and Laodicea (see Revelation 1:11). The leader of the Church at Ephesus, despite his shortcomings, was extolled for his patience and devoted labor—and especially for his discernment of those in his circle unrighteously claiming the truth: "But this thou hast, that thou hatest the deeds of the Nicolaitans, which I also hate" (Revelation 2:6). The leader at Pergamos is warned of practitioners of evil in his congregation: "So hast thou also them that hold the doctrine of the Nicolaitans, which thing I hate" (Revelation 2:15).

Who were the Nicolaitans? Elder Bruce R. McConkie identifies them as:

> Members of the Church who were trying to maintain their church standing while continuing to live after the manner of the world. They must have had some specific doctrinal teachings which they used to justify their course. In the counsel given to the Church in Pergamos, their doctrine is condemned as severely as that of Balaam who sought to lead Israel astray (Rev. 2:14-16; 2 Pet. 2:10-22; Num. 22, 23, and 24). Whatever their particular deeds and doctrines were, the designation has come to be used to identify those who want their names on the records of the Church, but do not want to devote themselves to the gospel cause with full purpose of heart. (*DNTC*, 3:446)

The term *Nicolaitane band* is used in the Doctrine and Covenants in the Lord's severe reprimand of Bishop Newel K. Whitney: "Let my servant Newel K. Whitney be ashamed of the Nicolaitane band and of all their secret abominations, and of all his littleness of soul before me, saith the Lord, and come up to the land of Adam-ondi-Ahman, and be a bishop unto my people, saith the Lord, not in name but in deed, saith the Lord" (D&C 117:11). Newel K. Whitney redirected his ways and remained valiant in the faith.

NICOLAS (MEANING: VICTORY OF THE PEOPLE.)

Nicolas was among the seven brethren called by the Apostles to help in Church service, including caring for the needs of the widows: "And they chose Stephen, a man full of faith and of the Holy Ghost, and Philip, and Prochorus, and Nicanor, and Timon, and Parmenas, and Nicolas a proselyte of Antioch" (Acts 6:5). The term *proselyte* (meaning "stranger") was a designation given to Gentile converts to the Jewish faith. (See also the entry for Proselytes.)

NOAH (MEANING: REST.)

Noah, the ancient patriarch, is referenced three times in the New Testament:

- in Paul's discourse on faith (see Hebrews 11:7)
- in Peter's words about the ministry of Christ in the spirit world (see 1 Peter 3:18-20)

- in Peter's warning about evil-doers creeping into the Church (see 2 Peter 2:4-5).

With the spelling *Noe*, there are also several other references to Noah in the New Testament, including the mention of his name in the genealogical lineage of Jesus (see Luke 3:36). In addition, the Savior likened the Second Coming to the sudden encompassing flood at the time of Noah, when the people ignored his warnings: "But of that day and hour knoweth no man, no, not the angels of heaven, but my Father only. But as the days of Noe were, so shall also the coming of the Son of man be. For as in the days that were before the flood they were eating and drinking, marrying and giving in marriage, until the day that Noe entered into the ark" (Matthew 24:36-38; see also Luke 17:26-27).

In historical terms, Noah was the son of Lamech (see Genesis 5:28-29; Luke 3:36). From latter-day scripture, we learn that Noah, when ten years old, was ordained to the priesthood by Methuselah (see D&C 107:52). From that moment on, he honored his priesthood calling with valor. The story of Noah and the ark is an intimate and revealing source of knowledge about the nature of spirituality and obedience to the covenants—precisely the kinds of qualities that are required for each of us to preserve life for ourselves and our families from day to day. Noah, like all the Lord's chosen prophets, was a just and righteous man (see Moses 8:27; see also Genesis 6:9). Noah was commanded to call the people to repentance so they might avoid being destroyed—something he did in strict obedience to the will of God, though his words were disdained by all beyond the circle of his immediate family (see Moses 8:20-30).

The Lord established a covenant with Noah, commanding him to build an ark, gather provisions and animals, and preserve his family (see Genesis 6:14-22; Hebrews 11:7; 1 Peter 3:20; 2 Peter 2:5). The flood came, universal in regard to its reach across the earth—the Book of Mormon also makes reference to the effects of the flood in the New World (see Ether 13:2). The waters flooded and surged for forty days (see Genesis 7:12, 17). Everything on the earth was destroyed—only Noah and those on the ark were preserved. The waters prevailed for another 150 days (see Genesis 8:3), eventually subsiding to allow the ark and its passengers to come to rest on "the mountains of Ararat" (Genesis 8:4). The Lord had preserved the life of mankind and earthly creatures. A new era of life was about to begin.

The Prophet Joseph Smith confirms Noah's greatness in a latter-day pronouncement, placing him next to Adam in authority: "Then to Noah, who is Gabriel; he stands next in authority to Adam in the Priesthood; he was called of God to this office, and was the father of all living in his day, and to him was given the dominion" (*HC*, 3:386).

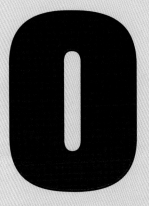

OBED (MEANING: SERVANT.)

Obed was the son of Ruth and Boaz: "And the women her neighbours [i.e., the neighbors of Naomi, Ruth's mother-in-law] gave it a name, saying, There is a son born to Naomi; and they called his name Obed: he is the father of Jesse, the father of David" (Ruth 4:17, 21–22; see also 1 Chronicles 2:12). Obed is listed in the genealogical lineage of Jesus Christ (see Matthew 1:5; Luke 3:2).

ONE HUNDRED AND FORTY-FOUR THOUSAND

John speaks of the servants of God with the seal of the living God: "And I saw another angel ascending from the east, having the seal of the living God: and he cried with a loud voice to the four angels, to whom it was given to hurt the earth and the sea, Saying, Hurt not the earth, neither the sea, nor the trees, till we have sealed the servants of our God in their foreheads. And I heard the number of them which were sealed: and there were sealed an hundred and forty and four thousand of all the tribes of the children of Israel" (Revelation 7:2–4;

see also Revelation 14:1–3). Twelve thousand are to come from each of the twelve tribes of Israel (see Revelation 7:5–8).

Section 77 of the Doctrine and Covenants provides inspired commentary on various passages written by John the Revelator, including the following reference: "And I heard the number of them which were sealed: and there were sealed an hundred and forty and four thousand of all the tribes of the children of Israel" (D&C 7:4). Latter-day scripture asks the question:

Q. What are we to understand by sealing the one hundred and forty-four thousand, out of all the tribes of Israel—twelve thousand out of every tribe?

A. We are to understand that those who are sealed are high priests, ordained unto the holy order of God, to administer the everlasting gospel; for they are they who are ordained out of every nation, kindred, tongue, and people, by the angels to whom is given power over the nations of the earth, to bring as many as will come to the church of the Firstborn. (D&C 77:11)

The 144,000 noble and righteous priesthood leaders are, therefore, apparently called to oversee the gathering of the faithful from the four quarters of earth in the final chapters of the earth's history.

ONESIMUS (MEANING: PROFITABLE.)

Onesimus was a faithful messenger mentioned by Paul in his epistle to the Colossians: "Let your speech be alway with grace, seasoned with salt, that ye may know how ye ought to answer every man. All my state shall Tychicus declare unto you, who is a beloved brother, and a faithful minister and fellowservant in the Lord: Whom I have sent unto you for the same purpose, that he might know your estate, and comfort your hearts; With Onesimus, a faithful and beloved brother, who is one of you. They shall make known unto you all things which are done here" (Colossians 4:6–9). It seems clear that Onesimus was a servant who had abandoned his master Philemon, but, through the intercession of Paul, his mentor in the gospel, was to be reinstated as a brother in the gospel (see Philemon 1:10–18).

The story of Onesimus is a touching account of how an Apostle teaches true principles of reconciliation and intercedes in kindness and gentleness with an appeal to the master, Philemon, to forgive and accept back his runaway servant—all with the guarantee from Paul to cover the expense of what the servant might have taken away. In like measure, the Lord pays the price for our misdeeds through the power and love of the Atonement.

PARTHIANS

On the Day of Pentecost, when the Holy Ghost was imparted to the gathering crowds, all were able to understand the messages in their own tongue: "And they were all amazed and marvelled, saying one to another, Behold, are not all these which speak Galilæans? And how hear we every man in our own tongue, wherein we were born? Parthians, and Medes, and Elamites, and the dwellers in Mesopotamia, and in Judæa, and Cappadocia, in Pontus, and Asia" (Acts 2:7-9). The Parthians mentioned in this passage were Jews who had settled in Parthia, a large region southeast of the Caspian Sea.

PATRIARCH/PATRIARCHS

The word *patriarch* is not used in the King James Version of the Old Testament; however, in reference to Old Testament figures, it is used twice in the New Testament concerning "the patriarch David" (Acts 2:12) and "the patriarch Abraham" (Hebrews 7:4)—a title that applies to all the early prophet-fathers in the Old Testament account

(see Bible Dictionary). The word *patriarchs* (plural) is likewise not used in the Old Testament but occurs twice in the New Testament, in Stephen's recounting of the history of Israel and the sons of Jacob, called "patriarchs," (Acts 7:8, 9). The word *patriarchs* is used once in the Pearl of Great Price in a statement by Abraham, where he refers to his fathers as "patriarchs" (Abraham 1:31; on patriarch—"evangelist"—as an ordained office in the Melchizedek Priesthood, see D&C 107:39-41).

PAUL

Paul is one of the Lord's greatest missionaries in any dispensation. From his intellectual and historical training as a Pharisee, including his studies under Gamaliel, he was intimately acquainted with the traditions and cultural nuances embraced by the Jewish leadership of his day. He could see through their window of view and understand their perspectives—thus, he was well prepared following his miraculous conversion to the Christian faith to address the concerns of his Jewish audience and frame the

PAUL TEACHES THE EPHESIANS.

truths of the new covenant in such a way that they could understand them and believe them, if their hearts were willing to embrace Jesus Christ as the long-heralded Messiah. Paul's record of intense persecution of the Church prior to his rebirth (like that of Alma the younger in the Book of Mormon) rendered his newfound devotion to the cause of the Savior even more passionate and vigorous. Having cultivated a multifaceted perspective on things spiritual, he emerged as a profoundly committed exponent of Christian views among the Gentile populations of his day. As a teacher, Paul was unsurpassed in the articulation of supernal gospel truths in a way that has lost none of its ardor and intensity even today. He traveled endless miles in the cause of the Lord; he fostered friendship among countless numbers of Saints; he endured inexpressibly painful hardship and tribulation; he resolved differences with his companions; he

continually practiced the art of communicating and cultivating understanding; he was inviolate in his witness of the divinity of the Savior; and he has left his legacy of love and devotion as the archetype of one who fulfilled an apostolic mission, for *Apostle* means, indeed, "messenger." According to tradition, he gave his life as a martyr for the cause of truth.

Some of the unforgettable milestones in his lifetime and tenure include the following:

- **his miraculous conversion:** "I am verily a man which am a Jew, born in Tarsus, a city in Cilicia, yet brought up in this city at the feet of Gamaliel, and taught according to the perfect manner of the law of the fathers, and was zealous toward God, as ye all are this day. And I persecuted this way unto the death, binding and delivering into prisons both men and women. As also the high priest doth bear me witness, and all the estate of the elders: from whom also I received letters unto the brethren, and went to Damascus, to bring them which were there bound unto Jerusalem, for to be punished. And it came to pass, that, as I made my journey, and was come nigh unto Damascus about noon, suddenly there shone from heaven a great light round about me. And I fell unto the ground, and heard a voice saying unto me, Saul, Saul, why persecutest thou me? And I answered, Who art thou, Lord? And he said unto me, I am Jesus of Nazareth, whom thou persecutest. And they that were with me saw indeed the light, and were afraid; but they heard not the voice of him that spake to me. And I said, What shall I do, Lord? And the Lord said unto me, Arise, and go into Damascus; and there it shall be told thee of all things which are appointed for thee to do" (Acts 22:3–10; see also Acts 6:1–8). Thereafter, Saul (Paul) hastened to Damascus where Ananias, already prepared for the assignment by vision, greeted him with the words: "The God of our fathers hath chosen thee, that thou shouldest know his will, and see that Just One, and shouldest hear the voice of his mouth. For thou shalt be his witness unto all men of what thou hast seen and heard" (Acts 22:14–15; 26:12–20).

- **his service as an Apostle:** Paul is identified as an Apostle in several passages (see Romans 1:1; 1 Corinthians 1:1; 9:1–2; Galatians 1:1; 1 Timothy 2:7). Besides Paul, two others not of the original Twelve were identified as Apostles—Barnabas (see Acts 14:14; see also 1 Corinthians 9:6) and "James the Lord's brother" (Galatians 1:19). Concerning the calling of Paul, James, and Barnabas as Apostles, the Bible Dictionary states, "The New Testament does not inform us whether these three brethren also served in the council of the Twelve as vacancies occurred therein, or whether they were apostles strictly in the sense of being special witnesses for the Lord Jesus Christ" (612). In the latter days, the Lord spoke of Paul as "Paul mine apostle" (D&C 18:9).

- **his missionary journeys:** Amidst a ceaseless array of trips and meetings throughout his career, Paul is noted for his three major missionary excursions in the lands to the east and north of the Mediterranean (see Acts 13:1–14:26; Acts 15:36–18:22; Acts 18:23–21:15).

- **his encounters with the authorities:** He was arrested in Jerusalem following his third missionary journey and was confined at Caesarea. Then, as a Roman citizen, he was sent to Rome for trial and additional confinement for a period of time (see Acts 21:17–23:35; Acts 24:1–26:32; Acts 27:1–28:10, 20).

- **his final years:** After his release from Rome, he apparently continued his travels until he was taken prisoner once more in Rome and, according to tradition, suffered death as a martyr during the reign of Nero.

Paul's writings contain an amazing abundance of scriptural gems to strengthen faith and inspire obedience in following the pathway set forth by the Savior. Here are just a few examples:

- Paul's sermon on Mars' Hill concerning the true God (see Acts 17:23–31)

PAUL PRAYS FOR GUIDANCE.

- Paul's actions in Corinth to institute the fulness of the baptismal covenant (see Acts 19:1–6)
- Paul's warning about impending apostasy (see Acts 20:28–31; 2 Timothy 3:1–13)
- Paul's self-defense when accused before Felix (see Acts 24:14–16; Paul's defense before Agrippa—Acts 26:12–23)
- Paul's testimony and witness to the Romans (see Romans 1:16)
- the power and efficacy of grace (see Romans 3:20–26).
- hope through the love of the Spirit (see Romans 5:3–5)
- power of the word (see Romans 10:14–17)
- Revelation of God's blessings through the Spirit (see 1 Corinthians 2:9–11)
- we are the temple of God (see 1 Corinthians 3:16–17)
- marriage appointed of God (see 1 Corinthians 11:11)
- testimony comes through the Spirit (see 1 Corinthians 12:3)
- the gifts of the Spirit come from God (see 1 Corinthians 12:4–31)
- Paul's discourse on charity (see 1 Corinthians 13:1, 8, 13)
- Paul's statement on baptism for the dead (see 1 Corinthians 15:29)
- Paul's reference to degrees of glory (see 1 Corinthians 15:40–41)
- conversion is inward commitment to the new covenant (see 2 Corinthians 3:3–6; Hebrews 8:10)
- Godly sorrow is fundamental to repentance (see 2 Corinthians 7:10)
- the Law of Moses as a schoolmaster preparing us for Christ (see Galatians 3:24–29)
- freedom through Christ (see Galatians 5:1)
- we reap what we sow (see Galatians 6:7–9)

- prophecy of the Restoration (see Ephesians 1:9–10)
- unity in the Church through Christ (see Ephesians 2:19–22)
- the strength of the Church organization (see Ephesians 4:11–13)
- the divinity of Christ (see Philippians 2:5–6)
- work out your own salvation in Christ (see Philippians 2:11–13)
- embrace honorable qualities (see Philippians 4:8; Article of Faith 1:13)
- labor of love (see 1 Thessalonians 1:2–3; Hebrews 6:10)
- have devotion (see 1 Thessalonians 5:21)
- counsel to youth (see 1 Timothy 4:12)
- caring for one's family (see 1 Timothy 5:8)
- the love of money (see 1 Timothy 6:10–11)
- overcome fear through Christ (see 2 Timothy 1:7–8)
- the blessing of scripture (see 2 Timothy 3:16–17)
- the good fight (see 2 Timothy 4:7)
- Called by authority (see Hebrews 5:4)
- the perfection of Christ (see Hebrews 5:9; 12:2)
- the mediator of the new testament (see Hebrews 9:14–16)
- on faith (see Hebrews 11:1; the entire chapter).
- on service (see Hebrews 12:12–13; D&C 81:5)

PETER (MEANING: ROCK.)

Peter ("rock," the meaning of the Greek equivalent of his Aramaic name, *Cephas*), along with his brother Andrew, was the first of the Twelve Apostles called by the Lord during

PETER DENIES CHRIST.

Some of the most memorable passages concerning the ministry of Peter include the following:

- Peter called as a "fisher of men" (see Matthew 4:18–19; Mark 1:18; Luke 5:1–11; John 1:40–42)
- Peter's witness of the divinity of the Savior (see Matthew 16:13–19)
- Peter's momentary lapse in denying the Savior (see Matthew 26:33–35, 69–75)
- at the time of the Resurrection (see John 20:3–9; Mark 16:7; 9:9; Luke 24:12, 34)
- With the risen Lord by the Sea of Galilee (see John 21:15–17)
- the emergence of Peter as the post-Resurrection leader of the Church (see Acts 2:37–40)
- the healing of the lame man (see Acts 3:1–9)
- the beginning of missionary work among the Gentiles (see Acts 10:34–43)
- statement of royal identity for the Church (see 1 Peter 2:9)
- declarations about the ministry of the Lord in the spirit world (see 1 Peter 3:18–20; 4:6)

His mortal ministry (Matthew 4:18–22; Mark 1:16–18; Luke 5:1–11; and John 1:40–42). He was the leading Apostle belonging to the inner circle of three Apostles (Peter, James, and John)—constituting, as it were, the First Presidency of the Church. All three were with the Savior on the Mount of Transfiguration (see Matthew 17: 1–13; Mark 9:2–9; Luke 4:28–36) and at Gethsemane (see Matthew 26:36–37; Mark 14:32–33; Luke 22:39). Peter's affirmation of the divine Sonship of Jesus (Matthew 16:16) preceded the Savior's celebrated declaration (see Matthew 16:17–19; the similar reference to Peter in D&C 128:10).

It was through Peter's missionary work that the gospel was introduced among the Gentiles (Acts 10–11). Peter's pronouncement to the people concerning the predicted "times of refreshing" and "times of restitution of all things" (Acts 3:19, 21) coming through the future ministry of the Lord foreshadowed the Restoration in the latter days.

Peter is also identified as the exemplary gospel messenger when the Lord instructed Sidney Rigdon, Parley P. Pratt, and Leman Copley to go among the Shakers and proclaim the truths of the restored gospel:

> Wherefore, I give unto you a commandment that ye go among this people, and say unto them, like unto mine apostle of old, whose name was Peter:
> Believe on the name of the Lord Jesus, who was on the earth,

138

and is to come, the beginning and the end;

Repent and be baptized in the name of Jesus Christ, according to the holy commandment, for the remission of sins;

And whoso doeth this shall receive the gift of the Holy Ghost, by the laying on of the hands of the elders of the church. (D&C 49:11–14)

Moreover, it was through pondering the writings of Peter that President Joseph F. Smith was granted his grand vision of the work of salvation taking place in the spirit world (D&C 138:5–6, 9–10, 28).

PHARISEES (MEANING: SEPARATED, FROM THE HEBREW WORD *PERUSHIM*.)

The Pharisees were one of the leading religious parties among the Jewish people of Christ's time. They observed strict separation from the Gentile strata of their day, placed as great an emphasis on the oral traditions and practices of their heritage as upon the written law, prescribed meticulous rules of outward observance for daily living, and proselyted zealously to convert people to their confined and narrow point of view. In opposition to the Sadducees, they did profess a belief in the resurrection and the afterlife as well as in the existence of angels and spirits (see Acts 23:8). In this they agreed with the Christian view, but their party still constituted one of the major impediments to the unfolding of the Church instituted by the Savior, who was repeatedly subjected to their conspiratorial onslaughts and attacks. Some of the passages showing the Savior's characterization of the Pharasitical philosophy are given below:

- **concerning salvation:** "For I say unto you, That except your righteousness shall exceed the righteousness of the scribes and Pharisees, ye shall in no case enter into the kingdom of heaven" (Matthew 5:20).
- **blind leading the blind:** "Then came his disciples, and said unto him, Knowest thou that the Pharisees were offended, after they heard this saying? But he answered and said, Every plant, which my heavenly Father hath not planted, shall be rooted up. Let them alone: they be blind leaders of the blind. And if the blind lead the blind, both shall fall into the ditch" (Matthew 15:12–14).
- **seeking for a sign:** "The Pharisees also with the Sadducees came, and tempting

CHRIST COMPARES THE PHARISEES AND THE PUBLICANS.

desired him that he would shew them a sign from heaven. He answered and said unto them, When it is evening, ye say, It will be fair weather: for the sky is red. And in the morning, It will be foul weather to day: for the sky is red and lowring. O ye hypocrites, ye can discern the face of the sky; but can ye not discern the signs of the times? A wicked and adulterous generation seeketh after a sign; and there shall no sign be given unto it, but the sign of the prophet Jonas. And he left them, and departed" (Matthew 16:1–4).

- **false doctrine:** "How is it that ye do not understand that I spake it not to you concerning bread, that ye should beware of the leaven of the Pharisees and of the Sadducees? Then understood they how that he bade them not beware of the leaven of bread, but of the doctrine of the Pharisees and of the Sadducees" (Matthew 16:11–12).

- **hypocrisy:** "Then spake Jesus to the multitude, and to his disciples, Saying, The scribes and the Pharisees sit in Moses' seat: All therefore whatsoever they bid you observe, that observe and do; but do not ye after their works: for they say, and do not" (Matthew 23:1–3).

- **obsession with external rules:** "But woe unto you, scribes and Pharisees, hypocrites! for ye shut up the kingdom of heaven against men: for ye neither go in yourselves, neither suffer ye them that are entering to go in. . . . Woe unto you, scribes and Pharisees, hypocrites! for ye pay tithe of mint and anise and cummin, and have omitted the weightier matters of the law, judgment, mercy, and faith: these ought ye to have done, and not to leave the other

undone. Ye blind guides, which strain at a gnat, and swallow a camel. Woe unto you, scribes and Pharisees, hypocrites! for ye make clean the outside of the cup and of the platter, but within they are full of extortion and excess. Thou blind Pharisee, cleanse first that which is within the cup and platter, that the outside of them may be clean also. Woe unto you, scribes and Pharisees, hypocrites! for ye are like unto whited sepulchres, which indeed appear beautiful outward, but are within full of dead men's bones, and of all uncleanness. Even so ye also outwardly appear righteous unto men, but within ye are full of hypocrisy and iniquity" (Matthew 23:13, 23–28; see also Luke 11:39–44).

- **obsession with the traditions and commandments of men:** "Then the Pharisees and scribes asked him, Why walk not thy disciples according to the tradition of the elders, but eat bread with unwashen hands? He answered and said unto them, Well hath Esaias [Isaiah] prophesied of you hypocrites, as it is written, This people honoureth me with their lips, but their heart is far from me [see Isaiah 29:13]. Howbeit in vain do they worship me, teaching for doctrines the commandments of men. For laying aside the commandment of God, ye hold the tradition of men, as the washing of pots and cups: and many other such like things ye do. And he said unto them, Full well ye reject the commandment of God, that ye may keep your own tradition" (Mark 7:5–9).

It is little wonder that the Savior declared to the Pharisees and their like, "O Jerusalem, Jerusalem, which killest the prophets, and stonest them that are sent unto thee; how often would I have gathered thy children together, as a hen doth gather her brood under her wings, and ye would not! Behold, your house is left unto you desolate: and verily I say unto you, Ye shall not see me, until the time come when ye shall say, Blessed is he that cometh in the name of the Lord" (Luke 13:34-35). Some of those of Pharasitical persuasion did indeed listen and believe–such as Nicodemus (see John 3) and Paul–after his miraculous conversion (see Acts 9:1-6; 17-18). But the Pharisees proved to be key in carrying out the Crucifixion of our Lord, a grim reminder of what Jacob prophesied in the Book of Mormon:

> Wherefore, as I said unto you, it must needs be expedient that Christ–for in the last night the angel spake unto me that this should be his name–should come among the Jews, among those who are the more wicked part of the world; and they shall crucify him–for thus it behooveth our God, and there is none other nation on earth that would crucify their God.
>
> For should the mighty miracles be wrought among other nations they would repent, and know that he be their God. (2 Nephi 10:3-4)

The reason for this gross offense is clearly laid at the feet of the religious leaders of the day: "But because of priestcrafts and iniquities, they at Jerusalem will stiffen their necks against him, that he be crucified" (Jacob 10:5). The result would be disastrous for the people: "Wherefore, because of their iniquities, destructions, famines, pestilences, and bloodshed shall come upon them; and they who shall not be destroyed shall be scattered among all nations" (Jacob 10:6).

Yet, the Lord, even He who was crucified, reserves a blessing unto those who return and believe:

> But behold, thus saith the Lord God: When the day cometh that they shall believe in me, that I am Christ, then have I covenanted with their fathers that they shall be restored in the flesh, upon the earth, unto the lands of their inheritance.
>
> And it shall come to pass that they shall be gathered in from their long dispersion, from the isles of the sea, and from the four parts of the earth; and the nations of the Gentiles shall be great in the eyes of me, saith God, in carrying them forth to the lands of their inheritance. (2 Nephi 10:7-8)

PHILEMON

Philemon was one of the Colossian Saints, being a convert brought into the Church by Paul: "Paul, a prisoner of Jesus Christ, and Timothy our brother, unto Philemon our dearly beloved, and fellowlabourer" (Philemon 1:1). Philemon was the master of a servant (or slave) named Onesimus who had deserted his post and taken away valuables. Paul interceded on behalf of Onesimus, whom he had brought into the fold, and reached out to Philemon with an invitation to receive his servant back as a brother in the gospel (see Philemon 1:8–21). (See the entry for Onesimus.)

PHILIP (MEANING: LOVER OF HORSES.)

1. Philip was one of the Twelve: "Now the names of the twelve apostles are these; The first, Simon, who is called Peter, and Andrew his brother; James the son of Zebedee, and John his brother; Philip, and Bartholomew; Thomas, and Matthew the publican; James the son of Alphæus, and Lebbæus, whose surname was Thaddæus; Simon the Canaanite, and Judas Iscariot, who also betrayed him" (Matthew 10:2–4; see also Mark 3:18; Luke 6:14). Philip was instrumental in bringing Nathanael (thought to be same person as Bartholomew) into the circle of followers of the Savior (see John 1:43–49).

Jesus tested Philip just prior to the miracle of the loaves and fishes:

When Jesus then lifted up his eyes, and saw a great company come unto him, he saith unto Philip, Whence shall we buy bread, that these may eat?

And this he said to prove him: for he himself knew what he would do. Philip answered him, Two hundred pennyworth of bread is not sufficient for them, that every one of them may take a little.

PHILIP TEACHES THE GOSPEL TO AN ETHIOPIAN EUNUCH.

One of his disciples, Andrew, Simon Peter's brother, saith unto him,

There is a lad here, which hath five barley loaves, and two small fishes: but what are they among so many?

And Jesus said, Make the men sit down. Now there was much grass in the place. So the men sat down, in number about five thousand.

And Jesus took the loaves; and when he had given thanks, he distributed to the disciples, and the disciples to them that were set down; and likewise of the fishes as much as they would.

When they were filled, he said unto his disciples, Gather up the fragments that remain, that nothing be lost.

Therefore they gathered them together, and filled twelve baskets with the fragments of the five barley loaves, which remained over and above unto them that had eaten.

Then those men, when they had seen the miracle that Jesus did, said, This is of a truth that prophet that should come into the world. (John 6:5–14)

Following the miracle in which Lazarus was restored to life, the fame and reputation of the Lord spread, with many seeking Him out after His triumphal procession into Jerusalem for the Passover feast. At that time, it was Philip who

directed some Greek visitors to the Lord: "And there were certain Greeks among them that came up to worship at the feast: The same came therefore to Philip, which was of Bethsaida of Galilee, and desired him, saying, Sir, we would see Jesus. Philip cometh and telleth Andrew: and again Andrew and Philip tell Jesus. And Jesus answered them, saying, The hour is come, that the Son of man should be glorified" (John 12:20–23). Philip was also instrumental in prompting a marvelous declaration by the Savior concerning His mission and His relationship with the Father (see John 14:6–15).

Philip was also present with the Apostles to receive instruction from the risen Lord and to witness the Ascension (see Acts 1:1–14). (See also the entry for Nathanael.)

2. Philip was one of the seven special ministers— "seven men of honest report" (Acts 6:3)—chosen to care for the needs of the widows and perform other works of service (see Acts 6:5). We learn also that Philip achieved success in his missionary labors in Samaria: "Then Philip went down to the city of Samaria, and preached Christ unto them. And the people with one accord gave heed unto those things which Philip spake, hearing and seeing the miracles which he did. . . . And there was great joy in that city" (Acts 8:5–6, 8).

Philip was later instrumental in baptizing an Ethiopian eunuch: The Spirit guided Philip to a place along a certain desert roadway where the eunuch was sitting alone in his chariot reading a passage from Isaiah that foretold the coming of one who would be sacrificed for mankind (see Acts 8:32–33; Isaiah 53:7–8). Responding to the eunuch's request for clarification of the passage, Philip bore witness of the divine mission of Jesus Christ as the fulfillment of Isaiah's prophecy: "And as they went on their way, they came unto a certain water: and the eunuch said, See, here is water; what doth hinder me to be baptized?" (Acts 8:35–36). Philip then baptized the man, who "went on his way rejoicing" (Acts 8:39; see also the entry for Eunuch). According to the record, Paul also stayed on one occasion with Philip and his family, including his daughters who manifested spiritual gifts: "And the next day we that were of Paul's company departed, and came unto Cæsarea: and we entered into the house of Philip the evangelist, which was one of the seven; and abode with him. And the same man had four daughters, virgins, which did prophesy" (Acts 21:8–9).

3. Philip was a son of Herod the Great (by Mariamne II) and the first husband of Herodias before she left him and joined with Herod Antipas (see Matthew 14:3; Mark 6:17; Luke 3:19). (See the entry for Herod and the entry for Herod Antipas.)

4. Philip was another son of Herod (by Cleopatra) and tetrarch of Ituraea and Trachonitis (see Luke 3:1). Philip was associated with the expansion of the city of Caesarea Philippi (see Matthew 16:13; Mark 8:27).

PHILIPPIANS

The Philippians were residents of the city of Philippi in Macedonia, a Greek colony re-established by Philip II (382–336 BC), who was the father of Alexander the Great of Macedon. When Paul visited the city during his second missionary journey, he was incarcerated by the authorities. Having been miraculously freed by an earthquake, Paul used the moment to preach the gospel to the terrified keeper of the prison (see Acts 16:28–33).

In his epistle to the Philippians, Paul confirmed his love and gratitude to the faithful Saints of the congregation he established in that area: "I thank my God upon every remembrance of you, Always in every prayer of mine for you all making request with joy, For your fellowship in the gospel from the first day until now; Being confident of this very thing, that he which hath begun a good work in you will perform it until the day of Jesus Christ" (Philippians 1:3–6; see also Philippians 4:9–15).

PILATE

Pontius Pilate was the Roman procurator in Judaea in the time frame AD 26–36: "Now in the fifteenth year of the reign of Tiberius Cæsar, Pontius Pilate being governor of Judæa, and Herod [Herod Antipas] being tetrarch of Galilee, and his brother Philip tetrarch of Ituræa and of the region of Trachonitis, and Lysanias the tetrarch of Abilene" (Luke 3:1). The role of Pilate in the Crucifixion of the Lord is well documented (see Matthew 27:2–26; 58–66; Mark 15:1–15, 42–47; Luke 23:1–25, 50–53; John 18:28–19:22, 31, 38). The Jewish conspirators in the Sanhedrin council had to appeal to Pilate for his consent to carry out the execution, but he at first demurred, having found no evidence to support the charges of sedition and concurring with the advice of his wife, who had had a troubling dream on the matter. Eventually, however, fearful of repercussions at higher levels of the Roman government, Pilate consented to the death of the Lord in place of the liberated Barabbas and ordered the action at the hands of his soldiers (see Matthew 27:11–25).

PRIEST/PRIESTS

Over the generations, the office of priest was bestowed upon the worthy sons of Aaron (see Numbers 18:1–2, 7; Numbers 16:5, 40;

PILATE PRESENTS CHRIST TO THE PEOPLE.

Hebrews 5:4) in connection with their rendering such services as blessing the people, offering sacrifices, teaching the principles of the law, and communicating the will of the Lord (see Leviticus 10:10–11; Numbers 6:22–27; 16:40, 18:2–7; 27:21; Deuteronomy 33:10; Malachi 2:7). The priests were supported from portions of the offerings given by the people (see Leviticus 7: 8, 34; 27:21, 27; Numbers 15:20–21; 18:9, 12–13, 15–17, 26–28; Deuteronomy 8:3–5; Nehemiah 10:35–37) and given certain cities in the Holy Land (see Numbers 18:20; Joshua 21:13–19).

In the New Testament the words *priest* and *priests* are used often, usually in connection with the term *high priest*. There is a great contrast in the portrayal of the office of high priest in the days of Jesus—being on the one hand a designation for the detractors of the Lord among the Jewish leadership who conspired against Him and on the other a designation for the glory and majesty of the Lord's own calling, as in the words of Paul: "Seeing then that we have a great high priest, that is passed into the heavens, Jesus the Son of God, let us hold fast our profession. For we have not an high priest which cannot be touched with the feeling of our infirmities; but was in all points tempted like as we are, yet without sin. Let us therefore come boldly unto the throne of

PRIESTS ACCEPTING AN OFFERING.

grace, that we may obtain mercy, and find grace to help in time of need" (Acts 4:14–16; see also Acts 5:1–10). (See the entry for High Priest.)

PRISCA/PRISCILLA (MEANING: ANCIENT.)

Priscilla (Priska in the Greek form, meaning "ancient") and her husband Aquila (Akyla in the Greek form, meaning "eagle") are noteworthy examples of devout Saints who served as missionaries of the gospel and made their home available for Church meetings. The first mention of Priscilla and Aquila is in this passage: "After these things Paul departed from Athens, and came to Corinth; And found a certain Jew named Aquila, born in Pontus [a Roman province in Asia Minor, on the southern coast of the Black Sea], lately come from Italy, with his wife Priscilla; (because that Claudius had commanded all Jews to depart from Rome:)

and came unto them. And because he was of the same craft, he abode with them, and wrought: for by their occupation they were tentmakers" (Acts 18:1–3). After a season they moved to Ephesus, accompanied by Paul (see Acts 18:18), where the couple met Apollo, an articulate spokesperson from Alexandria visiting there to discourse on gospel themes, and, having taken him aside, "expounded unto him the way of God more perfectly" (Acts 18:26). Thanks to Priscilla and Aquila, Apollo, a Jew who was accepting of the ministry of John the Baptist, was able to grasp the full measure of the Savior's atoning mission and carry the message to others. The couple's home at Ephesus served as a gathering place for Church activity, as Paul confirms: "The churches of Asia salute you. Aquila and Priscilla salute you much in the Lord, with the church that is in their house" (1 Corinthians 16:19). Subsequently, Priscilla and Aquila returned to

Rome, as inferred by this message of Paul to the Romans: "Greet Priscilla and Aquila my helpers in Christ Jesus: Who have for my life laid down their own necks [see Acts 19]: unto whom not only I give thanks, but also all the churches of the Gentiles. Likewise greet the church that is in their house" (see Romans 16:3–5). Apparently, they returned later on to Ephesus, for Paul asks Timothy to greet them: "Salute Prisca and Aquila, and the household of Onesiphorus" (2 Timothy 4:19).

Prophet/Prophets

The Old Testament provides comprehensive and compelling evidence of the divine commission and indispensable service of the prophets of the Lord in all ages—from Adam through Malachi and beyond. Amos confirmed, "Surely the Lord God will do nothing, but he revealeth his secret unto his servants the prophets" (Amos 3:7). The gift of a prophet is to confirm for mankind, through the power of the Holy Ghost, that God lives; to communicate God's divine will for the blessing of all His children; and to uphold, sustain, and further the designs of heaven for the eternal salvation and exaltation of the sons and daughters of God, all dimensions of the plan being empowered through the sacred Atonement of Jesus Christ.

In the New Testament the word *prophet* or *prophets* is used pervasively, for the most part in connection with citations from the ancient prophets, such as Jeremiah, Isaiah, Jonah, David, Elisha, Joel, and Samuel. John the Baptist was envisioned by his father, Zacharias, as a prophet: "And thou, child, shalt be called the prophet of the Highest: for thou shalt go before the face of the Lord to prepare his ways; To give knowledge of salvation unto his people by the remission of their sins" (Luke 1:76–77). The people whose lives were touched by John the Baptist also confirmed him as a prophet (see Matthew 11:9; 21:26; Mark 6:15; 11:32; Luke 7:26–28; 20:6).

The mission of the Savior as a prophet was foretold anciently, as Peter states, "For Moses truly said unto the fathers, A prophet shall the Lord your God raise up unto you of your brethren, like unto me; him shall ye hear in all things whatsoever he shall say unto you" (Acts 3:22; see also Acts 7:37). The Pharisees denied the prophetic calling of the Lord: "Search, and look: for out of Galilee ariseth no prophet" (John 7:52). The Lord Himself confirmed the misperception of His contemporaries: "A prophet is not without honour, but in his own country, and among his own kin, and in his own house" (Mark 6:4; see also Matthew 13:57; Luke 4:24; John 4:44). Nevertheless, many of the people observing the work of the Savior perceived the divinity of His calling as a prophet: "And the multitude said, This is Jesus the prophet of Nazareth of Galilee" (Matthew 21:11; see also Matthew 14:5; 21:46; John 6:14; 7:40; 9:17). The people were astounded at His power to restore life to the departed: "And there came a fear on all: and they glorified God, saying, That a great prophet is risen up among us; and, That God hath visited his people" (Luke 7:16). The Samaritan woman at the well, upon learning about the nature of living waters and listening to Jesus unfold to her the circumstances of her own life, pronounced the true identity of the Lord: "The woman saith unto him, Sir, I perceive that thou art a prophet" (John 4:19). The two disciples on the way to Emmaus told the risen Lord, not recognizing who He was, about the story of the Crucifixion: "And they said unto him, Concerning Jesus of Nazareth, which was a prophet mighty in deed and word before God and all the people: And how the chief priests and our rulers delivered him to be condemned to death, and have crucified him" (Luke 24:19–20). Thereupon He blessed them with prophetic teachings about the plan of happiness, supped with them, and, finally, revealed His identity to them before vanishing.

In the record of the New Testament are many warnings against the work of false prophets, for the past and present (see Matthew 7:15; 24:11, 24; Mark 13:22; Luke 6:26; Acts 13:6; 2 Peter 2:1; 1 John 4:1; Revelation 16:13; 19:20; 20:10). At the same time, by contrast, the ministry and service of Church leaders during apostolic days is at times characterized as the work of prophets (see Acts 11:27; 13:1; 15:32; 21:10). Paul makes clear the doctrine that the office of a prophet is central to the operation of the Church established by Christ:

- "And God hath set some in the church, first apostles, secondarily prophets, thirdly teachers, after that miracles, then gifts of healings, helps, governments, diversities of tongues" (1 Corinthians 12:28).
- "Now therefore ye are no more strangers and foreigners, but fellowcitizens with the saints, and of the household of God; And are built upon the foundation of the apostles and prophets, Jesus Christ himself being the chief corner stone; In whom all the building fitly framed together groweth unto an holy temple in the Lord" (Ephesians 2:19–21).
- "Whereby, when ye read, ye may understand my knowledge in the mystery of Christ. Which in other ages was not made known unto the sons of men, as it is now revealed unto his holy apostles and prophets by the Spirit" (Ephesians 3:4–5).

- "And he gave some, apostles; and some, prophets; and some, evangelists; and some, pastors and teachers; For the perfecting of the saints, for the work of the ministry, for the edifying of the body of Christ" (Ephesians 4:11–12).

When the Pharisees demanded of the Savior to know which was the greatest commandment in the law, He replied, "Thou shalt love the Lord thy God with all thy heart, and with all thy soul, and with all thy mind. This is the first and great commandment. And the second is like unto it, Thou shalt love thy neighbour as thyself. On these two commandments hang all the law and the prophets" (Matthew 22:37–40). That was His definitive summary of the Israelite tradition preserved in the law and the prophets, the former being the five books of Moses and the latter being the words of the subsequent prophets of God. The Savior lamented the tragic fate of the

PROPHETS ARE THE MOUTHPIECE OF GOD ON EARTH.

148

prophets of God: "O Jerusalem, Jerusalem, which killest the prophets, and stonest them that are sent unto thee; how often would I have gathered thy children together, as a hen doth gather her brood under her wings, and ye would not!" (Luke 13:34). Even into the last days, the fate of prophets was foretold (see Revelation 11:10).

At the same time, those who accept and follow the counsel of the prophets of the Lord are promised great blessings, as Peter declared, "Ye are the children of the prophets, and of the covenant which God made with our fathers, saying unto Abraham, And in thy seed shall all the kindreds of the earth be blessed. Unto you first God, having raised up his Son Jesus, sent him to bless you, in turning away every one of you from his iniquities" (Acts 3:25–26). The same glorious blessing was proclaimed by the risen Lord to the Saints in the New World: "And behold, ye are the children of the prophets; and ye are of the house of Israel; and ye are of the covenant which the Father made with your fathers, saying unto Abraham: And in thy seed shall all the kindreds of the earth be blessed. The Father having raised me up unto you first, and sent me to bless you in turning away every one of you from his iniquities; and this because ye are the children of the covenant" (3 Nephi 20:25–26). The entire latter-day canon, including the Book of Mormon, the Doctrine and Covenants, and the Pearl of Great Price, is a witness of the divinity of Jesus Christ as confirmed by the prophets of God and sustained through the voice of the living prophets of our day.

PROSELYTES

The term *proselyte* (meaning "stranger") was a designation given to Gentile converts to the Jewish faith (see Matthew 23:15; Acts 2:10; 13:43). For example, Nicolas was among the seven brethren called by the Apostles to help in Church service, including caring for the needs of the widows: "And they chose Stephen, a man full of faith and of the Holy Ghost, and Philip, and Prochorus, and Nicanor, and Timon, and Parmenas, and Nicolas a proselyte of Antioch" (Acts 6:5). The centurion Cornelius may be the first Gentile convert to Christianity who was not a proselyte; he did not first embrace fully the Jewish faith before coming into the Church: "There was a certain man in Cæsarea called Cornelius, a centurion of the band called the Italian band, A devout man, and one that feared God with all his house, which gave much alms to the people, and prayed to God always" (Acts 10:1–2). Nevertheless, Cornelius seemed to belong to the category of individuals known traditionally as a "God-fearer" or one who may have believed in the God of Israel without fully subscribing to the practices of the Jewish religion. Paul seems to have addressed this category while preaching in a synagogue in Antioch on one occasion: "Then Paul stood up, and beckoning with his hand said, Men of Israel, and ye that fear God, give audience" (see also Acts 13:16). At the same time, expressions referring to those who "fear God" can have a general application concerning the devout and righteous: "And a voice came out of the throne, saying, Praise our God, all ye his servants, and ye that fear him, both small and great" (Revelation 19:5; pervasively throughout the scriptures).

PUBLICANS

Publicans in the days of Jesus were those who were engaged in the government-sponsored business of collecting taxes and, as such, were not the most popular of careerists. Being disdained and cut off as sinners, the publicans became emblems of the category of humanity that Jesus sought to help. Thus, when Jesus associated with the publican Levi, the scribes and Pharisees objected, saying to the disciples, "Why do ye eat and drink with publicans and sinners? And Jesus answering said unto them, They that are whole need not a physician; but they that are sick. I came not to call the righteous, but sinners to repentance" (Luke 5:30–32). Such a platform of service set the stage for the reciting of powerful parables that addressed the needs of the lost, such as the parable of the lost sheep (see Luke 15:3–7), the lost piece of silver (see Luke 15:8–10), and the prodigal son (see Luke 15:11–32). In the latter, who might have qualified better than the scribes and Pharisees to play the role of the elder son who objected to the forgiving welcome of the father to his returning prodigal? Later, when the multitude objected to Jesus consorting with Zacchaeus, "chief among the publicans," they murmured, saying, "That he was gone to be guest with a man that is a sinner" (Luke 19:7). But the Savior, listening to the authentic witness of Zacchaeus, declared, "This day is salvation come to this house, forsomuch as he also is a son of Abraham. For the Son of man is come to seek and to save that which was lost" (Luke 19:9–10).

One of the Twelve, Matthew, was chosen at the time he was involved in the collection of taxes: "And as Jesus passed forth from thence, he saw a man, named Matthew, sitting at the receipt of custom: and he saith unto him, Follow me. And he arose, and followed him" (Matthew 9:9; see also Matthew 10:2–4; other references where he is called Levi—Mark 2:14; Luke 5:27–29). There are also other references concerning the willingness of publicans to receive the gospel (see Matthew 21:31–32; Luke 3:12; 7:29; 15:1; 18:13). (See also the entry for Matthew.)

QUATERNION

A quaternion consisted of a guard crew of four individuals assigned to confine and watch over a prisoner, as in the confinement of Peter: "And when he [Herod Agrippa I] had apprehended him, he put him in prison, and delivered him to four quaternions of soldiers to keep him; intending after Easter to bring him forth to the people" (Acts 12:4). Peter was subsequently liberated by an angel of the Lord and continued his ministry.

RABBI (MEANING: MY MASTER.)

The title *rabbi* was used by the Jewish people in the time of Christ to signify a teacher. The Lord was critical of the Pharisees for their obsession with such titles: "And to be called of men, Rabbi, Rabbi. But be not ye called Rabbi: for one is your Master, even Christ; and all ye are brethren" (Matthew 23:7–8). Two of the disciples of John the Baptist referred to Jesus as "Rabbi" (John 1:38), whereupon He invited them to follow Him. Nathanael said to Christ, "Rabbi, thou art the Son of God; thou art the King of Israel" (John 1:49). The Pharisee Nicodemus, coming secretly to Jesus at night, used the same title: "Rabbi, we know that thou art a teacher come from God: for no man can do these miracles that thou doest, except God be with him" (John 3:2). John the Baptist himself was addressed on occasion with the title *rabbi* (see John 3:26). The day after the miracle of the loaves and fishes, the multitude came seeking Jesus: "And when they had found him on the other side of the sea, they said unto him, Rabbi, when camest thou hither? Jesus answered them and said, Verily, verily, I say unto you, Ye seek me, not because ye saw the miracles, but because ye did eat of the loaves, and were filled. Labour not for the meat which perisheth, but for that meat which endureth unto everlasting life, which the Son of man shall give unto you: for him hath God the Father sealed" (John 6:25–27).

The title *master*, used by the disciples of Jesus to address Him on occasion (see Mark 9:5; 11:21; John 4:31; 9:2; 11:8) implies the same spirit of respect and deference as the title *rabbi*—except in the case where *Master* was used by Judas Iscariot: "The Son of man goeth as it is written of him: but woe unto that man by whom the Son of man is betrayed! it had been good for that man if he had not been born. Then Judas, which betrayed him, answered and said, Master, is it I? He said unto him, Thou hast said" (Matthew 26:24–25; see also Matthew 26:49; Mark 14:45).

RABBONI (MEANING: MY GREAT MASTER.)

The term *rabboni* was used on one occasion by Mary Magdalene. After her encounter with the angels at the empty tomb, the angels said to her,

Woman, why weepest thou? She saith unto them, Because they have taken away my Lord, and I know not where they have laid him.

And when she had thus said, she turned herself back, and saw Jesus standing, and knew not that it was Jesus.

Jesus saith unto her, Woman, why weepest thou? whom seekest thou? She, supposing him to be the gardener, saith unto him, Sir, if thou have borne him hence, tell me where thou hast laid him, and I will take him away.

Jesus saith unto her, Mary. She turned herself, and saith unto him, Rabboni; which is to say, Master. (John 20:13–16)

At that point, the resurrected Lord said to her, "Touch me not [JST: "Hold me not"]; for I am not yet ascended to my Father: but go to my brethren, and say unto them, I ascend unto my Father, and your Father; and to my God, and your God" (John 20:17). Thus, the news of the Resurrection was communicated to the rest of the fold of Christ.

RACHEL (MEANING: EWE.)

The name Rachel is used only once in the New Testament, in relationship to the devastating campaign of Herod to slay all the children in the area of Bethlehem two years of age and under (see Matthew 2:16). The author of the Gospel concludes, "Then was fulfilled that which was spoken by Jeremy the prophet, saying, In Rama was there a voice heard, lamentation, and weeping, and great mourning, Rachel weeping for her children, and would not be comforted, because they are not" (Matthew 2:17–18). The antecedent wording in Jeremiah is as follows: "Thus saith the Lord; A voice was heard in Ramah [the town of deportation into Babylonian captivity around 587 BC], lamentation, and bitter weeping; Rahel weeping for her children refused to be comforted for her children, because they were not" (Jeremiah 31:15). In the words of Jeremiah, Rahel (Rachel) is used symbolically to denote Israel as it undergoes the scattering and tribulation that flows unto it through the judgments of God; yet, as Jeremiah goes on to say, through the mercy and love of God, Israel will overcome its distress and be once again gathered together in glory and joy under the auspices of a new covenant in the future (see Jeremiah 31:27–34). Thus, despite the mourning in Bethlehem, the actual site of Rachel's grave, the rancor and murderous plot of Herod would not deter the design of the Almighty to bring about the divine Atonement essential for the immortality of all mankind and the exaltation of the obedient and righteous.

Historically, Rachel was the younger of the two daughters of Laban, son of Bethuel, the latter being the youngest son of Nahor, brother of Abraham (see Genesis 22:22–23). When Isaac sent his son Jacob to Laban (who was the brother of Rebekah, his mother), Jacob was well received. The story of his encounter with Rachel is a memorable courtship chronicled in the Old Testament (see Genesis 29). Laban required Jacob to marry his older daughter, Leah, before also receiving Rachel as his wife. Leah bore unto Jacob six sons: Reuben, Simeon, Levi, Judah, Issachar, and Zebulun (see Genesis 29:32–35; 30:17–20; 35:23). Leah also bore unto Jacob a daughter by the name of Dinah (see Genesis 30:21). All of these children were born before Rachel was able to conceive, so Rachel gave Jacob her maid

Bilhah, who bore two sons: Dan and Naphtali (see Genesis 30:1–8). Thereafter, Rachel was also blessed to have children: "And God remembered Rachel, and God hearkened to her, and opened her womb. And she conceived, and bare a son; and said, God hath taken away my reproach: And she called his name Joseph; and said, The Lord shall add to me another son" (Genesis 30:22–24). She later passed away in giving birth to Benjamin: "And Rachel died, and was buried in the way to Ephrath, which is Beth-lehem. And Jacob set a pillar upon her grave: that is the pillar of Rachel's grave unto this day" (Genesis 35:19–20; see also Genesis 46:19; 48:7).

Boaz's compatriots invoked the spirit of Rachel and Leah when he married Ruth and ensured that the lineage of Israel would be carried on down to the time of the Savior: "And all the people that were in the gate, and the elders, said, We are witnesses. The Lord make the woman that is come into thine house like Rachel and like Leah, which two did build the house of Israel: and do thou worthily in Ephratah, and be famous in Beth-lehem" (Ruth 4:11). In the same spirit, Jeremiah also used Rachel as an emblem of the lamentation of Israel in the face of calamites (see Jeremiah 31:15). The hope that Jeremiah unfolds for his listeners in reference to Rachel is none other than the Restoration of the gospel of Jesus Christ in the latter days (Jeremiah 31:31–34). It was especially through Joseph, son of Rachel and Jacob, that the power and blessings of the Abrahamic Covenant would be made available to all quarters of the earth in the latter days.

Rahab (Meaning: broad.)

Rahab, the woman who facilitated the invasion of Jericho by the forces of Israel, is referenced twice in the New Testament. Historically, Rahab sequestered the two spies sent by Joshua to survey the city in preparation for the Israelite advance into Canaan (see Joshua 2:1–3). Courageously, she, having concealed the men under stalks of flax on her roof, claimed that the fugitives had escaped in the night. Why would she have rescued the Israelite enemy spies in this fashion? According to her own witness to them, she and her household were persuaded that the Israelite cause was of divine making (see Joshua 2:9–11). She then requested of the men that they would spare her family during the impending invasion, something they agree to do in exchange for her silence concerning their mission. To secure the members of her family gathered within the walls of her house, which was located on the wall of the city, she was to tie a scarlet thread in the window through which she bid the spies escape (see Joshua 2:12–22). In honor of this oath, her family was withdrawn to safety on the day that Jericho was destroyed by the armies of Joshua (see Joshua 6:17–25).

Paul later recounted this event in his lecture on the principle of faith: "By faith the walls of Jericho fell down, after they were compassed about seven days. By faith the harlot Rahab perished not with them that believed not, when she had received the spies with peace" (Hebrews 11:30–31). In another passage, James uses the incident concerning Rahab's decisive initiative to illustrate the principle that "faith without works is dead" (James 2:26). In other passages of scripture, the word *Rahab* is used in a different sense—to identify, symbolically, a force of worldly pride, such as Egypt (see Psalm 87:4; 98:10; Isaiah 51:9).

Romans

Life at the time of Christ was defined and regulated by the empire-building momentum of the Romans on one hand and by the traditional

Jewish hegemony on the other. The blending of the two created the fabric of existence for the populations of the Holy Land as well as for those of the bordering Gentile provinces. In the same measure, it was the blending of the two that metastasized the cancerous growth of hatred against the cause of the Savior fomented by conspirators among the Jewish religious leadership—a hatred fulfilled in the Crucifixion carried out by the military men of the doubting but cooperative governor, Pontius Pilate. At the same time, and beyond, the Romans began to feel the Christian influence in their own homeland. During the decades following the Ascension, the Roman leadership served as a protecting influence for the growing Church until Nero began to institute a campaign of persecution against the Christians beginning in the mid 60s.

At one point in his apostolic career, when Paul was caught in the vortex of competing dangers from his most bitter enemies within the Jewish leadership, Paul was directed to turn his attention to the Romans: "And the night following the Lord stood by him, and said, Be of good cheer, Paul: for as thou hast testified of me in Jerusalem, so must thou bear witness also at Rome" (Acts 23:11). He wrote his epistle to the Romans while not yet having set foot there; he was possibly in Corinth. His letter is a doctrinal masterpiece that defends his theological perspective on the Christian faith

PAUL TESTIFIES BEFORE THE ROMANS.

and practice. Paul would soon visit Rome, not as an itinerant missionary, according to his desire, but as a prisoner of the state. After several years of enduring confinement and some concluding attempts to carry on his ministry, he would, as tradition claims, play the role of martyr among the Romans.

ROOT OF JESSE

The term *root of Jesse* is used one time in the New Testament, in a passage from Paul: "And again, Esaias [Isaiah] saith, There shall be a root of Jesse, and he that shall rise to reign over the Gentiles; in him shall the Gentiles trust" (Romans 15:12; see also Isaiah 11:10–12; 2 Nephi 21:10–12).

The Doctrine and Covenants provides the following commentary on the root of Jesse: "What is the root of Jesse spoken of in the 10th verse of the 11th chapter [of Isaiah]? Behold, thus saith the Lord, it is a descendant of Jesse, as well as of Joseph, unto whom rightly belongs the priesthood, and the keys of the kingdom, for an ensign, and for the gathering of my people in the last days" (D&C 113:6). The root of Jesse is most probably the Prophet Joseph Smith (see *DCE,* 479).

RUTH

Like Mary, the mother of the Lord, Ruth is mentioned in the genealogical lineage of Jesus Christ given in the Gospel of Matthew: "And Salmon begat Booz of Rachab; and Booz begat Obed of Ruth; and Obed begat Jesse" (Matthew 1:5). Ruth is not mentioned elsewhere in the New Testament.

Historically, Ruth was a Moabite woman who became the daughter-in-law of Naomi and a progenitor in the lineage leading to Jesus

RUTH GLEANS WHEAT FROM THE FIELD.

Christ. Compiled and authored by an unnamed writer, the book of Ruth, along with the book of Judges, presents all of the Hebrew history available concerning events during the period of time commencing with the death of Joshua and extending to the birth of Samuel. The time span of the book of Ruth was likely the middle part of the twelfth century BC, since Ruth was the great-grandmother of David (who was born around 1096 BC).

The book of Ruth is a story of unsurpassed beauty and tenderness illustrating loyalty and devotion within the family—especially in the context of the integration of a non-Israelite into the fold of Israel. As such, the story is an emblem of conversion and of setting aside one's former ways in favor of a new and higher pattern of living aligned with the spiritual laws of Jehovah. Moreover, the book provides a serene contrast to the pattern of turbulence and disorder that prevailed in cycles during the time of the judges. The book also highlights the continuity from the earlier times to the unfolding line of descent to Christ.

The four chapters of the book cover the transition of the Elimelech family to Moab, the marriages and deaths within the family, and the return of Naomi and Ruth to Bethlehem (chapter 1); the courtship of Boaz and Ruth (chapters 2–3); and the marriage of Boaz and Ruth, reflecting joy and unity (chapter 4). One of the key passages from the account is the determination of Ruth to remain with her mother-in-law, even after tragedy took the life of both Naomi's and Ruth's husbands: "And Ruth said, Intreat me not to leave thee, or to return from following after thee: for whither thou goest, I will go; and where thou lodgest, I will lodge: thy people shall be my people, and thy God my God" (Ruth 1:16).

A transcending truth unfolds when we recognize that Ruth was of the Moabite lineage, one of the indigenous cultures remaining in the Holy Land after the return of Israel from Egypt. The original Moab was the son of Lot's oldest daughter (see Genesis 19:37), and, thus, the Moabites were akin to the Israelites but represented a different way of life and religion. Ruth represented the local culture at its best, being a pure and virtuous individual with the highest aspirations and character, and she embraced wholeheartedly the Israelite way of life. She was welcomed into her new environment and became instrumental in continuing the promised lineage via David to the Savior Himself. What a fitting unfolding of history that the Author of universal salvation should have come from a line that united two cultures in Ruth and Boaz, one Israelite and the other non-Israelite— but both from the same Maker and Creator. It

is a reminder that converts to the Church and kingdom of God are welcome from all kindreds, nations, tongues, and peoples.

The short book of Ruth memorializes the qualities of loyalty, devotion, kindness, love, tolerance, and joy.

SABAOTH (MEANING: HOSTS.)

Sabaoth (pronounced sab'-ay-oth) refers to the armies arrayed to sustain the cause of the Lord—whether on earth or in heaven. *Lord of Sabaoth* as a title for Jehovah occurs six times in the scriptures (see Romans 9:29; James 5:4; D&C 87:7; 88:2; 95:7; 98:2). The more common equivalent title *Lord of hosts* occurs 309 times throughout holy writ, including 245 times in the Old Testament, as in the famous words of David spoken to Goliath and recorded in 1 Samuel 17:45: "I come to thee in the name of the Lord of hosts." The expression "Lord God of hosts" is also frequently encountered in the scriptures, some thirty-five times. However, neither "Lord of Hosts" nor "Lord God of hosts" occurs in the King James Version of the New Testament.

SADDUCEES

The Sadducees were a leading party among the Jews who held closely to the letter of the written Mosaic law rather than to the oral authority of traditional thought and practice. Unlike the Pharisees, they denied immortality and the resurrection and, thus, found no place for angels or spirits in their theological position: "For the Sadducees say that there is no resurrection, neither angel, nor spirit: but the Pharisees confess both" (Acts 23:8). In all, the Sadducees are mentioned fourteen times in the New Testament, always in the context of their antagonism for and conspiracy against Christ and His Church (see Matthew 3:7; 16:1, 6, 11–12; 22:23, 34; Mark 12:18; Luke 20:27; Acts 4:1; 5:17; 23:6–8). The Sadducees constituted the aristocracy of priestly endeavor associated with the temple, but they faded from view with the destruction of Jerusalem and the temple in AD 70.

The meaning of the name *Sadducees* is unclear. It may be related to the name Zadok (pronounced zay'-dok), one of the leaders in the Aaronic/Levitical Priesthood order in the days of David and Solomon (see 2 Samuel 8:17; 1 Chronicles 16:39) and a descendant in the line of priests stemming from Eleazar, son of Aaron (1 Chronicles 6:4–8; 24:3). The other leading priest during that time was Abiathar, of the line of

CHRIST TEACHES THE SADDUCEES.

descent from Ithamar, brother of Eleazar, through Eli (see 1 Samuel 23:6, 9; 30:7; 1 Chronicles 15:11; 27:33–34). During the rebellion by David's third son, Absalom (2 Samuel 15–18), Abiathar remained faithful to the king (see 2 Samuel 15:1); however, when Adonijah, fourth son of David, rose up and aspired to become king in the place of his aging father, Abiathar supported him as successor to the king rather than Solomon (1 Kings 1:7). By way of contrast, Zadok remained faithful to the cause of David and Solomon. After Solomon was anointed king, Adonijah was put to death as a schemer. Abiathar was stripped of his priestly authority and exiled, putting an end to the priestly service of the line descending from Eli (see 1 Kings 2:26–27; 1 Samuel 2:31–35). Zadok was made chief priest (1 Kings 2:34–35; 1 Chronicles 29:22; Ezekiel 40:46; 43:19; 44:15; 48:11).

SAINT/SAINTS (MEANING: SANCTIFIED.)

The word *saint* or *saints* occurs in the canon of scriptures frequently, including sixty-one times in the New Testament but only once in the Gospels, in relation to the resurrection: "And the graves were opened; and many bodies of the saints which slept arose, And came out of the graves after his resurrection, and went into the holy city, and appeared unto many" (Matthew 27:52–53). The word *saint* applies to all who have come into the fold of Christ by covenant through obedience to the principles and ordinances of the gospel.

Some beautiful examples of the use of the word *saints* are the following, each of which contributes to a fuller understanding of the implications and resonance of the word itself as an invitation of the Almighty to all of His children to become Saints:

- "And it came to pass, as Peter passed throughout all quarters, he came down also to the saints which dwelt at Lydda" (Acts 9:32).
- "To all that be in Rome, beloved of God, called to be saints: Grace to you and peace from God our Father, and the Lord Jesus Christ" (Romans 1:7).
- "But now I go unto Jerusalem to minister unto the saints" (Romans 15:25).
- "Unto the church of God which is at Corinth, to them that are sanctified in Christ Jesus, called to be saints, with all that in every place call upon the name of Jesus" (1 Corinthians 1:2).
- "For God is not the author of confusion, but of peace, as in all churches of the saints" (1 Corinthians 14:33).
- "The eyes of your understanding being enlightened; that ye may know what is the hope of his calling, and what the riches of the glory of his inheritance in the saints" (Ephesians 1:18).
- "Now therefore ye are no more strangers and foreigners, but fellowcitizens with the saints, and of the household of God" (Ephesians 2:19).

- "That Christ may dwell in your hearts by faith; that ye, being rooted and grounded in love, May be able to comprehend with all saints what is the breadth, and length, and depth, and height" (Ephesians 3:19).
- "And he gave some, apostles; and some, prophets; and some, evangelists; and some, pastors and teachers; For the perfecting of the saints, for the work of the ministry, for the edifying of the body of Christ" (Ephesians 4:11–12).
- "Salute every saint in Christ Jesus. The brethren which are with me greet you. All the saints salute you" (Philippians 4:21–22).
- "Giving thanks unto the Father, which hath made us meet to be partakers of the inheritance of the saints in light" (Colossians 1:12).
- "Whereof I am made a minister, according to the dispensation of God which is given to me for you, to fulfil the word of God; Even the mystery which hath been hid from ages and from generations, but now is made manifest to his saints" (Colossians 1:25–26).
- "And the Lord make you to increase and abound in love one toward another, and toward all men, even as we do toward you: To the end he may stablish your hearts unblameable in holiness before God, even our Father, at the coming of our Lord Jesus Christ with all his saints" (Thessalonians 3:12–13).
- "I thank my God, making mention of thee always in my prayers, Hearing of thy love and faith, which thou hast toward the Lord Jesus, and toward all saints" (Philemon 1:4–5).
- "And Enoch also, the seventh from Adam, prophesied of these, saying, Behold, the

Lord cometh with ten thousands of his saints" (Jude 1:4).

- "Here is the patience of the saints: here are they that keep the commandments of God, and the faith of Jesus" (Revelation 14:12).
- "And they sing the song of Moses the servant of God, and the song of the Lamb, saying, Great and marvellous are thy works, Lord God Almighty; just and true are thy ways, thou King of saints" (Revelation 15:3).

It is a blessing to the Saints of the Lord that He has named His Church and kingdom in an inclusive way—including not only His own divine name but also the name of those who belong to His fold: "For thus shall my church be called in the last days, even The Church of Jesus Christ of Latter-day Saints" (D&C 105:4).

SALOME

1. Salome was the wife of Zebedee and the mother of James and John, two of the original Apostles. Note the reference to "the mother of Zebedee's children" in the scripture identifying the women who witnessed the Crucifixion: "Among which was Mary Magdalene, and Mary the mother of James and Joses, and the mother of Zebedee's children" (Matthew 27:56). In the reference to the same occasion given in Mark, the following are mentioned: "There were also women looking on afar off: among whom was Mary Magdalene, and Mary the mother of James the less and of Joses, and Salome" (Mark 15:40). Thus, Salome is equivalent to "the mother of Zebedee's children." In a subsequent reference, we learn, "And when the sabbath was past, Mary Magdalene, and Mary the mother of James, and Salome, had bought sweet spices, that they might come and anoint him" (Mark 16:1).

An earlier reference in Matthew indicates that the mother of Zebedee's children joined with her sons to request that they be given a special favor: "Then came to him the mother of Zebedee's children with her sons, worshipping him, and desiring a certain thing of him" (Matthew 20:20). Her request, not out of keeping with the desire of a caring mother, was that the two sons be given a place of honor alongside the Savior, one on the right and one on the left—much to the annoyance of the other ten disciples. The Savior responded, "To sit on my right hand, and on my left, is not mine to give, but it shall be given to them for whom it is prepared of my Father" (Matthew 20:23). He then took the occasion to teach a lesson that service supersedes station: "But it shall not be so among you: but whosoever will be great among you, let him be your minister; And whosoever will be chief among you, let him be your servant" (Matthew 20:26-27).

2. Salome was also the daughter of Herodias, who was the sister of Marcus Julius Agrippa I, also known as Herod Agrippa I. (See the entries for Herod Antipas and Herodias.)

SAMARITANS

The Samaritans were a people who populated Samaria following the Assyrian captivity of the northern kingdom of Israel around 721 BC. Samaria, located in the mountainous region of Palestine, had originally been established as a stronghold capital by Omri, king of Israel (see 1 Kings 16:23-24). The Samaritans were, in general, descendants of the colonists placed in that territory by the Assyrian conquerors (see 2 Kings 17:23-24). Though incorrigibly idolatrous

A SAMARITAN HAS COMPASSION ON A FALLEN MAN.

Jewish people. It was to this site upon Gerizim that the Samaritan woman referred when she was being counseled by the Savior at the well: "The woman saith unto him, Sir, I perceive that thou art a prophet. Our fathers worshipped in this mountain; and ye say, that in Jerusalem is the place where men ought to worship" (John 4:19–20). Despite the intolerance of the Jewish people for the Samaritans living among them (see Matthew 10:5; Luke 9:51–56; 10:33; 17:16; John 4:9, 39; 8:48), the Samaritans were able, in their time, to receive the gospel message from the disciples of Jesus (see Acts 1:8; 8:4–15).

SAMSON (MEANING: OF THE SUN.)

Samson, ancient judge in Israel, is mentioned only one time by name in the New Testament, in Paul's discourse on faith: "And what shall I more say? for the time would fail me to tell of Gedeon, and of Barak, and of Samson, and of Jephthae; of David also, and Samuel, and of the prophets: Who through faith subdued kingdoms, wrought righteousness, obtained promises, stopped the mouths of lions" (Hebrews 11:32–33).

Historically speaking, Samson, known for his astounding strength, was the twelfth in a sequence of judges serving in Israel (see Judges 13–16). At a time when the Israelites had been in bondage to the Philistines for four decades, an angel of the Lord came to the wife of Manoah, a member of the tribe of Dan, and pronounced a wondrous blessing upon her head, for she had been barren: "For, lo, thou shalt conceive, and bear a son; and no razor shall come on his head: for the child shall be a Nazarite unto God from the womb: and he shall begin to deliver Israel out of the hand of the Philistines. . . . And the woman bare a son, and called his name Samson: and the child grew, and the Lord blessed him"

in character and incurring the judgments of heaven, these colonists were taught to fear the Lord by a priest sent from among the captive circle of Israelites by the Assyrian king (see 2 Kings 17:25–41). Generations later, upon the return of Judah from the Babylonian captivity of the sixth century BC, the Samaritans desired to assist in the rebuilding of the temple at Jerusalem—a privilege denied them by the Jewish leaders (see Ezra 4:1–3).

Angered, the Samaritans turned against Judah with much animosity and later erected a temple of their own on Mount Gerizim (pronounced gair'-uh-zim). Gerizim became for the Samaritans what Jerusalem was for the

(Judges 13:5, 24). The rise of Samson was marked by several notable milestones:

- his slaying of a lion with his bare hands during the time he was courting a Philistine woman (see Judges 14)
- his slaying of a thousand Philistines with the jawbone of an ass in connection with bitter disappointments concerning his marriage (see Judges 15)
- his fatal interaction with Delilah, a woman from the valley of Sorek whom he loved (see Judges 16:4)

The Philistines bribed Delilah to discover the secret of Samson's astounding strength. Three times in sequence she induced him deceitfully to share the information with her, but each time it proved to be fiction. She persisted: "And it came to pass, when she pressed him daily with her words, and urged him, so that his soul was vexed unto death; That he told her all his heart,

Delilah tries to persuade Samson to share his secret of strength.

and said unto her, There hath not come a razor upon mine head; for I have been a Nazarite unto God from my mother's womb [see Judges 13:5; Numbers 6:1–8]: if I be shaven, then my strength will go from me, and I shall become weak, and be like any other man" (Judges 16:16–17).

Then Delilah made her move by causing his hair to be shaved, leaving him enervated and powerless: "And he wist not that the Lord was departed from him" (Judges 16:20). The Philistines then put out Samson's eyes and imprisoned him at Gaza. Later, after Samson's hair had grown long once again (Judges 16:22), the Philistines assembled a vast throng of people to celebrate their victory and to make sport of Samson. It was then that he called one last time upon the Lord and pulled down the pillars of the house, destroying himself and all three thousand of the celebrants who were there (see Judges 16:28–30).

SAMUEL (MEANING: NAME OF GOD.)

Samuel the prophet is mentioned by name twice in the New Testament:

- **In Paul's sermon in the synagogue at Antioch, giving an interesting synopsis of the history of the Israelite people down to Christ:** "The God of this people of Israel chose our fathers, and exalted the people when they dwelt as strangers in the land of Egypt, and with an high arm brought he them out of it. And about the time of forty years suffered he their manners in the wilderness. And when he had destroyed seven nations in the land of Chanaan, he divided their land to them by lot. And after that he gave unto them judges about the space of four hundred and fifty years, until

SAMUEL HEARS THE VOICE OF THE LORD.

Samuel the prophet. And afterward they desired a king: and God gave unto them Saul the son of Cis, a man of the tribe of Benjamin, by the space of forty years. And when he had removed him, he raised up unto them David to be their king; to whom also he gave testimony, and said, I have found David the son of Jesse, a man after mine own heart, which shall fulfil all my will. Of this man's seed hath God according to his promise raised unto Israel a Saviour, Jesus" (Acts 13:17–23).

• **In Paul's discourse on faith:** "And what shall I more say? for the time would fail me to tell of Gedeon, and of Barak, and of Samson, and of Jephthae; of David also, and Samuel, and of the prophets: Who through faith subdued kingdoms, wrought righteousness, obtained promises, stopped the mouths of lions, Quenched the violence of fire, escaped the edge of the sword, out of weakness were made strong, waxed valiant in fight, turned to flight the armies of the aliens" (Hebrews 11:32–34).

Historically speaking, Samuel was the son of Elkanah and Hannah. The story of his birth is remarkable—Hannah's heartfelt desire to become a mother and her devotion and pleading before the Lord near the temple were heard, and the Lord's servant, Eli, promised her that her prayers would be answered. She conceived and bear Samuel, the coming prophet of the Lord, and was filled with joy and thanksgiving, pleased to dedicate her son to the service of holiness (see 1 Samuel 1:27–28). Hannah gave praise to the Lord for His goodness as her son Samuel grew and prospered, ministering before the Lord and increasing in favor and righteousness: "And the child Samuel grew on, and was in favour both

164

with the Lord, and also with men" (1 Samuel 2:26).

Having come under the care of the priest Eli, Samuel hears a voice during the night: "The Lord called Samuel: and he answered, Here am I" (1 Samuel 3:4). Samuel inquires of Eli who it might be, but Eli has him return to his bed. When this scene repeats itself twice more, Eli tells him to listen, for it is the Lord calling. The Lord reveals to Samuel the sad news of Eli's sons and their unrighteousness: "For I have told him that I will judge his house for ever for the iniquity which he knoweth; because his sons made themselves vile, and he restrained them not. And therefore I have sworn unto the house of Eli, that the iniquity of Eli's house shall not be purged with sacrifice nor offering for ever" (1 Samuel 3:13–14). Eli's sons are killed in battle (see 1 Samuel 4:11), and Eli, as a blind, feeble ninety-eight-year-old, passes away in a tragic accident (see 1 Samuel 4:18).

The examples in Samuel's story teach the power of prayer, devotion in giving oneself to the service of God, and in the case of Eli, the price we pay for permissiveness in failing to correct our children properly. The Lord hears and answers prayers of the righteous even as He heard Hannah's. The blessings of prayer truly empower us to do all things in the strength of the Lord. The Psalmist remembered Samuel in this inspiring exhortation: "Exalt ye the Lord our God, and worship at his footstool; for he is holy. Moses and Aaron among his priests, and Samuel among them that call upon his name; they called upon the Lord, and he answered them" (Psalm 99:5–6). In giving testimony of His own redeeming mission to the assembled Saints in Bountiful, the resurrected Lord included a reference to Samuel: "Verily I say unto you, yea, and all the prophets from Samuel and those

that follow after, as many as have spoken, have testified of me" (3 Nephi 20:24). These words are similar to those given by the Apostle Peter in bearing witness to the divinity of the Savior (see Acts 4:24).

SANHEDRIN (MEANING: COUNCIL OR A COMING TOGETHER.)

The Sanhedrin was the leading Jewish council for civil and ecclesiastic matters. The word *sanhedrin* itself does not occur in the New Testament. (See entry for Council.)

SAPPHIRA (MEANING: BEAUTIFUL.)

Sapphira is the wife of Ananias. (See the entry for Ananias.)

SARAH (MEANING: PRINCESS.)

Sarah, the wife of Abraham, is mentioned four times in the New Testament (always as *Sara*), first of all in a passage from Paul's epistle to the Romans (see Romans 4:16–20).

Paul continues the same theme in his epistle to the Hebrews, where he invokes the promise of the Abrahamic Covenant to expand the chosen people to an innumerable multitude: "Through faith also Sara herself received strength to conceive seed, and was delivered of a child when she was past age, because she judged him faithful who had promised. Therefore sprang there even of one, and him as good as dead, so many as the stars of the sky in multitude, and as the sand which is by the sea shore innumerable" (Hebrews 11:11–12). It was the design of the Almighty to pour out His blessings upon His chosen people "to whom pertaineth the adoption, and the glory, and the covenants, and the giving of the law, and the service of God, and the promises" (Romans 9:4), and He made Abraham and Sarah the fountain of multitudes through Isaac: "For this is the word of promise, At this time will I come, and Sara shall have a son" (Romans 9:9).

Peter also used the example of Sara as a faithful companion to Abraham and Abraham as one who honored his wife, they being together heirs of grand blessings (see 1 Peter 3:5–7).

From the historical perspective—well understood by Peter, Paul, and their associates—Sarah was known originally as Sarai (pronounced sair'-eye or sair'-ay-eye). She and Abraham were married in Ur of Chaldees: "And Abram and Nahor took them wives: the name of Abram's wife was Sarai; and the name of Nahor's wife, Milcah, the daughter of Haran. . . . But Sarai was barren; she had no child" (Genesis 11:29–

30). The childless state of Sarai was a continual burden to her until she was blessed, eventually, to conceive and give birth to Isaac. Meanwhile, Abram (Abraham) journeyed with his family circle toward Canaan, dwelling for a time en route at Haran (see Genesis 11:31). It was there that the Lord blessed Abram with a magnificent covenant blessing: "And I will make of thee a great nation, and I will bless thee, and make thy name great; and thou shalt be a blessing: And I will bless them that bless thee, and curse him that curseth thee: and in thee shall all families of the earth be blessed" (Genesis 12:2–3; see also Abraham 2:8–12).

The famine in Canaan caused Abram and Sarai to move onward for a time to the land of Egypt. Upon returning to Canaan, Abram yearned for his promised posterity, and the Lord sent words of comfort: "And he brought him forth abroad, and said, Look now toward

SARAH SHOWS FAITH IN THE LORD AND THE TEACHINGS OF HER HUSBAND.

heaven, and tell the stars, if thou be able to number them: and he said unto him, So shall thy seed be. And he believed in the Lord; and he counted it to him for righteousness" (Genesis 15:5–6).

After ten years in Canaan with no children, Sarai, in accordance with the cultural practice of her time, gave unto Abram her Egyptian handmaid, Hagar, as a wife. The Doctrine and Covenants confirms, "God commanded Abraham, and Sarah gave Hagar to Abraham to wife. And why did she do it? Because this was the law; and from Hagar sprang many people. This, therefore, was fulfilling, among other things, the promises. Was Abraham, therefore, under condemnation? Verily I say unto you, Nay; for I, the Lord, commanded it" (D&C 132:34–35; see also D&C 132:65). Subsequently, Hagar gave birth to Ishmael (see Genesis 16). Several years later, the Lord confirmed to Abraham the covenant promise of great increase and changed his name to Abraham, "father of many nations" (Genesis 17:5). Sarai, too, received the new name of Sarah and was promised she would bear a son (see Genesis 17:15–19).

Somewhat later, three holy men visiting Abraham and Sarah at their encampment confirmed the promise of Sarah's motherhood. When the aged Sarah overheard the statement that she would conceive and bear a son, she responded with understandable incredulity, "Therefore Sarah laughed within herself, saying, After I am waxed old shall I have pleasure, my lord being old also? And the Lord said unto Abraham, Wherefore did Sarah laugh, saying, Shall I of a surety bear a child, which am old? Is any thing too hard for the Lord? At the time appointed I will return unto thee, according to the time of life, and Sarah shall have a son" (Genesis 18:12–14). In accordance with the principle that nothing is "too hard for the Lord," Sarah did indeed bear a son, who was given the name Isaac, meaning "he laughed" (see Genesis 21:1–3). In due time, a divine commandment was given to Abraham—and by extension, to Sarah—to relinquish Isaac through a sacrificial offering. That extraordinary test in the land of Moriah, calling forth every fiber of obedience and valor on the part of Abraham—and Isaac—proved to be the sealing grace upon the future unfolding of the Abrahamic Covenant. The Lord had prepared a ram in the thicket as the offering that day, and Abraham and Isaac could then move onward down the pathway as principals in the process leading to the blessing of all mankind through the spreading of the gospel message about the ultimate sacrifice of the Lamb of God (see Genesis 22:15–18).

Sarah passed away some time later at age 127: "Abraham came to mourn for Sarah, and to weep for her" (Genesis 23:2). She was buried "in the cave of the field of Machpelah before Mamre: the same is Hebron in the land of Canaan" (Genesis 23:19; see also Isaiah 51:2; 2 Romans 4:19; Nephi 8:2).

SAREPTA, WIDOW OF

At the commencement of His ministry, Jesus came to Nazareth, the community where He had been raised, and went to the local synagogue on the Sabbath day. The passage He chose to read aloud that day was from the prophet Isaiah (see Luke 4:18–21).

When the assembled audience greeted His words with doubt, assuming that no one from Nazareth could actually be the promised Messiah, He responded by citing two well-known illustrations: "But I tell you of a truth, many widows were in Israel in the days of Elias, when the heaven was shut up three years and six months, when great famine was throughout all the land; But unto none of them was Elias [Elijah] sent, save unto Sarepta, a city of Sidon, unto a woman that was a widow. And many lepers were in Israel in the time of Eliseus [Elisha] the prophet; and none of them was cleansed, saving Naaman the Syrian" (Luke 4:25–27).

His listeners were outraged at the implication of His saying, since the widow of Sarepta (Greek for Zarephath) lived in a Phoenician city between Tyre and Sidon on the Mediterranean Sea, above Galilee, and Naaman was a Syrian. Those of faith were, therefore, from outside the Israelite sphere—just as the Savior confirmed concerning the incredulity of His own neighbors: "And he said, Verily I say unto you, No prophet is accepted in his own country" (Luke 4:24). As a result of their anger, Jesus's audience "rose up, and thrust him out of the city, and led him unto the brow of the hill whereon their city was built, that they might cast him down headlong. But he passing through the midst of them went his way" (Luke 4:29–30).

The historical background of the Savior's reference to the widow of Sarepta is contained in 1 Kings 17, where the Lord, through Elijah, sealed the heavens to bring on a famine for the correction of a perverse and wayward house of Israel. To preserve the life of His prophet, the Lord commanded him as follows: "Arise, get thee to Zarephath, which belongeth to Zidon, and dwell there: behold, I have commanded a widow woman there to sustain thee" (1 Kings 17:9). Elijah did as he was told, and, having come to the widow, performed a miracle in her household by multiplying her meager store of flour and oil as needed for the support of herself, her son, and the prophet sent from the Lord. Later, after the son had taken ill and died, Elijah, by the power of the Lord, restored him

to life. The widow then exclaimed, "Now by this I know that thou art a man of God, and that the word of the Lord in thy mouth is truth" (1 Kings 17:24). It was this witness that served as a perfect contrast to the doubt and blindness of the Lord's neighbors in Nazareth, who, though closely associated with His upbringing, failed to believe His word.

Satan (Meaning: adversary.)

Satan, the devil, appears early in the New Testament record, having come forth to tempt the Savior in the wilderness at the dawning of

Satan is cast down.

His ministry. The dialogue between the son of the morning (the primordial Lucifer) and the Son of God is replete with doctrinal truth:

Then was Jesus led up of the Spirit into the wilderness to be tempted of the devil.

And when he had fasted forty days and forty nights, he was afterward an hungred.

And when the tempter came to him, he said, If thou be the Son of God, command that these stones be made bread.

But he answered and said, It is written, Man shall not live by bread alone, but by every word that proceedeth out of the mouth of God.

Then the devil taketh him up into the holy city, and setteth him on a pinnacle of the temple,

And saith unto him, If thou be the Son of God, cast thyself down: for it is written, He shall give his angels charge concerning thee: and in their hands they shall bear thee up, lest at any time thou dash thy foot against a stone.

Jesus said unto him, It is written again, Thou shalt not tempt the Lord thy God.

Again, the devil taketh him up into an exceeding high mountain, and sheweth him all the kingdoms of the world, and the glory of them;

And saith unto him, All these things will I give thee, if thou wilt fall down and worship me.

Then saith Jesus unto him, Get thee hence, Satan: for it is written, Thou shalt worship the Lord thy God, and him only shalt thou serve.

Then the devil leaveth him, and, behold, angels came and ministered unto him. (Matthew 4:1–11; see also Mark 1:12–13)

The truths taught by the Savior on this occasion are simple but important: live by the word of God, tempt not God with unseemly and inappropriate requests, and worship and serve God alone. Abiding by this divine counsel dispels the forces of darkness and opens the doorway to service by the angels of heaven. Such is in keeping with the promises made to Peter by the Lord: "And I say also unto thee, That thou art Peter, and upon this rock I will build my church; and the gates of hell shall not prevail against it" (Matthew 16:18, the "rock" being Jesus Christ as the divine empowerment of revelation to guide the kingdom of God). The same promise was given again in the latter days concerning the need to follow the word of the Lord as given by His living prophet: "For his word ye shall receive, as if from mine own mouth, in all patience and faith. For by doing these things the gates of hell shall not prevail against you; yea, and the Lord God will disperse the powers of darkness from before you, and cause the heavens to shake for your good, and his name's glory" (D&C 21:5–6).

In addition to the references cited above, Satan is mentioned fairly often in the New Testament:

- when he entered into the person of Judas Iscariot to impel him to proceed with the deception and Crucifixion of the Lord (see John 13:26-27)

- in the counsel and warning of the Lord to Peter on that occasion (see Luke 22:31-32)
- in the observation by Paul concerning the deceptions of Satan and his followers (see 2 Corinthians 11:13-14)
- in the book of Revelation concerning his initial fall from heaven (see Revelation 12:7-9)
- concerning Satan's ultimate fate through the justice of God (see Revelation 20:10)

Satan, who is Lucifer, the principal devil and primordial enemy to God, is mentioned in the Old Testament some nineteen times—including fourteen times in the book of Job, beginning with Job 1:6. Satan, as the enemy of all righteousness, is referenced frequently in the Doctrine and Covenants under various names. In one central passage (D&C 75:25-29), he is mentioned no fewer than seven times, with different designations: "fallen angel," "Perdition," "Lucifer," "son of the morning," "Satan," "old serpent," and "devil."

The word *perdition* in English usage comes from the Latin verb *perdere*, meaning "to lose." Assuredly, Satan is the archetype of the loser, for as an angel in authority in the premortal realm who rebelled against the Almighty God, he lost forever the divinely appointed opportunity to receive an inheritance of glory and exaltation (see Isaiah 14:12-15; Luke 10:18). The word *lucifer* means literally "the shining one" or "the lightbringer" (see Bible Dictionary, 726). This name, which derives from the Latin word for "light" (see also the related word *lucid*), is the equivalent of the appellation "son of the morning." The word *satan* in its Greek, Latin,

and Hebrew sources, means "adversary"—the perfect characterization of the fallen angel's defining role in opposing the Father's plan of redemption and rejecting the choice of Jehovah as Redeemer from the foundations of the world. The word *devil* in its Latin and Greek etymological derivation means "slanderer"—a further characterization of the fallen angel's strategy in opposing the eternal source of truth.

The case of Lucifer (Perdition, Satan, devil, etc.) is the most fundamental example of irony in the scriptures, for how could a being of light (son of the morning) transform himself into the archetypal representative of darkness? The benighted personality of Satan stands in infinite contrast to the grandeur of the eternal source of light and truth, even the Father and the Son.

The heavens wept over Lucifer, for he was an angel "in authority in the presence of God" (D&C 76:25). He held high office. It was this tragic transformation, this total abdication of godly potential in one of the leading sons of God in the spirit realm, that caused the heavens to weep (see D&C 76:26). In the visions of eternity granted unto the prophet Enoch, he also beheld Satan: "And he had a great chain in his hand, and it veiled the whole face of the earth with darkness; and he looked up and laughed, and his angels rejoiced" (Moses 7:26; see also D&C 29:36; Moses 1:19; 4:1-3). The condition of those who followed Satan caused God to weep (see Moses 7:28), much to the discomfort of Enoch—until he was told the reason why: "Behold, their sins shall be upon the heads of their fathers; Satan shall be their father, and misery shall be their doom; and the whole heavens shall weep over them, even all the workmanship of mine hands; wherefore should not the heavens weep, seeing these shall suffer?" (Moses 7:37). It is the inevitable suffering of the wicked, brought about by their own choice, that causes the heavens to weep—seeing that the divine plan of the atoning sacrifice would otherwise save God's children through the grace and truth of the Almighty and the obedience and righteousness of the faithful. But Lucifer and his followers would not have it so—hence the triumphant campaign of heaven to thwart his designs. No wonder his diabolical work is mentioned so frequently in the Doctrine and Covenants: the word *Satan* occurs thirty-five times, *devil* twenty-five times, *Perdition* three times, *serpent* twice, *son of the morning* twice, and *Lucifer* once.

To this day, the hosts of Satan—he who would usurp the honor of God (see Moses 4:1)—rage in the cauldron of darkness that recoils from the power of the glory of heaven. Ultimately, Michael (Adam) and his armies will dispel Satan and his benighted minions forever (see D&C 88:111–116).

SAUL (MEANING: ASKED.)

1. Saul, first king of Israel, is mentioned once in the New Testament, in a passage in which Paul is giving a summary of the history of the house of Israel: "And afterward they desired a king: and God gave unto them Saul the son of Cis, a man of the tribe of Benjamin, by the space of forty years" (Acts 13:21). His reign lasted from around 1095 BC to the middle of that century. His history is recorded in 1 Samuel, this chronicle constituting the beginning of the historical account of the kings of Israel and covering the time period from the birth of Samuel to the death of Saul and his sons. Against the backdrop of intrigue and pride reflected in the vacillating character of Saul, we perceive the principled ministry of the prophet Samuel as a

SAUL BEING REBUKED BY THE PROPHET.

mirror of divine purpose and truth. We also see the magnanimous character of the young David as he emerges from obscurity to a position of prominence as a great leader in Israel.

The story of Saul, gripping and tragic, is a reminder of the peril arising from the influence of a king or ruler who falls dangerously short of the measure of righteousness exemplified in the stature and glory of the Lord of Lords, Jesus Christ. Samuel had adjured the people to relent in demanding that a king be placed over them, rehearsing before them the burdens such a ruler can impose when the people choose a worldly sovereign rather than the Lord (1 Samuel 8:6–18; see also Mosiah 23:7; 29:13, 16–17, 23). But when Israel rejected the Lord as their king, insisting on having a worldly king like the neighboring cultures, the Lord caused the prophet Samuel to anoint the young Saul to be king of Israel. Saul had many good qualities, including (at the beginning) a humble nature. As part of his transition to leadership, the Lord gave him "another heart" (1 Samuel 10:9); thus Saul was illuminated by divine purpose and became spiritually committed. But Saul soon turned to his own devices and allowed pride to control his actions. Eventually, he fell from the Lord's favor. When Saul defeated the Amalekites, he disobeyed the Lord's command by taking the spoils and failing to slay their king; hence, he was rejected as king: "And Samuel said, Hath the Lord as great delight in burnt offerings and sacrifices, as in obeying the voice of the Lord? Behold, to obey is better than sacrifice, and to hearken than the fat of rams. For rebellion is as the sin of witchcraft, and stubbornness is as iniquity and idolatry. Because thou hast rejected the word of the Lord, he hath also rejected thee from being king" (1 Samuel 15:22–23).

2. Saul is Paul the Apostle: In the record of the New Testament, Paul was known by the name Saul (his original Jewish name) up until the following passage: "Then Saul, (who also is called Paul,) filled with the Holy Ghost, set his eyes on him [Elymus]" (Acts 13:9). Thereafter, except in Paul's later recounting of his miraculous conversion (see Acts 22, 26), the name of Paul is used.

SCRIBES

Scribes are often mentioned in the New Testament, frequently in connection with the Pharisees, high priests, and elders—the prevailing religious and civil leadership of the Jewish people at a time when the Romans were in control. The duty of the scribes, often lawyers, was to maintain and teach the doctrines and provisions of the law, including oral traditions, and then to help apply the law to the circumstances of their day. The scribes were part of the leadership conspiracy against Jesus and His followers. Though they constituted a negative and viral force against the Church, they also unwittingly provided the platform for the teaching of powerful and useful lessons by the Savior:

- **the Law:** The scribes and their associates maintained that Jesus's teachings violated the law. In fact, the opposite was true (see Matthew 5:17–20).
- **authority:** The scribes and their associates rejected the authority of Jesus, though His manner discredited their assertion of false authority (see Matthew 7:24–29; Mark 1:22). On another occasion the chief priests, scribes, and elders attempted to trap Jesus on the issue of authority (see Mark 11:27–33; 20:1–8).
- **forgiveness of sins:** The scribes found Jesus guilty of blasphemy for claiming to forgive sins, but he refuted them (see Mark 2:3–12; Luke 5:18–32). On another occasion the scribes and Pharisees accused a woman of adultery and wanted the Savior to agree to the Mosaic requirement that she be stoned (see John 8:6–11).
- **charity toward sinners:** The scribes and Pharisees murmured that Jesus associated with tax collectors and sinners, but He used this occasion to teach a gospel lesson (see Mark 2:15–17; Luke 5:27–32; 15:1–7).
- **the law of the fast:** The scribes and Pharisees complained that Jesus and His disciples were observed to eat together.

THE SCRIBES ACCUSE AN ADULTEROUS WOMAN.

The Savior corrected their traditional interpretation of the practice of fasting (see Luke 5:33–39).

- **the Sabbath:** The scribes and Pharisees were watchful to catch Jesus healing on the Sabbath, but He silenced them concerning this issue (see Luke 6:5–11).

- **the claim that Jesus's miracles were of the devil:** The scribes imputed evil powers to the Lord when He cast out devils, but He refuted their logic (see Mark 3:22–30).

- **seeking a sign:** The scribes and Pharisees demanded of Jesus a sign of His authenticity, and He responded that sign seekers are evil (see Matthew 12:38–40).

- **washing of hands:** The scribes and Pharisees were obsessed with outward rules and superficial regulations. Jesus reminded them of their hypocrisy and hardness of hearts (see Matthew 15:1–9; Mark 7:1–13).

- **interpreting scripture:** The Lord helped His disciples understand the scriptures more wisely than the scribes could do so (see Matthew 17:10–13; Mark 8:11–12).

- **purifying the temple and healing the sick— invoking the praise of the people:** When the people rejoiced over the miraculous actions of Jesus and praised Him, Christ refuted the murmuring scribes and chief priests (see Matthew 21:12–16; Mark 11:15–19; Luke 19:45–48).

- **the first commandment:** The scribes prided themselves on knowing the law intimately. The Savior taught one of the scribes that he was coming close to the truth (see Mark 12: 28–34; Deuteronomy 6:4–5; 11:13; 13:3; 30:6; Joshua 22:5; Matthew 22:37–40; Luke 10:25–37).

- **love of the honor of men:** The scribes and their companions treasured worldly honors, and Jesus characterized their behavior (see Mark 12:38-40; Luke 20:45-47).
- **tribute to the government:** The chief priests and scribes attempted to trap Jesus into committing treason against the Roman government, but Jesus silenced them (see Luke 20:19-26).
- **do not follow their works:** The Savior honored the spirit of the law coming down from Moses, but He warned the people against the unrighteousness of the scribes and Pharisees (see Matthew 22:13-39; Luke 11:44-55).
- **identifying and recognizing your enemies:** The Lord was explicit in knowing the enemies of the Church (see Matthew 16:21-23; 20:17-19; 26:3-5; Mark 8:31-33; 10:32-34; 14:1-2; Luke 9:22; 22:1-2).

  See also the persecution against Church leaders by the scribes and their associates after the Ascension: Peter and John (see Acts 4:5-12), Stephen (Acts 6:9-15; 7), and Paul (Acts 23:1-11).
- **the accuracy of the Lord's judgment of the scribes, chief priests, and elders:** The Lord discerned with complete accuracy the role that would be played by His Jewish detractors (see Matthew 27:39-43; Mark 15:1, 29-32). (See also the entry for Pharisees.)

SCYTHIANS

The Scythians (pronounced sith'-ians) were a pastoral people living north of the Black Sea and Caspian Sea. In his message about the universality of the brotherhood of Christ—where all those who believe are of the same family—Paul gave a panoramic picture of humanity in all its dimensions and then witnessed that all are to be in Christ (see Colossians 3:10-14; 12:13; Ephesians 6:8; Revelation 13:16; 19:18).

The passage from Paul is reminiscent of the words of Nephi: "For he [the Lord] doeth that which is good among the children of men; and he doeth nothing save it be plain unto the children of men; and he inviteth them all to come unto him and partake of his goodness; and he denieth none that come unto him, black and white, bond and free, male and female; and he remembereth the heathen; and all are alike unto God, both Jew and Gentile" (2 Nephi 26:33).

SEED OF ABRAHAM

The expression *seed of Abraham*, referring to the heirs of the promises and covenants made by the Lord unto the patriarch Abraham, is used by Paul four times:

- in connection with those who are of the house of God because they are chosen of God, whether literally of the seed of Abraham or righteous Gentiles adopted into the fold (see Romans 9:6-7)
- to indicate the lineage of Paul (see Hebrews 11:1)
- an expression of boldness in the face of reproach (see 2 Corinthians 11:22-23)
- in recognition of the mercy and love of the Savior for His people, the seed of Abraham (see Hebrews 2:15-17)

Seer

The word *seer* is not used in the King James Version of the New Testament; however in the Joseph Smith Translation for John 1:42, concerning the calling of Peter, we read, "And he brought him to Jesus. And when Jesus beheld him, he said, Thou art Simon, the son of Jona, thou shalt be called Cephas, which is, by interpretation, a seer, or a stone. And they were fishermen. And they straightway left all, and followed Jesus." In the Old Testament, *seer* is used as a title for Samuel, Zadok, Gad, Heman, Iddo, Hanani, Asaph, Jeduthun, and Amos.

Seth

Seth, son of Adam and Eve, is mentioned once in the New Testament, at the end of Luke's summary of the genealogical lineage of Jesus Christ: "Which was the son of Enos, which was the son of Seth, which was the son of Adam, which was the son of God" (Luke 3:38).

According to the biblical account, his mother "called his name Seth: For God, said she, hath appointed me another seed instead of Abel, whom Cain slew" (Genesis 4:25; see also Moses 6:2). Seth was "in his [Adam's] own likeness, after his image" (Genesis 5:3). Seth, who lived 912 years, was the father of Enos as well as other sons and daughters (see Genesis 5:6–8; Luke 3:38; Moses 6:16). From latter-day scripture, we have a fuller understanding of the character and importance of Seth. He is mentioned five times in the Doctrine and Covenants. The following passage indicates the pathway of priesthood lineage through Seth, and also gives a profile of his character:

This order [of the priesthood] was instituted in the days of Adam, and came down by lineage in the following manner:

From Adam to Seth, who was ordained by Adam at the age of sixty-nine years, and was blessed by him three years previous to his (Adam's) death, and received the promise of God by his father, that his posterity should be the chosen of the Lord, and that they should be preserved unto the end of the earth;

Because he (Seth) was a perfect man, and his likeness was the express likeness of his father, insomuch that he seemed to be like unto his father in all things, and could be distinguished from him only by his age. (D&C 107:41–43; see also D&C 107:51)

Additionally, Seth is mentioned as a participant in the august assembly of elect individuals gathered together by Adam to receive his benedictory blessing: "Three years previous to the death of Adam, he called Seth, Enos, Cainan, Mahalaleel, Jared, Enoch, and Methuselah, who were all high priests, with the residue of his posterity who were righteous, into the valley of Adam-ondi-Ahman, and there bestowed upon them his last blessing" (D&C 107:53). Seth is also mentioned as one of the noble personages President Joseph F. Smith viewed in his vision of the spirit realm: "Abel, the first martyr, was there, and his brother Seth, one of the mighty ones, who was in the express image of his father, Adam" (D&C 138:40). Moreover, the Pearl of Great Price confirms that "God revealed himself unto Seth," he having offered "an acceptable sacrifice, like unto his brother Abel" (Moses 6:3).

SEVEN ANGELS

The book of Revelation speaks fairly often about the presence and actions of "seven angels" (see Revelation 8:2, 6; 15:1, 6–8; 16:1; 17:1; 21:9). Section 77 of the Doctrine and Covenants provides inspired commentary on various passages written by John the Revelator, including the following reference: "And I saw the seven angels which stood before God; and to them were given seven trumpets" (Revelation 8:2). Latter-day scripture asks,

> Q. What are we to understand by the sounding of the trumpets, mentioned in the 8th chapter of Revelation?
>
> A. We are to understand that as God made the world in six days, and on the seventh day he finished his work, and sanctified it, and also formed man out of the dust of the earth, even so, in the beginning of the seventh thousand years will the Lord God sanctify the earth, and complete the salvation of man, and judge all things, and shall redeem all things, except that which he hath not put into his power, when he shall have sealed all things, unto the end of all things; and the sounding of the trumpets of the seven angels are the preparing and finishing of his work, in the beginning of the seventh thousand years—the preparing

of the way before the time of his coming. (D&C 77:12)

SHEM (MEANING: NAME.)

The New Testament contains only one reference to Shem, son of Noah (rendered *Sem*), in the genealogical lineage of Jesus Christ given by Luke: "Sem, which was the son of Noe, which was the son of Lamech" (Luke 3:36). Shem is the first mentioned of Noah's three sons (see Genesis 5:32; 6:10; 1 Chronicles 1:4) and one of the eight individuals who embarked on the journey to preserve humankind: "In the selfsame day entered Noah, and Shem, and Ham, and Japheth, the sons of Noah, and Noah's wife, and the three wives of his sons with them, into the ark" (Genesis 7:13; see also Genesis 9:18, 26). The descendants of Shem are listed in the scriptural text (see Genesis 10:21–31; 11:10–27, 1 Chronicles 1:17–28) and include Abram, (Abraham). Shem is traditionally considered to be the ancestor of the Semitic races, including the Hebrews, Phoenicians, Arabs, Aramaeans (or Syrians), and the Babylonians and Assyrians—all of these belonging to the Semitic language family of nations.

Shem is mentioned only once in the Doctrine and Covenants, in connection with the elect personalities observed by President Joseph F. Smith in his vision of the work of salvation in the spirit world, including "Noah, who gave warning of the flood; Shem, the great high priest; Abraham, the father of the faithful; Isaac, Jacob, and Moses, the great law-giver of Israel" (D&C 138:41). Shem is also mentioned in the Pearl of Great Price, where his position as the middle of the three sons of Noah (not the firstborn) is confirmed: "And Noah was four hundred and fifty years old, and begat Japheth; and forty-two years afterward he begat Shem of her who was the mother of Japheth, and when he was five hundred years old he begat Ham" (Moses 8:12). We also have the statement concerning the righteous nobility of Noah and his sons: "And thus Noah found grace in the eyes of the Lord; for Noah was a just man, and perfect in his generation; and he walked with God, as did also his three sons, Shem, Ham, and Japheth" (Moses 8:27; see also Genesis 9:18–27).

Silas

Silas was one of the chief leaders among the Christians at Jerusalem: "Then pleased it the apostles and elders, with the whole church, to send chosen men of their own company to Antioch with Paul and Barnabas; namely, Judas surnamed Barsabas, and Silas, chief men among the brethren" (Acts 15:22). The purpose for the delegation to Antioch was to resolve a dispute among the Saints there concerning circumcision—that it was no longer required of those coming into the fold: "We have sent therefore Judas and Silas, who shall also tell you the same things by mouth" (Acts 15:27). Silas and Judas were characterized as being prophets: "And Judas and Silas, being prophets also themselves, exhorted the brethren with many words, and confirmed them. And after

PAUL AND SILAS PREACH TO THE JAILER.

they had tarried there a space, they were let go in peace from the brethren unto the apostles. Notwithstanding it pleased Silas to abide there still" (Acts 15:32–34). Silas participated with Paul in missionary assignments (see Acts 15:40; 16:19–40; 17:1–15; 18:5). In addition, he is sometimes referred to as Silvanus: "By Silvanus, a faithful brother unto you, as I suppose, I have written briefly, exhorting, and testifying that this is the true grace of God wherein ye stand" (1 Peter 5:12; see also 1 Thessalonians 1:1; 2 Thessalonians 1:1).

Silvanus

Silvanus is another name for Silas. (See the entry for Silas.)

Simeon (Meaning: that hears.)

1. Simeon, son of Jacob, is mentioned once in the New Testament, in Luke's genealogical lineage of Jesus Christ: "Simeon, which was the son of Juda, which was the son of Joseph, which was the son of Jonan, which was the son of Eliakim" (Luke 3:30). Simeon was the second son of Jacob by his wife Leah (see Genesis 29:33; 35:23; Exodus 1:2). Of note in the life of Simeon is the drastic retribution inflicted upon the Shechemites by him and his brother Levi for the mistreatment of Dinah, daughter of Jacob and Leah (see Genesis 34:26, 30; 35:1–5). Simeon also figures into the dramatic encounter between Joseph of Egypt and his brothers, by whom Joseph had been sold into slavery and who now came appealing for provisions during the famine in Canaan. Simeon was retained by Joseph—still not recognized by his brothers—as hostage collateral to guarantee the delivery of Benjamin, being eventually released when reconciliation and forgiveness came about (see Genesis 42:24, 36; 43:23). The inheritance of the tribe of Simeon in the promised land is indicated in Joshua 19:1–9 and 1 Chronicles 4:24–33.

2. Simeon was a righteous man of senior years in Jerusalem who was inspired to come to the temple on the day Joseph and Mary brought their babe to that holy place, in keeping with Mosaic practice:

> And, behold, there was a man in Jerusalem, whose name was Simeon; and the same man was just and devout, waiting for the consolation of Israel: and the Holy Ghost was upon him.
>
> And it was revealed unto him by the Holy Ghost, that he should not see death, before he had seen the Lord's Christ.
>
> And he came by the Spirit into the temple: and when the parents brought in the child Jesus, to do for him after the custom of the law,
>
> Then took he him up in his arms, and blessed God, and said,
>
> Lord, now lettest thou thy servant depart in peace, according to thy word:
>
> For mine eyes have seen thy salvation,
>
> Which thou hast prepared before the face of all people;
>
> A light to lighten the Gentiles, and the glory of thy people Israel.
>
> And Joseph and his mother marvelled at those things which

were spoken of him. (Luke 2:25–33)

Then Simeon pronounced a prophetic blessing upon the family: "And Simeon blessed them, and said unto Mary his mother, Behold, this child is set for the fall and rising again of many in Israel; and for a sign which shall be spoken against; (Yea, a sword shall pierce through thy own soul also,) that the thoughts of many hearts may be revealed" (Luke 25:24–25).

3. Simeon was a prophet and teacher at Antioch who participated in the calling of Barnabas and Saul (Paul) for the ministry: "Now there were in the church that was at Antioch certain prophets and teachers; as Barnabas, and Simeon that was called Niger, and Lucius of Cyrene, and Manaen, which had been brought up with Herod the tetrarch, and Saul. As they ministered to the Lord, and fasted, the Holy Ghost said, Separate me Barnabas and Saul for the work whereunto I have called them. And when they had fasted and prayed, and laid their hands on them, they sent them away" (Acts 13:1–3).

4. Simeon is an alternate rendition of the name for Simon Peter: "And after they had held their peace, James answered, saying, Men and brethren, hearken unto me: Simeon hath declared how God at the first did visit the Gentiles, to take out of them a people for his name" (Acts 15:13–14).

SIMON

1. Simon is identified as the brother of Jesus: "Is not this the carpenter's son? is not his mother called Mary? and his brethren, James, and Joses,

and Simon, and Judas?" (Matthew 13:55; see also Mark 6:3).

2. Simon, called "the Canaanite," is identified as one of the original Twelve Apostles: "Now the names of the twelve apostles are these; The first, Simon, who is called Peter, and Andrew his brother; James the son of Zebedee, and John his brother; Philip, and Bartholomew; Thomas, and Matthew the publican; James the son of Alphæus, and Lebbæus, whose surname was Thaddæus; Simon the Canaanite, and Judas Iscariot, who also betrayed him" (Matthew 10:2–4; see also Mark 3:16–19). Simon is also referred to by Luke as Simon Zelotes (see Luke 6:15; Acts 1:13), apparently in reference to the "Zealots," or followers of the Cananaean persuasion, referring to those with an attachment to certain political leanings in favor of an independent Israel in the days of Roman imperial sovereignty. The word *cananaean* derives from an Aramaic word *kanan*, equivalent to the Greek word *zelotes*. Thus "Cananaean" rather than "Canaanite" appears to be the more accurate translation in Matthew 10:4 and Mark 3:18.

3. Simon of Cyrene was the man compelled to carry the cross of the Lord on the way to Golgotha: "And when they had mocked him, they took off the purple from him, and put his own clothes on him, and led him out to crucify him. And they compel one Simon a Cyrenian, who passed by, coming out of the country, the father of Alexander and Rufus, to bear his cross" (Mark 15:20–21; see also Matthew 27:32; Luke 23:26).

4. Simon the leper was a man in whose house Mary, sister of Martha and Lazarus, anointed the Lord in anticipation of His sacrifice as the Lamb of God (see Matthew 26:6–13; Mark 14:3).

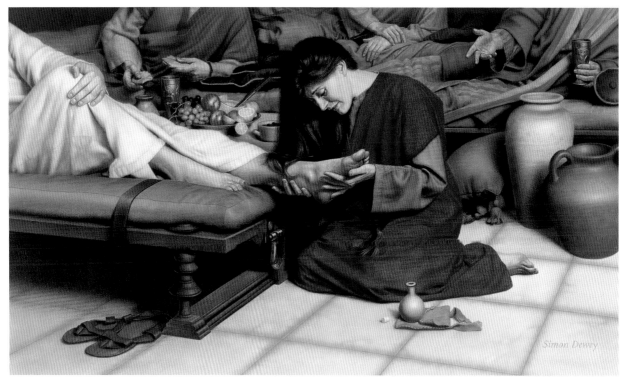

MARY WASHES THE SAVIOR'S FEET IN THE HOUSE OF SIMON, THE PHARISEE.

5. Simon Magus was a sorcerer who came into the Church through the preaching of Philip. His story illustrates the principle that the blessings of heaven cannot be obtained through earthly means but only upon principles of righteousness (see Acts 8:9–13).

When the Apostles Peter and John came to Samaria to bestow the gift of the Holy Ghost upon the newly baptized converts there, Simon observed a wondrous outpouring of heavenly blessings and wanted the power to do the same (see Acts 8:18–24).

6. Simon is another name for Peter, the Apostle: "And Jesus, walking by the sea of Galilee, saw two brethren, Simon called Peter, and Andrew his brother, casting a net into the sea: for they were fishers. And he saith unto them, Follow me, and I will make you fishers of men. And they straightway left their nets, and followed him" (Matthew 4:18–20).

7. Simon was a Pharisee to whom the Savior taught a grand lesson on forgiveness and faith (see Luke 7:36–40). The Savior, having discerned Simon's thoughts, related the parable of the creditor who forgave a debtor of five hundred pence and a debtor of fifty pence, with the follow-up question: "Tell me therefore, which of them will love him most?" (Luke 7:42). Simon, supposing the answer to be the creditor who was forgiven the most, then heard from the Savior these compelling words:

> Seest thou this woman? I entered into thine house, thou gavest me no water for my feet: but she hath washed my feet with tears, and wiped them with the hairs of her head.
>
> Thou gavest me no kiss: but this woman since the time I came in hath not ceased to kiss my feet.

My head with oil thou didst not anoint: but this woman hath anointed my feet with ointment.

Wherefore I say unto thee, Her sins, which are many, are forgiven; for she loved much: but to whom little is forgiven, the same loveth little.

And he said unto her, Thy sins are forgiven.

And they that sat at meat with him began to say within themselves, Who is this that forgiveth sins also?

And he said to the woman, Thy faith hath saved thee; go in peace. (Luke 7:44–50)

8. Simon was a tanner at Joppa, at whose house Peter stayed following his miracle of restoring life to the deceased Tabitha (see Acts 9:43). It was to this location that Cornelius the centurion, at the bidding of an angel of God, sent an invitation to Peter to come to him in Caesarea: "And now send men to Joppa [said the angel], and call for one Simon, whose surname is Peter: He lodgeth with one Simon a tanner, whose house is by the sea side: he shall tell thee what thou oughtest to do" (Acts 10:5–6; see also Acts 10:17–18, 32). It was the coming together of Peter and Cornelius by divine design that launched the missionary program to the Gentiles.

SION (See the entry for Zion.)

SISTERS OF THE LORD

The New Testament makes clear that Jesus Christ had both brothers and sisters who were children of Joseph and Mary after Jesus was born (see Matthew 13:54–57).

According to the Bible Dictionary in the entry for "Brethren of the Lord," "The number of girls is not specified, but the Greek text makes it clear that there were more than two. Since the exact number is not known, this is presented in the King James Version as 'all his sisters'" (627).

SOLOMON (Meaning: peaceable.)

Solomon, son of David and king of Israel, is mentioned several times in the New Testament, initially in Matthew's summary of the genealogical lineage of Jesus Christ: "And Jesse begat David the king; and David the king begat Solomon of her that had been the wife of Urias; And Solomon begat Roboam" (Matthew 1:6–7). In addition, the Savior referred to Solomon in the Sermon on the Mount: "And why take ye thought for raiment? Consider the lilies of the

Solomon rules over Israel.

field, how they grow; they toil not, neither do they spin: And yet I say unto you, That even Solomon in all his glory was not arrayed like one of these. Wherefore, if God so clothe the grass of the field, which to day is, and to morrow is cast into the oven, shall he not much more clothe you, O ye of little faith?" (Matthew 6:28–30; see also Luke 12:27–28). When the scribes and Pharisees—in such close proximity to the Savior and yet so far away in judgment and perception—asked Him for a sign, He declared, "The queen of the south shall rise up in the judgment with this generation, and shall condemn it: for she came from the uttermost parts of the earth to hear the wisdom of Solomon; and, behold, a greater than Solomon is here" (Matthew 12:42; see also Luke 11:31). Finally, Stephen, prior to his martyrdom, evoked the memory of Solomon as the builder of the temple (see Acts 7:44–49).

From the historical perspective, Solomon, son of David and Bathsheba, was the successor to David on the throne of Israel, reigning from around 1015 BC until his death around 975 BC. The story of Solomon is presented in 1 Kings 1–11. Two elements of truth radiate from the life of Solomon with special significance: wisdom anchored in principles of righteousness and the power and glory of the holy temple. We now consider each of these elements in turn.

Concerning the wisdom of Solomon, we read, "And Solomon loved the Lord, walking in the statutes of David his father" (1 Kings 3:3). Consequently, Solomon received a glorious blessing from the Lord: "Lo, I have given thee a wise and an understanding heart" (1 Kings 3:12). "And there came of all people to hear the wisdom of Solomon, from all kings of the earth, which had heard of his wisdom" (1 Kings 4:29–34), including the queen of Sheba (see 1 Kings 10:1–13). The book of Proverbs was authored by Solomon and successors who imitated his craft. Proverbs is one of the eleven books of the Old Testament that belong to the so-called Hagiographa ("sacred writings") of the Jewish canon, along with the books of Job, Psalms, Song of Solomon, Ruth, Lamentations, Ecclesiastes, Daniel, Esther, Ezra-Nehemiah (counted as one book in the Jewish canon), and Chronicles (also counted as one book). The proverbs of Solomon include a veritable garden of wisdom in the form of cogent maxims, exhortations, and poems for governing one's life. There are, in general, four principal themes running through Proverbs: (1) trusting in God is the foundation of wisdom, (2) a willingness to be entreated is the key to cultivating wisdom, (3) the flowering of wisdom is to bring forth good fruit unto the Lord, and (4) pride leads to folly—"Pride goeth before destruction, and a haughty spirit before a fall" (Proverbs 16:18).

Solomon was enormously prolific: "And he spake three thousand proverbs: and his songs were a thousand and five" (1 Kings 4:32). He is also traditionally considered to be the author of Ecclesiastes; however, the writing of Ecclesiastes appears to have occurred much later, in the time frame of 300 BC to 250 BC. In the course of his own life, as it turned out, Solomon was rather better at conveying wisdom than in becoming its leading practitioner. Despite his enormous wisdom and his triumph in building the great temple, Solomon eventually allowed his interests to shift unwisely to behaviors that violated his sacred trust, for he married outside Israel and his heart turned to idolatry (see 1 Kings 11). In his example, we can perceive with clarity the opposing principles of wisdom and worldliness. Through his example, we can learn important lessons about seeking to make wise choices and avoiding the pitfalls of temptation, for there is much in his legacy that can benefit and instruct the honest seeker after truth.

In regard to the temple, the Lord had promised David that his son would build a house to the Lord (see 1 Kings 5:5). Solomon followed through with this destined project and erected a magnificent temple complex for sacred worship. The dedicatory program (see 1 Kings 8) is replete with utterances importuning the Lord to accept His people as His own and prosper their way as long as they heeded His word and kept His commandments, looking toward the temple as a continual reminder of their covenant commitments. The temple edifice became renowned throughout the region, and rulers and potentates came from all around to admire it and bask in the opulence and wisdom of Solomon's court.

SON OF GOD

Son of God is one of many titles of the Savior. It was used in the annunciation by Gabriel: "And the angel answered and said unto her, The Holy Ghost shall come upon thee, and the power of the Highest shall overshadow thee: therefore also that holy thing which shall be born of thee shall be called the Son of God" (Luke 1:35). It was used by Jesus in His instructions to Nicodemus: "For God so loved the world, that he gave his only begotten Son, that whosoever believeth in him should not perish, but have everlasting life. For God sent not his Son into the world to condemn the world; but that the world through him might be saved. He that believeth on him is not condemned: but he that believeth not is condemned already, because he hath not believed in the name of the only begotten Son of God" (John 3:16–18). To the Jews who were going to stone Him, He said,

Many good works have I shewed you from my Father; for which of those works do ye stone me?

The Jews answered him, saying, For a good work we stone thee not; but for blasphemy; and because that thou, being a man, makest thyself God.

Jesus answered them, Is it not written in your law, I said, Ye are gods [Psalm 82:6]?

If he called them gods, unto whom the word of God came, and the scripture cannot be broken;

Say ye of him, whom the Father hath sanctified, and sent into the world, Thou blasphemest; because I said, I am the Son of God?

If I do not the works of my Father, believe me not.

CHRIST WITH THE CHILDREN

But if I do, though ye believe not me, believe the works: that ye may know, and believe, that the Father is in me, and I in him. (John 10:32–38)

Many other individuals throughout the record of the New Testament referred to Jesus as the Son of God, including Paul in the following familiar statement concerning the Church: "And he gave some, apostles; and some, prophets; and some, evangelists; and some, pastors and teachers; For the perfecting of the saints, for the work of the ministry, for the edifying of the body of Christ: Till we all come in the unity of the faith, and of the knowledge of the Son of God, unto a perfect man, unto the measure of the stature of the fulness of Christ" (Ephesians 4:11–13). Jesus is verily the Son of God, as confirmed throughout all of holy writ.

Son of Man

Son of Man is an additional title for the Lord, one He used frequently in the Gospels, initially in this passage: "Now when Jesus saw great multitudes about him, he gave commandment to depart unto the other side. And a certain scribe came, and said unto him, Master, I will follow thee whithersoever thou goest. And Jesus saith unto him, The foxes have holes, and the birds of the air have nests; but the Son of man hath not where to lay his head" (Matthew 8:18–20). Later, the Lord said, concerning the parable of the wheat and the tares, "He that soweth the good seed is the Son of man" (Matthew 13:37). Of His disciples, the Lord inquired, "Whom do men say that I the Son of man am?" (Matthew 16:13); to which Peter gave his sincere reply, "Thou art the Christ, the Son of the living God" (Matthew 16:16). Jesus declared to His disciples, "Behold, we go up to Jerusalem; and the Son of man shall be betrayed unto the chief priests and unto the scribes, and they shall condemn him to death, And shall deliver him to the Gentiles to mock, and to scourge, and to crucify him: and the third day he shall rise again" (Matthew 20:18–19). These and many other similar references throughout the scriptures confirm the divine calling of Jesus as the Only Begotten Son of God, and—through the condescension of the Father and the Son—as the Son of Man.

In some cases in the scriptures, "son of man" is used to denote humankind, as in this example: "God is not a man, that he should lie; neither the son of man, that he should repent" (Numbers 23:19). "Son of man" can also denote a prophet, as throughout Ezekiel: "Moreover, thou son of man, take thee one stick, and write upon it, For Judah, and for the children of Israel his companions: then take another stick, and write upon it, For Joseph, the stick of Ephraim, and for all the house of Israel his companions" (Ezekiel 37:16).

Sons of God

The expression "sons of God" is used six times in the New Testament, in the following four passages:

- the witness of John the Baptist concerning the Lord (see John 1:9–12)
- the witness of Paul about the confirming testimony received through the Spirit of God (see Romans 8:14–19)
- the counsel of Paul about the walk of life of the righteous (see Philippians 2:14–15)
- the promise of John about our future meeting of the Lord (see 1 John 3:1–2)

Sons of Levi

The expression "sons of Levi" is used only one time in the New Testament, in a passage from Paul concerning Jesus Christ as the supreme High Priest of salvation in contrast to the preparatory service of the Levites in their priesthood calling: "And verily they that are of the sons of Levi, who receive the office of the priesthood, have a commandment to take tithes of the people according to the law, that is, of their brethren, though they come out of the loins of Abraham" (Hebrews 7:5). Thus, "If therefore perfection were by the Levitical priesthood, (for under it the people received the law,) what further need was there that another priest should rise after the order of Melchisedec, and not be called after the order of Aaron?" (Hebrews 7:11).

The background for this comparison comes from the Old Testament, where the expression "sons of Levi" is used occasionally in connection with the priesthood commission given to the descendants of Levi—Aaron being the first appointed—concerning the assignment to assist in the work of the sacred rites of sacrifice and worship. For example, "And the priests the sons of Levi shall come near; for them the Lord thy God hath chosen to minister unto him, and to bless in the name of the Lord" (Deuteronomy 21:5; see also Deuteronomy 31:9). In addition, "These were the sons of Levi after the house of their fathers; even the chief of the fathers, as they were counted by number of names by their polls, that did the work for the service of the house of the Lord, from the age of twenty years and upward" (1 Chronicles 23:24; see also Nehemiah 12:23; Ezekiel 40:46; Malachi 3:3; Hebrews 7:5; 3 Nephi 24:3).

Sons of Men

The expression "sons of men" occurs twice in the New Testament: once in the Savior's statement to the murmuring scribes—"Verily I say unto you, All sins shall be forgiven unto the sons of men, and blasphemies wherewith soever they shall blaspheme: But he that shall blaspheme against the Holy Ghost hath never forgiveness, but is in danger of eternal damnation" (Mark 3:28-29)—and once by Paul—"Whereby, when ye read, ye may understand my knowledge in the mystery of Christ Which in other ages was not made known unto the sons of men, as it is now revealed unto his holy apostles and prophets by the Spirit" (Ephesians 3:4-5). The expression "sons of men" is used pervasively in the other standard works to denote mortals in general.

Sorcerer/Sorcerers

The New Testament refers to a "sorcerer" on one occasion, during the missionary work of Paul (see Acts 13:6-11).

In general, a sorcerer is one who claims the power to foretell future events, such as the sorcerers at the court of Pharaoh during the days of Moses (see Exodus 7:11) or those during the days of Jeremiah who gave counsel in opposition to the word of the Lord (see Jeremiah 27:9). Sorcerers were active during the days of Daniel, attempting without success to interpret the dreams of Nebuchadnezzar (see Daniel 2:2). Malachi prophesies divine judgment against sorcerers and other evil-doers (see Malachi 3:5; Revelation 21:8; 22:15; 3 Nephi 24:5; D&C 76:103).

Spirit of God/Spirit of the Lord (See the entry for Holy Ghost.)

Stephen

Stephen was a bold and devout defender of the cause of the Church, one of the seven special ministering leaders chosen to serve the needs of the Saints (see Acts 6:3–6).

For his witness of Christ, Stephen was called before the Sanhedrin to face charges of blasphemy: "And all that sat in the council, looking stedfastly on him, saw his face as it had been the face of an angel" (Acts 6:15). His self-defense, eloquent and impassioned (see Acts 7:1–53), was also filled with bold recriminations against the authorities who were attacking him: "Ye stiffnecked and uncircumcised in heart and ears, ye do always resist the Holy Ghost: as your fathers did, so do ye. Which of the prophets have not your fathers persecuted? and they have slain them which shewed before of the coming

Stephen becomes a martyr for the gospel's sake.

of the Just One; of whom ye have been now the betrayers and murderers: Who have received the law by the disposition of angels, and have not kept it" (Acts 7:51–53). Following his delivery, he was subjected to stoning and became a martyr, with Saul (Paul) present as an observer (see Acts 7:54–60).

Stoics

Both the Stoics and the Epicureans are mentioned once in the New Testament, in connection with the visit of Paul to Mars' Hill in Athens: "Then certain philosophers of the Epicureans, and of the Stoicks, encountered him. And some said, What will this babbler say? other some, He seemeth to be a setter forth of strange gods: because he preached unto them Jesus, and the resurrection" (Acts 17:18). (Concerning the Epicureans, see the entry on the Epicureans.)

The Stoics, as a school of philosophy, elevated virtue as the primary duty of man and believed in a divine force of reason governing the universe according to absolute laws. It held to the view that individuals, to be happy, needed to harmonize their lives with this grand order by overcoming negative emotions and wicked impulses and accepting their lot in life with a kind of fatalistic nobility—hence the implication of the adjective *stoic*, as it has come to be understood in our time. The Stoic school was founded by the philosopher Zeno around 300 BC, the name of his movement deriving from the Greek word *stoa* or *portico*, and is where he taught in Athens. Stoicism was an ethical philosophy known to or followed by many of those whom Paul taught (not just in Athens)—hence, the importance of his understanding and knowing this lifestyle just as he intimately understood and knew the written law and oral traditions the Jewish people followed. Such a familiarity with one's missionary audience is a principal dimension of successful missionary work.

SYRIANS

The Syrians were a people of Semitic origin (see Genesis 10:22; 22:21) living in the ancient realm of Syria, north and northeast of Palestine, originally called Aram, meaning "highlands" (see Numbers 23:7)—hence, the term *Aramaeans* is a general equivalent to the term *Syrians*. Aramaic became the language of diplomatic communication in the days of Hezekiah and gradually became the language of daily life among the Jewish people and the native language Jesus spoke. The Syrians (or Aramaeans) were generally rivals of Israel (see 2 Samuel 8:3-6; 1 Kings 11:23-25; 15:18; 20:34; 22; 2 Kings 6:24 to 7:20; 8:28-29; 10:32-33; 13:3-7, 25; 14:28; 16:7-9). At the time of Jesus, Syria was a Roman province (see Matthew 4:24; Luke 2:2; Acts 15:23, 41; 18:18; 20:3; 21:3; Galatians 1:21). The Syrians are also mentioned one time in the Book of Mormon, in a passage quoting the prophet Isaiah (see 2 Nephi 19:12; Isaiah 9:12).

SYROPHENICIAN

The term *Syrophenician* is used only once in the New Testament, concerning a woman descended from the Phoenicians of Syria: "The woman was a Greek, a Syrophenician by nation; and she besought him that he would cast forth the devil out of her daughter" (Mark 7:26). Though the Lord's ministry was to the Israelites (the Apostles would be called to those of other origin), He nevertheless blessed the woman's family and liberated the daughter from her malaise.

THADDAEUS

Thaddaeus, or Lebbaeus, was one of the original Twelve: "Now the names of the twelve apostles are these; The first, Simon, who is called Peter, and Andrew his brother; James the son of Zebedee, and John his brother; Philip, and Bartholomew; Thomas, and Matthew the publican; James the son of Alphæus, and Lebbæus, whose surname was Thaddæus; Simon the Canaanite, and Judas Iscariot, who also betrayed him" (Matthew 10:2-4; see also Mark 3:18; Luke 6:16 and Acts 1:13, where the reference to "Judas the brother of James" is most likely the same as Thaddaeus; see the entry for Judas, item 3).

THEOPHILUS (MEANING: FRIEND OF GOD.)

Theophilus is the individual to whom Luke addressed his writings—the Gospel of Luke and the Acts of the Apostles. The wording at the beginning of the Gospel is as follows: "Forasmuch as many have taken in hand to set forth in order a declaration of those things which are most surely believed among us, Even as they delivered them unto us, which from the beginning were eyewitnesses, and ministers of the word; It seemed good to me also, having had perfect understanding of all things from the very first, to write unto thee in order, most excellent Theophilus, That thou mightest know the certainty of those things, wherein thou hast been instructed" (Luke 1:1-4).

The implication is that the "most excellent Theophilus" is an actual person. We learn also that Luke is depending on the testimony of eyewitnesses to prepare his history, he himself not being directly involved—at least not until he became Paul's companion during the period the Acts was written (see Acts 16:9-10, when the first use of the first person plural form *we* indicates that Luke was indeed a fellow traveler with Paul at that point and on number of occasions beyond). In reference to Theophilus, the introduction to the Acts reads, "The former treatise [Gospel of Luke] have I made, O Theophilus, of all that Jesus began both to do and teach" (Luke 1:1). The Joseph Smith Translation includes an additional reference to Theophilus: "For it is well known unto you, Theophilus, that after the manner of the Jews, and according to the custom of their law in receiving money into the treasury, that out of the abundance which was received, was appointed unto the poor, every man his portion; And after this manner did the publicans also, wherefore John said unto them, Exact no more than that which is appointed you" (JST Luke 3:19-20).

THESSALONIANS

The Thessalonians were residents of the Macedonian city of Thessalonica, founded in the fourth century BC and named in honor of Thessalonica, sister of Alexander the Great and wife of Cassander, a Greek military leader. Paul and his companion Silas taught the gospel there, assisted by Timothy (see Acts 16:1-3) and, for a time, possibly the physician and author Luke (see the "we" form of address that commenced with Acts 16:10-11). Their arrival in Thessalonica was perhaps around AD 50: "Now when they had passed through Amphipolis and Apollonia, they came to Thessalonica, where was a synagogue of the Jews" (Acts 17:1). The message to the Thessalonians from Paul and his companions (see the two epistles to the Thessalonians) is to strengthen their faith, sanctify themselves and others, prepare for the Second Coming, look forward to the reward of heavenly glory, and pray for the gospel cause.

THOMAS (MEANING: TWIN.)

Thomas was one of the Twelve and is identified as such in the record (see Matthew 10:2-4; Mark 3:18; Luke 6:15; Acts 1:13). Thomas is mentioned several other times in the New Testament:

- when Jesus learned of the passing of Lazarus (see John 11:14-16)
- when Jesus was teaching His disciples about the coming world (see John 14:1-7)
- the account of "doubting Thomas," which occurred after the risen Lord had appeared to His disciples, Thomas being absent at the time (see John 20:24-29)

Thereafter, Thomas is identified as being present when the Savior was with some of His Apostles near the shores of the Sea of Tiberias (Galilee): "After these things Jesus shewed himself again to the disciples at the sea of Tiberias; and on

CHRIST APPEARS TO THE DOUBTING THOMAS.

this wise shewed he himself. There were together Simon Peter, and Thomas called Didymus, and Nathanael of Cana in Galilee, and the sons of Zebedee, and two other of his disciples" (John 21:1–2). Thomas was, therefore, also a witness to the wonderful dialogue where the Lord instructed Peter, "Feed my lambs. . . . Feed my sheep. . . . Feed my sheep" (John 20:15–17).

TIBERIUS (SEE THE ENTRY FOR AUGUSTUS–ITEM 2.)

TIMOTHEUS

Timotheus, mentioned frequently in the New Testament, is the Greek form of the name Timothy. (See the entry for Timothy.)

TIMOTHY (MEANING: HONORED OF GOD.)

Timothy, trusted young companion to Paul, is mentioned by name seven times in the New Testament—and seventeen more times as Timotheus.

Paul accords Timothy—whom he identifies as "my workfellow" (Romans 16:21), "my own son in the faith" (1 Timothy 1:20), "my beloved son, and faithful in the Lord" (1 Corinthians 4:17), and "our fellowlabourer in the gospel of Christ" (1 Thessalonians 3:2)—with a magnificent expression of admiration (see 2 Timothy 1:1–8, 13).

Timothy served as Paul's emissary or companion in multiple projects (see Acts 17:14; 19:22; 20:4–5; Romans 16:21; 1 Corinthians 16:10; 2 Corinthians 1:1, 19; Philippians 1:1; 2:19–23; Colossians 1:1; 1 Thessalonians 1:1; 3:2; 2 Thessalonians 1:1; 1 Timothy 1:3; 2 Timothy 4:9, 21; Philemon 1:1). Timothy was at one point apparently imprisoned and then set free: "Know ye that our brother Timothy is set

at liberty; with whom, if he come shortly, I will see you" (Hebrews 13:23).

Some of the most memorable passages of counsel in the post-Gospel writings of the New Testament emanated from the relationship between Paul and Timothy. Consider these examples:

- hold to the faith (see 1 Timothy 1:18–19)
- working the cause of the Lord (see 1 Corinthians 16:10–11)
- an example of the believers (see 1 Timothy 4:12–16)
- avoid material things; follow after godliness (see 1 Timothy 6:9–12)
- be strong in the grace of Christ (see 2 Timothy 2:1–3)
- wisdom through the scriptures (see 2 Timothy 3:14–17)

Perhaps the best summary statement from Paul about his love for Timothy is this one: "But ye know the proof of him, that, as a son with the father, he hath served with me in the gospel" (Philippians 2:22).

TITUS

Of Titus's and Paul's other companions, Paul said, "Whether any do enquire of Titus, he is my partner and fellowhelper concerning you: or our brethren be enquired of, they are the messengers of the churches, and the glory of Christ" (2 Corinthians 8:23). Titus, a Greek (see Galatians 2:3), probably converted by Paul himself, was an exceptional missionary and representative of the gospel of Jesus Christ. The affection and respect Paul had for Titus comes through in the opening passage from the Epistle to Titus (see Titus 1:1–4).

Titus's ministry in support of the cause of Christ—whether in Corinth, Crete, or elsewhere—is set forth in these additional scriptures: 2 Corinthians 7:6, 13–14; 2 Corinthians 8:6, 16; 12:18; Galatians 2:1; and 2 Timothy 4:10.

TWELVE APOSTLES

The original Apostles in the meridian of time, emissaries or messengers from God, were chosen and empowered by the Savior personally. The following chart identifies each one, according to the precise wording in the record of the New Testament. (See the entries for the individual Apostles.)

During His visit to the New World, the resurrected Christ organized His Church, calling twelve men—Twelve Disciples—to lead the affairs of the kingdom of God in that part of the world. The Savior instructed the people concerning these authorized representatives (see 3 Nephi 12:1).

No.	Matthew 10:2–4	Mark 3:16–19	Luke 6:13–16	John 1:40–49 (not a full listing)	Acts 1:13
1	Simon (who is called Peter)	Simon (surnamed Peter)	Simon (whom he also named Peter)	Thou art Simon the son of Jona: thou shalt be called Cephas, which is by interpretation, A stone	Peter
2	Andrew (his brother)	Andrew (4th in Mark)	Andrew (his brother)	Andrew (Simon Peter's brother)	Andrew (4th in this listing)
3	James (the son of Zebedee)	James (the son of Zebedee [2nd in Mark])	James	-	James (2nd in this listing)
4	John (his brother)	John (the brother of James [3rd in Mark]; and he surnamed them Boanerges, which is, The sons of thunder)	John	-	John (3rd in this listing)
5	Philip	Philip	Philip	Philip	Philip

191

6	Bartholomew	Bartholomew	Bartholomew	Nathanael	Bartholomew (7th in this listing)
7	Thomas	Thomas (8th in Mark)	Thomas (8th in Luke)	-	Thomas (6th in this listing)
8	Matthew (the publican)	Matthew (7th in Mark)	Matthew (7th in Luke)	-	Matthew
9	James (the son of Alphæus)	James (the son of Alphæus)	James (the son of Alphæus)	-	James (the son of Alphæus)
10	Lebbæus (whose surname was Thaddæus)	Thaddæus	Judas (the brother of James [11th in Luke])	-	Judas (the brother of James [11th in this listing])
11	Simon (the Canaanite)	Simon (the Canaanite)	Simon (called Zelotes [10th in Luke])	-	Simon (Zelotes [10th in this listing])
12	Judas Iscariot (who also betrayed him)	Judas Iscariot (which also betrayed him)	Judas Iscariot (which also was the traitor)	-	Defected; deceased; replaced by Matthias (Acts 1:26)

The Lord gave special instructions to these disciples, beginning with Nephi, the son of Nephi, who was the son of Helaman (see 3 Nephi 11:18-41; 13:25-34). We are given the names of the members of this sacred quorum: "Nephi and his brother whom he had raised from the dead, whose name was Timothy, and also his son, whose name was Jonas, and also Mathoni, and Mathonihah, his brother, and Kumen, and Kumenonhi, and Jeremiah, and Shemnon, and Jonas, and Zedekiah, and Isaiah—now these were the names of the disciples whom Jesus had chosen—and it came to pass that they went forth and stood in the midst of the multitude" (3 Nephi 19:4).

Great and glorious were the experiences of these men: they taught the people with power and authority, received and administered the ordinances of the gospel, enjoyed angelic ministrations, administered the sacrament to the people, radiated light in their countenances as they prayed, determined from the Savior the proper name of the Church, received the commission to be judges of the Nephites, and reflected the Spirit of the Lord in all of their service (see 3 Nephi 18-20, 26-27). The work of the Twelve Disciples following the Ascension of the Savior contributed to an era of unprecedented peace among the people, one that endured for some four generations, in accordance with the promises

CHRIST WALKS WITH HIS APOSTLES.

of the Lord (see 3 Nephi 27:30–32). By the end of the first century, "the disciples of Jesus, whom he had chosen, had all gone to the paradise of God, save it were the three who should tarry; and there were other disciples ordained in their stead; and also many of that generation had passed away" (4 Nephi 1:14). Thus, the work of the Lord continued, through times of peace and times of war, times of righteousness and times of spiritual decay, times of the outpouring of the Spirit and times where it was withheld due to wickedness—until the chronicle of the Book of Mormon came to an end and the plates were consigned to their earthly vault to await the dawning of the Restoration in our day.

The institution of the Twelve Apostles was to play a key role, once again, in the operation of the Church in the dispensation of the fulness of times. In the revelation known as section 29 of the Doctrine and Covenants, the Lord refers to His original Twelve Apostles in connection with the Second Coming as follows:

> And again, verily, verily, I say unto you, and it hath gone forth in a firm decree, by the will of the Father, that mine apostles, the Twelve which were with me in my ministry at Jerusalem, shall stand at my right hand at the day of my coming in a pillar of fire, being clothed with robes of righteousness, with crowns upon their heads, in glory even as I am, to judge the whole house of Israel, even as many as have loved me and kept my commandments, and none else. (D&C 29:12)

Concerning the Twelve Apostles of the Restoration, the original members of the latter-day Quorum of the Twelve Apostles (called in February 1835) included Lyman E. Johnson, Brigham Young, Heber C. Kimball, Orson Hyde, David W. Patten, Luke S. Johnson, William E. McLellin, John F. Boynton, Orson Pratt, William Smith, Thomas B. Marsh, and Parley P. Pratt (see *HC* 2:187; the "Testimony of the Twelve Apostles to the Truth of the Doctrine and Covenants" included in the introduction to that sacred volume of scripture). By January 1841, the Quorum had been adjusted (see D&C 124:127–130).

Thus, Lyman E. Johnson, Luke S. Johnson, William E. McLellin, John F. Boynton, and Thomas B. Marsh had been replaced by John Taylor, John E. Page, Wilford Woodruff, Willard Richards, and George A. Smith. David Patten died as a martyr on October 25, 1838, at the battle of Crooked River while defending the Saints in Missouri from attacks by the mobs.

The Doctrine and Covenants frequently refers to the office and duties of the Twelve (see D&C 18:27 [three times], 31, 37; 102:30; 107:23 [twice], 26, 33–35, 39, 58, 98; 112:12, 14, 16, 21, 30; 114:1; 118:1; 124:127, 128; 135:2; 136:3). The Twelve are called to be "special witnesses of the name of Christ in all the world—thus differing from other officers in the church in the duties of their calling" (D&C 107:23). As such, the Twelve "hold the keys to open up the authority of my kingdom upon the four corners of the earth, and after that to send my word to every creature" (D&C 124:128; see also D&C 107:35).

Two Witnesses

Doctrine and Covenants section 77 provides inspired commentary on various passages John the Revelator wrote, including the following reference: "And I will give power unto my two witnesses, and they shall prophesy a thousand two hundred and threescore days, clothed in sackcloth" (Revelation 11:3). Latter-day scripture asks, "Q. What is to be understood by the two witnesses, in the eleventh chapter of Revelation? A. They are two prophets that are to be raised up to the Jewish nation in the last days, at the time of the restoration, and to prophesy to the Jews after they are gathered and have built the city of Jerusalem in the land of their fathers" (D&C 77:15).

Elder Bruce R. McConkie comments, "'In the mouth of two or three witnesses shall every word be established.' (2 Corinthians 13:1.) Such is God's eternal law. And these two shall be followers of that humble man, Joseph Smith, through whom the Lord of Heaven restored the fulness of his everlasting gospel in this final dispensation of grace. No doubt they will be members of the Council of the Twelve or of the First Presidency of the Church. Their prophetic ministry to rebellious Jewry shall be the same in length as was our Lord's personal ministry among their rebellious forebears" (*DNTC*, 3:510; see also 2 Nephi 8:18–20; Isaiah 51:17–20; Ezekiel 38:17–23).

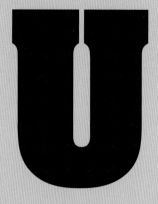

Unjust Judge

On one occasion, the Lord told the parable of the unjust judge and the importunate widow. The circumstances were as follows:

And he spake a parable unto them to this end, that men ought always to pray, and not to faint;

Saying, There was in a city a judge, which feared not God, neither regarded man:

And there was a widow in that city; and she came unto him, saying, Avenge me of mine adversary.

And he would not for a while: but afterward he said within himself, Though I fear not God, nor regard man;

Yet because this widow troubleth me, I will avenge her, lest by her continual coming she weary me.

And the Lord said, Hear what the unjust judge saith. And shall not God avenge his own elect, which cry day and night unto him, though he bear long with them?

I tell you that he will avenge them speedily. Nevertheless when the Son of man cometh, shall he find faith on the earth? (Luke 18:1–8)

The Savior penetrated to the heart of the matter: If the earthly judge, not fearing God nor having regard for man, would respond finally to the insistent pleas of the mistreated widow, then what higher degree of faith and hope should we have—while supplicating our Father in Heaven, whose mercy extends to all—that He would hear our prayers and extend blessings without measure? To cultivate this degree of faith is what the Savior was teaching.

What is unusual about this parable is that the Savior presented a sequel to it in the days of the Restoration. The unjust judge in the parable the Lord gave in section 101 of the Doctrine and Covenants is a figurative representation of the civil leadership to which the Saints of the Restoration appealed as they sought for redress in the face of daunting suffering and persecution (see D&C 101:81–85).

The lesson of the Savior's parable in the meridian of time resonated with equal poignancy and truth in the dispensation of the fulness of times. If the unjust judge would give relief to the widow, how much more would the Almighty, in His perfection and majesty, hear the pleas of His righteous Saints and grant them relief in their time of misery as they appealed to their civil leaders for help. In this revelation, the Lord invokes the spirit of the parable of the woman and unjust judge given in New Testament times to provide a spiritual framework in which the beleaguered Saints could proceed in faith to seek redress from the unconstitutional attacks being leveled against them. If the Saints were righteous and wholly dependent upon the Lord—and continued their petitions for redress in good faith—then relief would come, or the perpetrators would be punished in the due time of the Lord.

W

WIDOW OF SAREPTA (SEE THE ENTRY FOR SAREPTA, WIDOW OF.)

WISE MEN OF THE EAST

The story of the wise men who came from the East seeking the promised King is iconic in its status and impact even today. It begins, "Now when Jesus was born in Bethlehem of Judæa in the days of Herod the king, behold, there came wise men from the east to Jerusalem, Saying, Where is he that is born King of the Jews? for we have seen his star in the east, and are come to worship him" (Matthew 2:1–2). When Herod, distressed over the news, inquired of the chief priests and scribes where the foretold King should be born, they referred him to the prophecy of Micah: "But thou, Beth-lehem Ephratah, though thou be little among the thousands of Judah, yet out of thee shall he come forth unto me that is to be ruler in Israel; whose goings forth have been from of old, from everlasting" (Micah 5:2; see also Matthew 2:7–10).

The scene must have been extraordinarily touching as the men from the East paid homage to the child: "And when they were come into the house, they saw the young child with Mary his mother, and fell down, and worshipped him: and when they had opened their treasures, they presented unto him gifts; gold, and frankincense, and myrrh. And being warned of God in a dream that they should not return to Herod, they departed into their own country another way" (Matthew 2:11–12).

Concurrently, Joseph was warned in a dream to flee with his wife and child into Egypt for safety. Then Herod, angry over the action of the wise men, perpetrated his murderous horror by ordering death to all children two years old and

THE WISE MEN FOLLOW THE STAR TO THE BABY JESUS.

under in Bethlehem and its environs—giving us the approximate age range for the child Jesus he was determined to slay (see Matthew 2:16). We know nothing more of the wise men or their number, except the legendary supposition that the three gifts of gold, frankincense, and myrrh might suggest a party of three. We know only that they must have been receptive to the inspiration of God concerning the coming Messiah and sufficiently full of faith to journey so far to witness the miracle that had come into the world and then return "into their own country" to bear witness to their people of what they had seen.

ZACCHAEUS

Zacchaeus of Jericho was "chief among the publicans [tax collectors], and he was rich"

(Luke 19:2). He desired to observe Jesus, who was passing through Jericho at the time, but because Zacchaeus was small of stature, he could not fight his way through the crowds surging around the Lord. Thus, he climbed high into a sycamore tree for a better view, and what followed revealed the character of the Lord—and of Zacchaeus (see Mark 2:15–17; Luke 5:27–32; 15:1–7; 19:5–10).

ZACHARIAS

1. Zacharias was a priest in the days of king Herod and husband to Elisabeth. Zacharias and his wife "were both righteous before God, walking in all the commandments and ordinances of the Lord blameless. And they had no child, because that Elisabeth was barren, and they both were now well stricken in years" (Luke 1:6–7). During his time of annual service in the temple, Zacharias was suddenly visited by the angel Gabriel (see Luke 1:13–17).

Being of senior years, Zacharias did not immediately receive the news with faithful acceptance and, inquiring how he might with certainty know of its truth, was consigned to be rendered speechless for a time: "And, behold, thou shalt be dumb, and not able to speak, until the day that these things shall be performed, because thou believest not my words, which shall be fulfilled in their season" (Luke 1:20). As predicted, Elisabeth conceived and, over six months later, was visited by her relative Mary, who shared the joyous news of her own miraculous conception (see Luke 1:39–56). After Elisabeth had given birth to her son, Zacharias proclaimed in prophetic language his joy about the blessing that had come into the family (see Luke 1:68–80; D&C 27:7).

2. Zacharias (or Zechariah), from a priestly family during the time of king Joash of Judah (ninth century BC), was inspired by the Spirit of the Lord to call the royal leadership to repentance and was consequently stoned to death. Jesus Christ may have been invoking the memory of this Zacharias in condemning His detractors among the scribes and Pharisees in His powerful "woe unto you" speech (see Matthew 23:13–37; Luke 11:51).

In the Old Testament account, Zacharias was referred to as Zechariah and was identified as the son of Jehoiada, the high priest who was instrumental in overthrowing wicked Queen

ZACHARIAS PROPHECIES ABOUT AND REJOICES IN THE BIRTH OF HIS SON.

Athaliah—daughter of Ahab (king of Israel in the days of Elijah) and successor to her son Ahaziah, king of Judah—and elevating Joash (or Jehoash), surviving son of Ahaziah, to the throne (see 2 Kings 11:12–21; 2 Chronicles 22:10–12; 23:15). King Joash (or Jehoash) worked with Jehoiada diligently to repair and restore the house of the Lord (see 2 Chronicles 24:1–14). However, after the death of Jehoiada, the king, having submitted to the demands of the princes of the land to turn away from the house of the Lord and return to idolatry (see 2 Chronicles 24:18–19), was boldly called to repentance by Zechariah, son of Jehoiada (or historically, perhaps, his grandson), who pronounced upon the king the impending judgments of God: "And the Spirit of God came upon Zechariah the son of Jehoiada the priest, which stood above the people, and said unto them, Thus saith God, Why transgress ye the commandments of the Lord, that ye cannot prosper? because ye have forsaken the Lord, he hath also forsaken you. And they conspired against him, and stoned him with stones at the commandment of the king in the court of the house of the Lord" (2 Chronicles 24:20–21). Judea was soon thereafter invaded and despoiled by the Syrians, leaving Joash (or Jehoash) in a diseased state before he was slain by his own servants angered over the murder of the righteous Zechariah (see 2 Chronicles 24:24–27). Thus, this chapter of the Old Testament account, if indeed Jesus was referring to it in His chastisement of the scribes and Pharisees, was particularly applicable to conditions of the time, since His very audience of scribes and Pharisees would shortly be instrumental in His Crucifixion. It is possible that Jesus had another more contemporary Zacharias in mind, one unknown to us (see *DNTC*, 1:624).

ZEBEDEE

Zebedee was the father of James and John, two of the original members of the Twelve: "And when he had gone a little further thence, he saw James the son of Zebedee, and John his brother, who also were in the ship mending their nets. And straightway he called them: and they left their father Zebedee in the ship with the hired servants, and went after him" (Mark 1:19–20). The account implies that Zebedee, having hired servants, was a fairly successful professional (see Matthew 10:2; 26:37; Mark 3:17; 10:35; Luke 5:10; John 21:2). Zebedee's wife was Salome (see the entry for Salome, item 1).

ZELOTES (MEANING: ZEALOT.)

Zelotes was one of Simon's names, Simon being one of the original Twelve. (See the entry for Simon, item 2.)

ZERUBBABEL/ZOROBABEL (MEANING: BORN IN BABYLON.)

Zerubbabel (Zorobabel in the New Testament) is mentioned in the genealogical lineage of Jesus Christ (see Matthew 1:12–13; Luke 3:27). Zerubbabel, grandson of Jehoiachin, king of Judah, and son of Pedaiah (see 1 Chronicles 3:16–19), was appointed governor over Judea by the Persian authorities when Cyrus issued his decree in 537 BC, allowing the captive Jewish people to return to Palestine (see Ezra 1:8). Zerubbabel rebuilt the altar and the temple in Jerusalem (see Ezra 3:2, 8; 4:2–3; 5:2), aided by the prophets Haggai (see Haggai 1:1–15; 2:1–23) and Zechariah (see Zechariah 4:6–10)—despite much opposition from the local tribes, including the Samaritans (see the entry for the

Samaritans). Scholar Sydney B. Sperry indicates the nature of the rebuilt temple: "The plan of Solomon's temple was followed in general, but due to the poverty of the people, not on such a lavish scale. Many of the vessels used in the former temple were restored. (Ezra 1:7–11.) The Holy of Holies was empty, for the Ark of the Covenant disappeared when Nebuchadnezzar's forces invaded Palestine. This temple, called after Zerubbabel, and sometimes known as the Second Temple, was completed in the sixth year of Darius, 515 BC (Ezra 3:8; Ezra 6:15)" (Sidney B. Sperry, "Ancient Temples and Their Functions," *Ensign*, Jan. 1972, 67).

ZION

The word *Zion* is rendered *Sion* in the New Testament. Zion (Sion) refers to a place as well as to a people, with the word *Sion* occurring seven times in the New Testament, including these examples:

- the triumphal entry of Jesus into Jerusalem (see Matthew 21:5; John 12:15; Zechariah 9:9)
- Paul's discourse on following faith in the Lord, rather than robotic obedience to the law (see Romans 9:31–33; Isaiah 8:14)
- Paul's reference to Christ as the Deliverer of Zion (see Romans 11:26–27; Psalm 14:7; 53:6; Joel 2:32; Obadiah 1:17; Micah 4:10)
- Paul's edifying statement about the ultimate gathering of the hosts of heaven (see Hebrews 12:22–24; D&C 76:66–69)
- Peter's glorious characterization of the people of the Lord (see 1 Peter 2:6–9; Isaiah 28:16; 2 Nephi 18:14)
- John's vision of the assembly of great

leaders in the last days assembled on mount Zion (see Revelation 14:1)

These references to Sion (Zion) as the family of God—redeemed in righteousness through the Atonement of the Lord Jesus Christ and assembled on the temple-like mount with the angels of heaven radiating the glory and spirit of a chosen generation and a royal priesthood—echo the same edifying light that the word *Zion* radiates throughout all of the holy scriptures.

The name *Zion* appears 150 times in the Old Testament—mostly as a term indicating the place where the Lord's people dwell. However, in certain magnificent passages in Isaiah, the word takes on the nature of an appellation for the people themselves: "And I have put my words in thy mouth, and I have covered thee in the shadow of mine hand, that I may plant the heavens, and lay the foundations of the earth, and say unto Zion, Thou art my people" (Isaiah 51:16; see also Isaiah 52:1–2, 6–7).

Using the word *Zion* in this sense, as a name for the people of the Lord, is reinforced in latter-day scripture, as in the following passage from the Doctrine and Covenants: "Therefore, verily, thus saith the Lord, let Zion rejoice, for this is Zion—the pure in heart; therefore, let Zion rejoice, while all the wicked shall mourn" (D&C 97:21; see also D&C 100:16). The pure people constitute Zion, upon which the Lord bestows marvelous blessings: "For, behold, I say unto you that Zion shall flourish, and the glory of the Lord shall be upon her; And she shall be an ensign unto the people, and there shall come unto her out of every nation under heaven. And the day shall come when the nations of the earth shall tremble because of her, and shall fear because of her terrible ones. The Lord hath spoken it. Amen" (D&C 64:41–43; see also

D&C 105:5–6). Zion consists of a people unified in the discipleship of the Redeemer, like unto the people of Enoch: "And the Lord called his people Zion, because they were of one heart and one mind, and dwelt in righteousness; and there was no poor among them" (Moses 7:18). What are the implications of being such a people? Centrally, the unspeakable gift of being in the presence of the Lord continually and of being elevated above the plane of mortal existence into the bosom of God: "And Enoch and all his people walked with God, and he dwelt in the midst of Zion; and it came to pass that Zion was not, for God received it up into his own bosom; and from thence went forth the saying, Zion is fled" (Moses 7:69).

The term *Zion* draws the mind heavenward toward God, the spirit inward toward a state of worthiness and gratitude, the heart outward in service toward others, and the feet onward toward a "place of refuge, and for a covert from storm and rain" (Isaiah 4:6). Zion is a place, an institution, a state of mind, a noble destination, a people, a vision of perfection, an abode of God, an encapsulating summary of everything that is "honest, true, chaste, benevolent, virtuous . . . lovely, or of good report or praiseworthy" (Article of Faith 1:13). Zion is not a utopia ever nestled beyond mortal access; it is a reality that has already been manifested at times upon the earth among mortals who have risen to such a noble level of covenant righteousness that their exemplary level of peace, unity, and spiritual attainment have evoked upon them the highest blessings of our Father in Heaven. The dispensation of the fulness of times provides the unique framework for the unfolding of a Zion people and a Zion city in these latter days. It is the will of the Lord that such an establishment be forthcoming, prospered by the grace and beneficence of His loving care, overshadowed by His merciful Spirit, drawn on by His promised blessings, and secured by the inexorable finality of His word. What a glorious destiny is hereby proffered the Saints of God to be enlisted in such a magnificent work of edification and eternal progression. What a great responsibility to be engaged in the Lord's errand during the final period of the earth's history leading up to the inauguration of the millennial reign.

Appendix A

Notes on the Chronology of the New Testament Events

Historical dating of the events that transpired during New Testament times is often a difficult task for scholars and historians, given the paucity, or absence, of original documentation and the complexity of the process of rendering authentic judgments about the calendar origins of primary sources of which only later copies are available. The following chart gives approximations for the dates of important happenings. In the absence of dating certainty, often, at least, the relative sequencing of key events is helpful in placing them correctly into the developing saga of how the Christian cause unfolded from the birth of the Savior until the final stages of the Apostasy brought the dispensation to a close.

Decade	Events and Approximate Dates
First Decade BC	• When was the Savior born? There is agreement that the death of Herod the Great took place in 4 BC, ending a reign that began in 37 BC. When the wise men of the East arrived on scene to honor the young child whose birth was announced by the new star, Herod took notice of the emerging royal competition by ordering an egregious act: "And sent forth, and slew all the children that were in Bethlehem, and in all the coasts thereof, from two years old and under, according to the time which he had diligently enquired of the wise men" (Matthew 2:16). The targets of his campaign, which took place shortly before Herod's death in 4 BC, were children from under two years old and up to nearly three years old, indicating that the child Jesus, deemed part of this group, was likely born in the year 7 BC, 6 BC, or as late as 5 BC—not in the year 0 or AD 1, as commonly assumed. The conclusion that Jesus was born around 7–6 BC is supported by many commentators, as confirmed by the following bibliography shared with the author by Alonzo Gaskill, at the time Associate Professor of Church History and Doctrine at Brigham Young University: Joseph Fielding McConkie, *Witnesses of the Birth of Christ* (Salt Lake City, UT: Bookcraft, 1998), 25; Raymond E. Brown, *The Birth of the Messiah* (New York: Doubleday, 1993), 166–167; William F. Albright & C. S. Mann, *The Anchor Bible: Matthew* (New York: Doubleday, 1971), 12; Bruce R. McConkie, *The Mortal Messiah*, four volumes (Salt Lake City, UT: Deseret Book, 1980–1981), 1:349–350, n. 2; J. Reuben Clark, Jr., *Our Lord of the Gospels* (Salt Lake City, UT: Deseret Book, 1974), 168–174; Alfred Edersheim, *The Life and Times of Jesus the Messiah* (Grand Rapids, MI: Associated Publishers and Authors, Inc., n. d.), 164. • John the Baptist, being slightly older than Jesus, was born in the same time frame as Jesus (see Luke 1:36, 56; 2:5–7).

| AD First Decade | • In the middle part of this decade, Mary and Joseph took the twelve-year-old Jesus to Jerusalem for the Passover feast (see Luke 2:42). |
	• During the rest of the decade and the decade beyond, we learn that "Jesus increased in wisdom and stature, and in favour with God and man" (Luke 2:52).
AD Second Decade	• Jesus continued His growth and maturing.
AD Third Decade	• The baptism of the Savior and the beginning of His ministry would likely have taken place in the mid 20s, some thirty years after His birth (see Luke 3:23). Not long thereafter, Herod Antipas executed John the Baptist.
	• The Crucifixion and Resurrection would have taken place around the end of this decade or the beginning of the next. The death sentence was authorized by Pontius Pilate, who was in power as the fifth governor of Judea in the time frame AD 26 to AD 36. Perhaps the Crucifixion and Resurrection took place around AD 30 or somewhat earlier—though no absolute certainty for the dating can be determined.
AD Fourth Decade	• If the Crucifixion and Resurrection took place around AD 30 (the beginning of the fourth decade), then Paul's vision and conversion on the road to Damascus would likely have taken place around AD 32–33. The ministry of Paul extends from that time until the mid 60s, when, according to traditional sources, he was martyred.
AD Fifth Decade	• AD 44 was the year of the martyrdom of James, brother of John, by Herod Agrippa I, shortly before the latter's death at the hands of an angel of God (see Acts 12:1–3).
	• The mid 40s is the time frame for Paul's first missionary journey.
	• The celebrated Jerusalem Conference of the Apostles and other priesthood leaders took place in AD 49.
	• Paul's second missionary journey commenced in the late 40s and extended into the early years of the next decade.
AD Sixth Decade	• The 50s saw the emergence of the earliest New Testament writings:
	• 1 and 2 Thessalonians were written around AD 50–51. (Note: as a cross-reference to known historical events of the time, Paul went before Gallio likely in the fall of AD 51—see Acts 18:12.)
	• The Epistle of James may also date from this early period, though some place it around AD 60.
	• Galatians, 1 and 2 Corinthians, and Romans were written in the mid 50s, although, it is possible that Galatians dates from even before the Jerusalem meeting.
	• The mid 50s is the time of Paul's third missionary journey.
	• In the late 50s, Paul is imprisoned at Caesarea and also in Rome.

AD Seventh Decade	• Around AD 60 is the possible dating of the Gospel of Mark, the earliest of the Gospels. The Gospel of John, in its earliest dating, might have originated around this time as well, though an alternative position is that it was written in the 90s. The Epistle of James may also date from around this time (AD 60), though some scholars place it earlier, around AD 50–51. • According to historical accounts, AD 62 was the date of the martyrdom of James, brother of Jesus; thus, the Epistle of James must predate this year. • Philippians, Colossians, Ephesians, Hebrews, Philemon were written in the early 60s. • Titus, 1–2 Timothy, 1 Peter, Jude, 2 Peter were written in the mid 60s. (Note: around AD 64 is the traditional dating of the martyrdom of Peter—thus, the letters of Peter must have originated earlier than this.) • Around AD 64–67 is the traditional dating of the martyrdom of Paul. • Approximately AD 64–68 is the reign of Nero and the time frame for the early dating of Revelation. The later possibility for Revelation is AD 92–96, concurrent with the last years of the reign of Domitian.
AD Eighth Decade	• AD 70 is the date of the destruction of Jerusalem. • The Gospel of Matthew was likely written soon after AD 70. • Hebrews may date from just before or after AD 70—the origination date is not known for certain. • Around AD 75 is a possible dating of the Gospel of Luke. Acts, as the sequel to Luke, would have a date subsequent to this.
AD Ninth Decade	• AD 81–96 was the span of time during which Domitian reigned; Revelation might have originated during the latter part of this period, perhaps AD 92–96. Revelation was most likely not the last written of the books of the New Testament. The earlier possibility for the writing of Revelation was AD 64–68.
AD Tenth Decade	• A late dating for the Gospel of John is the 90s. • A possible dating for 1–3 John is the late 90s. • When John completed his earthly mission, he was translated in fulfillment of his request to the Savior (see D&C 7; 3 Nephi 28:1–12). Thus, the dispensation of the gospel in the meridian of time came to an end, and the glorious illumination of the gospel of Jesus Christ upon the earth was dimmed—until the coming dawning of the Restoration, nearly two millennia in the future, would usher in once more the fulness of the gospel of salvation.

Appendix B
Thematic Index

The following index is designed as a reference guide for personal study or to be used in preparing talks, lessons, or discussions. Each theme or item in the alphabetical inventory is followed by a list of the entries in the book where that theme or idea is discussed or referenced. By reviewing the entries associated with a given theme or item, the reader can gain a more thorough understanding of how that theme or item is developed and explained in the New Testament and associated cross-references in the LDS canon of scripture. A number after an entry refers to a sub-item within the main entry.

Aaronic Priesthood: Aaron, Bishop, High Priest, John the Baptist, Levi-1, Messiah, Peter, Priest/Priests, Sadducees, Sons of Levi

abduction: Lot

Abrahamic Covenant: Abraham, Cornelius, Heathen/Heathens, Jacob-1, Joseph, Melchizedek, Moses, Rachel, Sarah

accuser: Ananias-3

adoption: Isaac, Ishmael, Israel, Seed of Abraham

adversary: Satan

adversity: Job

Advocate: Jesus Christ

agency: Eve, Father in Heaven, Jesus-1, Lazarus-2, Lot

angel/angels: Cherub/Cherubim/Cherubims, Cornelius, Elisabeth, Gabriel, Gamaliel, Herod Agrippa I, Holy Ghost, Ishmael, Jesus-3, John the Baptist, Mary-1, Mary-2, Mary-6, Messiah, Noah, One Hundred and Forty-Four Thousand, Pharisees, Quaternion, Sadducees, Samson, Satan, Seven Angels, Stephen, Twelve Apostles, Zacharias-1

annunciation: Jesus Christ, Mary-1

anointed/anointing: Jesus Christ, Lazarus-1, Martha, Mary-3, Mary-4, Nazarene, Saul-1, Simon-4

anthem: Barak

apocalyptic writing: Daniel, Enoch

apostasy: High Priest, Paul

Apostle/Apostles: Apostle, Barnabas, Bartholomew, Boanerges, Canaanite, Cephas, Church, Didymus, Elder/Elders, Gamaliel, Gentile/Gentiles, High Priest, Holy Ghost, James-1, James-2, James-3, Joanna-2, John, Joseph-4, Judas-1, Judas-3, Levi-4, Mary-4, Mary-6, Matthew, Matthias, Moses, Nathanael, Onesimus, Paul, Peter, Philip-1, Publicans, Romans, Saint/Saints, Salome-1, Silas, Simon-2, Simon-5, Thaddaeus, Thomas, Timothy, Twelve Apostles, Zebedee, Zion

Aramaic: Hebrews, Syrians

ark: Noah

Ascension: Jesus Christ, Mary-1, Philip-1, Romans

Atonement: Adam, Father in Heaven, High Priest, Holy One of Israel, Isaac, Isaiah, James-1, Jesus Christ, Jonah, Lamb of God, Mark, Messiah, Moses, Nazarene, Nicodemus, Prisca/Priscilla, Prophet/Prophets, Zion

authority: Aaron, Abraham, Apostle, Church,

Hannah, James-1, Jesus Christ, John, Michael, Paul, Satan, Scribes, Twelve Apostles

Baal: Elijah, Gideon

baptism: Eunuch, Father in Heaven, Gentile/Gentiles, Holy Ghost, Israel, Jesus Christ, John the Baptist, Matthias, Nicodemus, Paul, Philip-2, Sons of Levi, Twelve Apostles

baptism for the dead: Paul

belief: Damaris, Dionysius the Areopagite, John, Martha

beloved: John

betrayal: Judas-1, Rabbi

birthright: Esau, Jacob-1, Joseph-1, Juda (Judah)

blasphemy: Holy Ghost, Stephen

blessings: Father in Heaven, Holy Ghost, Isaiah, Moses, Prophet/Prophets

blind leading the blind: Pharisees

body is a temple: Holy Ghost

bold: Boanerges, John, Stephen

Book of Mormon: Isaiah, Jeremias or Jeremy, Jesus Christ, John, Joseph-1, Juda (Judah), Malachi, Mary-1, Messiah, Moses

born again: Israel, Nicodemus

brazen serpent: Moses

brother/brothers: Brethren of the Lord

Cananaean: Simon-2

captain: Naaman

celestial glory: Father in Heaven, Sons of God

celestial marriage: Eunuch

celestial realm: Enoch, Michael

centurion: Cornelius, Julius

character: Joseph-1

chariots of fire: Elijah, Elisha

charity: Paul, Scribes, Sons of God

chastening: Abraham, Jeremias or Jeremy

chief captain: Claudius-2

chief corner stone: Jesus Christ, Zion

chief priests: Sanhedrin

children of the covenant: Prophet/Prophets

children of the prophets: Prophet/Prophets

Christian (the name): Christian/Christians

Church: Nicolaitans, Prophet/Prophets, Saint/Saints, Sanhedrin

commandments: Prophet/Prophets, Scribes

commandments of men: Pharisees, Scribes

compassion: Hannah, Joseph-1

compassionate: Eve

condescension: Jesus Christ, Son of Man

consecration: Barnabas

conspiracy: Caiaphas, Cain, Judas-1, Nazarene, Pharisees, Pilate, Romans, Sadducees, Salome-2, Sanhedrin, Satan, Scribes

conversion: Holy Ghost, Paul

correcting children: Samuel, Eli

council: Gamaliel, James-3, Joseph-3, Sanhedrin

counselor: Joseph-3

courage: Barak, Barnabas, David, Elisha, Jesus-1, Rachel, Rahab

covenant: Abraham, Esau, Eunuch, Father in Heaven, Heathen/Heathens, Hebrews, Holy Ghost, Isaac, Isaiah, Ishmael, Israel, Jacob-1, Jeremias or Jeremy, Jesus Christ, Juda (Judah), Melchizedek, Moses, Noah, Paul, Prophet/

Prophets, Rachel, Saint/Saints, Sarah, Zion

Creation: Father in Heaven, Holy Ghost, Jesus Christ

cross: Jesus Christ, Simon-3

Crucifixion: Centurion-2, Herod Agrippa I, James-4, Jesus Christ, Jew/Jews, John, Joseph-3, Judas-1, Mary-1, Mary-2, Mary-4, Mary-5, Nicodemus, Pharisees, Pilate, Prophet/Prophets, Romans, Salome-1, Sanhedrin, Satan, Simon-3, Zacharias-2

David: David, Ruth

deceit: Samson, Satan

defense: Paul, Nicodemus, Stephen

degrees of glory: Isaiah, Paul

deliverance: Ishmael, Jesus Christ, Jonah

Deliverer: Jesus Christ, Zion

denial: Peter, Satan

Devil: Satan, Scribes

devotion: Apollos, Aquila, Cornelius, Epaphras, Epaphroditus, Job, Paul, Prisca/Priscilla, Ruth, Samuel

devout: Stephen

discernment: Balaam, Beelzebub, Eve

dispensations: Adam, Malachi, Moses, Zion

dispensation of the fulness of times: Isaiah

disputation: Libertines

divine conception: Holy Ghost, Mary

divorce: Eunuch

doubting: Thomas

dove: Father in Heaven, John the Baptist

dragon: Michael

drought: Elias-1

elders: Sanhedrin, Scribes

Elias, spirit of: John the Baptist

eloquence: Apollos, Paul, Stephen

Emmanuel: Jesus Christ, Joseph-2

endurance: Job

envy: Joseph-1

eternal life: Eve, Father in Heaven, Jesus Christ, Melchizedek, Moses, Nazarene

eternal progression: Job, Zion

evil spirits: Gergesenes

exaltation: Father in Heaven, Isaac, Ishmael, Jacob-1, Jeremias or Jeremy, Jesus Christ, Michael, Moses, Prophet/Prophets, Satan

example: Scribes, Timothy

excellent: Theophilus

external rules: Pharisees

eyewitness: Luke, Theophilus

faith: Bartimaeus, Church, Elisha, Enoch, Esau, Eunice, Galatians, Gideon, Isaac, Israel, Jacob-1, Jesus-1, Jesus Christ, Jude, Mary-1, Melchizedek, Mercurius, Moses, Naaman, Nicolas, Noah, Paul, Saint/Saints, Samson, Samuel, Sarah, Sons of God, Thessalonians, Thomas, Titus, Unjust, Judge, Zion

faithful: Onesimus, Silas

fallen angel: Satan

false Christs: Christs, False; Anti-Christ

false prophet/false prophets: Bar-jesus, Prophet/Prophets, Sorcerer/Sorcerers

family: Moses, Paul

famine: Joel, Joseph-1; Sarepta, Woman of

fasting: Scribes

father: Adam, Abraham, Jacob-1

Father: Father in Heaven, John the Baptist, Rabboni, Stephen

father of many nations: Abraham, Sarah

favor: Salome-1

fear: Paul, Proselytes

First Vision: James-3

fishers of men: Apostle

flood: Noah

foreordination: Esau

forerunner: Elias-2, John the Baptist

forgiveness: Benjamin, David, Holy Ghost, Joseph-1, Moses, Onesimus, Publicans, Scribes, Simeon-1, Simon-7

fought a good fight: Paul

freedom: Paul

gathering: Holy Ghost, Isaiah, Juda (Judah), Malachi, Moses, One Hundred and Forty-Four Thousand, Pharisees, Zion

Gentile missionary service: Barsabas-2, Cornelius, Eunuch, Jonah, Nicolas, Paul, Peter, Philip-2, Proselytes, Ruth, Scythians, Simon-8

Gethsemane: James-1, Jesus Christ, John, Peter

gift of the Holy Ghost: Church, Holy Ghost, Jesus Christ

gifts: Epaphroditus, Moses

gifts of the Spirit: Bishop, Church, Holy Ghost, Paul

glorious: Eve, Mary-1

glory: Father in Heaven, Jesus Christ, Moses, Satan, Thessalonians

God-fearer: Proselytes

godliness: Timothy, Titus

godly sorrow: Paul

Golgotha: Jesus Christ

Good Shepherd: Jesus Christ

gospel: Baal, Gentile/Gentiles, Heathen/Heathens, Jesus Christ, Melchizedek, Moses, Nicodemus, One Hundred and Forty-Four Thousand, Paul, Saint/Saints, Timothy

gospel instruction from parents: Abel, Adam, Cain, Eve

Gospels composed in Greek: Grecians/Greeks

grace: Jesus Christ, Mary-1, Noah, Sarah, Timothy, Zion

gracious: Joseph-3

grandmother: Timothy

gratitude: Jonah, Philippians, Zion

greed: Ananias-1, Cain, Sapphira

guidance: Holy Ghost

guile (no guile): Nathanael

Hagiographa: Job, Solomon

happiness: Isaiah, Melchizedek

harmless as doves: Sanhedrin

hatred: Jacob-1

healing: Aeneas, Bartimaeus, Centurion-1, Elder/Elders, Elisha, Herodians, Isaiah, Joanna-2, Mary-2, Mercurius, Moses, Naaman, Peter, Scribes

high priest: Annas, Bishop, Jesus Christ, Caiaphas, Enoch, Gamaliel, Moses, Nazarene, One Hundred and Forty-Four Thousand, Priest/Priests, Scribes, Sons of Levi

high priesthood: Melchizedek

holy: Jesus Christ, Jude, Saint/Saints

Holy Ghost: Cornelius, Elisabeth, Father in Heaven, Joel, John the Baptist, Joseph-2, Mary-1, Nicolas, Parthians, Prophet/Prophets, Simon-5

home church meetings: Aquila, Mary-6, Prisca/Priscilla

honor: Salome-1, Sarah

honor of men: Scribes

honorable: Naaman

hope: Moses, Paul, Rachel, Saint/Saints, Unjust Judge

humility: Elisha, Isaiah, Naaman, Saul-1

hymns: David

hypocrisy: Pharisees

idol worship: Baal, Beelzebub, Diana, Demetrius-1, Ephesians, Gideon, Mercurius

idolatry: Isaiah, Samaritans, Solomon

image of God: Adam, Eve, Father in Heaven

Immanuel: Jesus Christ

immortality: Jesus Christ, Moses

industrious: Eve

integrity: Eunuch, Job, Joseph-1

irony: Satan

jealousy: Cain, Joseph-1

Jehovah: Father in Heaven, Jehovah, Jesus Christ

Jesus Christ: Father in Heaven, Jehovah, Jesus Christ, Lamb of God, Messiah, Prophet/Prophets

Jesus of Nazareth: Nazarene

Jews: Jew/Jews, Messiah

John Mark: Mark

John the Baptist: John the Baptist, Nazarite/Nazirite

joint-heirs with Christ: Abba, Ishmael, Sons of God

Joseph Smith: Joseph-1, John the Baptist, Peter, John, James-1, Moses, Noah, Root of Jesse, Seer

joy: Isaiah, Messiah, Ruth

judge: Gideon, Samson

judge in Israel: Bishop

judges: Twelve Apostles

judgment: Jesus Christ, Lot, Malachi, Scribes

judgment of God: Herod Agrippa I

just: Noah

justification: Moses, Paul

keys: Adam, Apostle, Bishop, Elias-4, Elijah, James-1, Jesus Christ, John the Baptist, John, Lazarus-2, Malachi, Melchizedek, Messiah, Michael, Moses, Peter

keys of salvation: Michael

kindness: Epaphroditus, Father in Heaven, Jonah, Julius, Mary-7, Onesimus

king: David, Melchizedek, Moses, Nathanael, Saul-1, Solomon

King: Jesus Christ

knowledge: Eve

labor of love: Paul

Lamb of God: Abel, Jesus Christ, John, John the Baptist, Lamb of God, Mark, Mary-1, Mary-3, One Hundred and Forty-Four Thousand, Sarah, Simon-4

laugh: Abraham, Sarah

law: Jesus-1, Melchizedek, Moses, Paul,

Pharisees, Prophet/Prophets, Sadducees, Sarah, Scribes, Stoics

lawyers: Scribes

leadership: David, High Priest, James-3, John, Juda (Judah), Levites, Melchizedek, Moses, One Hundred and Forty-Four Thousand, Peter, Prophet/Prophets, Saul-1, Silas, Twelve Apostles

leper: Bartimaeus, Eliseus, Mary-3, Naaman, Simon-4

Levitical Priesthood: Aaron, High Priest, Levi-1, Melchizedek, Sadducees, Sons of Levi

liberation: Moses, Quaternion

liberty: Holy Ghost

light: Jesus Christ

lineage of Christ: David

living water: Holy Ghost, Jacob-1, Jesus Christ, Moses, Prophet/Prophets

Lord of Sabaoth: Sabaoth

love: Church, Epaphras, Father in Heaven, Holy Ghost, Isaac, Jesus Christ, John, Jonah, Judas-3, Mary-1, Mary-3, Martha, Moses, Paul, Philippians, Prophet/Prophets, Saint/Saints, Seed of Abraham, Timothy

love of money: Paul

loyalty: Ruth

Lucifer: Satan

lying: Ananias-1, Sapphira

magicians: Jannes and Jambres

mankind: Son of Man, Sons of Men

manna: Moses

marriage: Esau, Eunuch, John the Baptist, Malachi, Mary-1, Paul, Rachel, Salome-2, Samson, Sarah, Solomon

martyr/martyrdom: Abel, Herod Agrippa I, Herod Antipas, Herodias, Holy Ghost, James-1, James-3, John the Baptist, Mark, Moses, Paul, Romans, Salome-2, Sanhedrin, Seth, Stephen, Zacharias-2

Mediator: Jesus Christ

meek: Moses

Melchizedek Priesthood: Bishop, James-1, John, Peter

mercy: Epaphroditus, Father in Heaven, Isaiah, Jesus Christ, Job, Jonah, Joseph-1, Lot, Seed of Abraham, Zion

messenger: Apostle, Malachi

Messiah: Hannah, Isaiah, Jesus Christ, John the Baptist, Melchizedek, Moses, Paul; Sarepta, Woman of; Wise Men of the East

millennium: Gog, Jesus Christ, Jew/Jews, Zion

miracle/miracles: Elisha, Eutychus, Jesus Christ, Mary-1, Philip-1; Sarepta, Woman of; Scribes

missionary work: Church, Cornelius, Ephesians, Eunuch, Gentile/Gentiles, Heathen/Heathens, Holy Ghost, Jonah, Melchizedek, Paul, Peter, Philippians, Silas, Stoics, Thessalonians, Timothy, Titus

moderation: Gamaliel

money: Paul

mother: Elisabeth, Eunice, Eve, John, Mary-1, Samuel, Sarah, Timothy

motherhood: Eve

motivation, misguided: Balaam

Mount of Transfiguration: Elias-1, Elijah, Father in Heaven, Fuller/Fullers, James-1, Jesus Christ, John, John the Baptist, Moses, Peter

murder: Abel, Barabbas, Cain, Joseph-2, Moses, Rachel, Wise Men of the East

murmur: Moses, Pharisees, Scribes

mythology: Castor and Pollux, Diana

Nazarite: Hannah, Samson

Noah: Gabriel

noble: One Hundred and Forty-Four Thousand, Seth

oath and covenant of the priesthood: Abraham, Father in Heaven, Seed of Abraham

obedience: Eve, Isaac, Abraham, Isaac, Isaiah, Jeremias or Jeremy, Jonah, Lot, Moses, Naaman, Noah, Paul, Sarah, Saul-1, Sons of God

old serpent: Satan

oral traditions: Pharisees, Scribes, Stoics

ordain/ordination: James-1, John, Melchizedek, Methuselah, Noah, One Hundred and Forty-Four Thousand

ordinances: Elijah, Holy Ghost

organization of the Church: Apostle, Bishop, Church, Elder/Elders, Holy Ghost, Paul, Prophet/Prophets

other sheep: Jesus Christ

outward regulations: Scribes

parables: Isaiah, Jesus Christ, Lazarus-2, Moses, Publicans, Scribes, Simon-7, Unjust Judge

parental instruction: Adam, Eunice, Eve, Mary-1, Timothy

partisanship: Apollos

patience: Job, Saint/Saints

patriarch: Abraham, High Priest, Jacob-1, Joseph-1, Melchizedek, Methuselah, Noah, Patriarch/Patriarchs, Seed of Abraham

Paul: Gamaliel, Saul-2

peace: Esau, Holy Ghost, Isaiah, Jesus Christ, Judas-5, Melchizedek, Saint/Saints

Perdition: Satan

perfect : Job, Melchizedek, Noah, Seth

perfection: Father in Heaven, Paul, Saint/Saints, Zion

persecution: Romans

perseverance: Samuel

personal revelation: Holy Ghost

persuade ("almost thou persuadest me"): Agrippa (Herod Agrippa II), Festus

Peter: Simeon-4, Simon-6

Pharisees: Gamaliel, Hebrews, Herodians, Isaiah, Matthew, Nicodemus, Paul, Pharisees, Prophet/Prophets, Publicans, Sadducees, Sanhedrin, Scribes, Simon-7, Solomon, Zacharias-2

philosophers: Epicureans, Stoics

plan of happiness: Prophet/Prophets

plan of salvation: Eve, Isaiah, Ishmael, Jacob-1, Jesus Christ

plural marriage: David, Isaac, Solomon

poetry: David, Job, Jonah

pottage: Esau, Jacob-1

power: Timothy, Twelve Apostles

prayer: Eve, Father in Heaven, Holy Ghost, Jesus Christ, Jonah, Joseph-4, Jude, Mary-6, Matthias, Moses, Samuel, Thessalonians, Unjust Judge, Zacharias-1

precious: Mary-1

premortal existence: Michael

president of the high priesthood: Moses

pride: Diotrephes, Isaiah, Saul-1, Solomon

priest/priests: Captain of the Temple, John the Baptist, Malachi, Melchizedek, Michael, Priest/Priests, Sadducees

priestcraft: Pharisees

priesthood: Abraham, Bishop, Elder/Elders, Elijah, Enoch, Enos, Father in Heaven, High Priest, Jacob-1, John, John the Baptist, Lazarus-2, Levi-1, Michael, Moses, Noah, One Hundred and Forty-Four Thousand, Peter, Seed of Abraham

prince: Michael

principles of the gospel: Church

priorities: Lot

promises: Malachi

prophecy: Agabus, Elisabeth, Isaiah, Jeremias or Jeremy, Methuselah, Moses, Naaman, Nazarene, Paul, Philip-2, Prophet/Prophets, Simeon-2, Zacharias-1

prophet: Elijah, Elias-4, Eliseus, Elisha, Esaias, Hannah, Holy Ghost, Isaiah, Ishmael, Jacob-1, Jeremias or Jeremy, Jesus-1, Jesus Christ, Joel, John the Baptist, Jonah, Joseph-1, Judas-5, Lot, Malachi, Melchizedek, Moses, Naaman, Noah, Paul, Prophet/Prophets, Samaritans, Samson, Samuel; Sarepta, Woman Of; Satan, Saul-1, Seer, Seth, Silas, Son of Man, Stephen, Simeon-3

proselyte: Nicolas

proverbs: Solomon

provocation: Jesus Christ

Psalms: David

pseudepigraphical writings: Enoch

publican/publicans: Matthew, Zacchaeus

pure: Nathanael, Ruth

pure in heart: Zion

purification: Holy Ghost, Sons of Levi

qualities of service: Bishop

reap what we sow: Paul

reconciliation: Onesimus

Redeemer: Isaiah, Jeremias or Jeremy, Jesus Christ, Job

redemption: Eve, Holy Ghost, Mary-1

redress: Unjust Judge

rejoice: Mary-1

remission of sins: Jesus Christ, Melchizedek

remorse: David

repentance: Church, David, Isaac, Jesus Christ, Jonah, Malachi, Matthew, Melchizedek, Noah, Paul, Zacharias-2

rescue: Lot

resolving a dispute: Judas-5

respect: Abel, Cain

Restoration: Church, Elijah, Epaphroditus, Gentile/Gentiles, High Priest, Isaiah, James-1, Jesus Christ, Joel, John, John the Baptist, Lazarus-2, Levi-1, Messiah, Moses, Paul, Peter, Pharisees, Rachel, Sanhedrin, Sons of Levi, Twelve Apostles, Two Witnesses, Unjust Judge

restoring of life: Dorcas, Eutychus, James-1, John, Lazarus-1, Martha, Mary-3, Prophet/Prophets; Sarepta, Woman of; Simon-8

resurrection: Abraham, Adam, Epicureans, Jesus Christ, Jonah, Martha, Mary 2, Matthias, Moses, Peter, Pharisees, Rabboni, Sadducees, Saint/Saints

revelation: Church, Holy Ghost, Moses, Paul

righteous: Simeon-2, Sons of God, Unjust

Judge, Zacharias-1

righteousness: Melchizedek, Zion

Roman citizen (Paul): Festus

royal priesthood: Peter, Zion

Sabbath: Abiathar, Jesus Christ; Sarepta, Widow of; Scribes

sacrament: James-1, Jesus Christ

sacrifice: Abel, Abraham, Barnabas, Cain, Eve, High Priest, Isaac, Lamb of God, Sarah, Sons of Levi

Saints: Zion

salvation: Jeremias or Jeremy, Mary-1, Melchizedek, Michael, Nazarene, Paul, Pharisees, Prophet/Prophets, Publicans, Zacchaeus

sanctification: Thessalonians

sanctified: Saint/Saints, Seed of Abraham

sanctify: Moses

Sanhedrin: Gamaliel, Joseph-3, Pilate, Stephen

Savior: Abraham, Isaiah, Holy One of Israel, Immanuel, Emmanuel, Jehovah, Jesus Christ, Rachel, Son of God, Son of Man

scattering: Rachel

schoolmaster: Moses, Paul

scribes: Isaiah, Matthew, Publicans, Sanhedrin, Solomon, Zacharias-2

scriptures: Cleopas, Eunice, Holy Ghost, Jesus Christ, Moses, Paul, Satan, Timothy

seal: One Hundred and Forty-Four Thousand

sealing : Church, Holy Ghost, Malachi, Moses, Peter

Second Coming: Daniel, Enoch, Gog, Isaac, Isaiah, Jeremias or Jeremy, Jesus Christ, Jew/Jews, Lot, Magog, Malachi, Noah, Peter, Seven

Angels, Thessalonians, Twelve Apostles

secret combinations: Cain

seed: Abraham, Eve, Father in Heaven

Semitic languages: Shem

Semitic race: Shem

Sermon on the Mount: Jesus Christ, Solomon

service: Epaphras, Epaphroditus, Judas-5, Paul, Salome-1, Samuel, Timothy

seven special ministering leaders: Philip-2, Stephen

seventies: Elder/Elders

Seventy: Church

sign: Jonah, Moses, Pharisees, Scribes, Solomon, Zacharias-1

sin: David

sing: Moses

sins, remitting of: Holy Ghost

sisters: Sisters of the Lord

slanderer: Satan

Sodom and Gomorrah: Lot

Son: Bar, Ben, John

son of the morning: Satan

sons of Levi: Malachi

sons of Moses: Moses

sorcerer/sorcerers: Jannes and Jambres, Simon-5

Spirit: Holy Ghost

spirit realm: Isaac, Isaiah, Lazarus-2, Michael, Noah, Peter, Seth

spirituality: Galatians, Noah

spokesman: Aaron

star: Wise Men of the East

stature: Joseph-2, Jesus Christ

stick of Joseph: Joseph-1

stick of Judah: Joseph-1

stone: Cephas

strength: Samson, Zion

succession in leadership: Apostle, Barsabas-1, Church, Elisha, High Priest, Joseph-4, Matthias

suffer: Satan

synoptic: John

Tabernacle: Moses

tax collectors: Zacchaeus, Publicans

teacher: Rabbi

teachers, false: Balaam

temple: Babylonia/Babylonians, Captain of the Temple, Cherub/Cherubim/Cherubims, Elijah, Holy Ghost, James-1, Jesus Christ, John the Baptist, Joseph-2, Juda (Judah), Malachi, Moses, Paul, Samaritans, Scribes, Simeon-2, Solomon, Sons of Levi, Zacharias-1, Zerubbabel (Zorobabel), Zion

temple work for the dead: Church

temptation: Satan

Ten Commandments: Moses

ten tribes: Moses

tent makers: Aquila, Paul

testament: Jesus Christ, Melchizedek, Moses

testimony: Paul

thanksgiving: Jonah

the way: Felix

theft: Onesimus

tithing: Bishop, Levi-1, Malachi, Melchizedek

tolerance: Jonah, Ruth

tomb: Joanna-2, John, Joseph-3, Mary-2, Mary-4, Rabboni

traditions: Moses, Pharisees, Prophet/Prophets, John, Michael, Moses

treason: Scribes

tribulation: Paul

tribute: Scribes

triumph of good: Isaiah

trust: Solomon

trusted: Timothy

truth: Jesus Christ

Twelve: Apostle, Church, Disciple, Holy Ghost, James-1, Jesus Christ, Judas-1, Judas-3, Mary-2, Matthew, Matthias, Nathanael, Paul, Peter, Philip-1, Publicans, Simon-2, Thaddaeus, Thomas, Twelve Apostles

Twelve Disciples: Twelve Apostles

twelve tribes of Israel: Jacob-1, Moses, One Hundred and Forty-Four Thousand

unity: Paul, Ruth, Zion

unity of the Godhead: Holy Ghost

uprising: Ephesians, Demetrius-1, Gaius-2

valiant: Jacob-1

valor: Isaac, Noah

vengeance: Simeon-1

vicarious work for the dead: Elijah

victory: Gideon, Gog

virgin: Mary-1, Nazarene

virtue: Joseph-1, Stoics

virtuous: Ruth

war: Isaac

washing of hands: Scribes

way: Felix, Philip-1

wickedness: Isaiah

widow: Sarepta, Widow of; Unjust Judge

wife: Eve, Rachel, Sarah

wisdom: Eve, Holy Ghost, Job, Joseph-2, Jesus Christ, Mary-1, Solomon, Timothy

wise as serpents: Sanhedrin

witness: John the Baptist, Luke, Matthias, Paul, Peter, Prophet/Prophets, Romans, Samuel, Stephen

witnesses: Two Witnesses

woman/women: Elisabeth, Herodias, Joanna-2, Lot's Wife, Martha, Mary-1, Mary-2, Mary-3, Mary-4, Mary-5, Mary-6, Mary-7, Messiah, Naaman, Nazarene, Philip-2, Prophet/Prophets, Rabboni, Rachel, Rahab, Ruth, Salome-1, Salome-2, Samson, Samuel, Sarah; Sarepta, Widow of; Scribes, Simon-4, Simon-7, Sisters of the Lord, Syrophenician, Timothy, Unjust Judge, Zacharias-1

Word: Father in Heaven, Holy Ghost, Jesus Christ

works: Isaac, James-3, Paul,

worldliness: Babylon

worship: Holy Ghost, Isaac, Mary-1, Satan

worthy: Zion

youth, counsel to: Paul

zealotry: Eunuch

Zealots: Simon-2

Zion: Enoch, Isaiah, Israel, Sanhedrin, Zion

ART CREDITS

Page 1: *Moses Calls Aaron to the Ministry* by Harry Anderson © Intellectual Reserve, Inc. Courtesy of the Church History Museum.

Page 3: *Abraham and Isaac* © William Whitaker

Page 5: *Leaving the Garden of Eden* © Joseph F. Brickey. For more information, go to www.josephbrickey.com.

Page 7: *Death of Ananias* by Gustave Doré, *The Doré Bible Illustrations*, Dover Publications, 1974.

Page 7: *Moses Seeing Jehovah* © Joseph F. Brickey. For more information, go to www.josephbrickey.com.

Page 11: *Christ Washing the Apostles Feet* by Del Parson © Intellectual Reserve, Inc

Page 12: *Christ Ordaining the Twelve Apostles* by Harry Anderson © Intellectual Reserve, Inc. Courtesy of the Church History Museum.

Page 17: *Babylon Fallen* by Gustave Doré, *The Doré Bible Illustrations*, Dover Publications, 1974.

Page 19: *Paul and Barnabas at Antioch*, from *The New Testament: A Pictorial Archive from Nineteenth-Century Sources*, Dover Publications, 1986.

Page 20: *The Last Supper* by Harry Anderson © Pacific Press Publishing Association, Nampa, Idaho.

Page 23: *The Lord Accused before Caiaphas* by Frank Adams.

Page 24: *Where Is Thy Brother?* © Walter Rane. For more information, visit www.walterrane.com.

Page 29: *Jesus Dies on the Cross* by Julius Schnorr von Carolsfeld, *Treasury of Bible Illustrations Old and New Testaments*, Dover Publications, 1999.

Page 30: *St. Peter in the house of Cornelius* by Gustave Doré, *The Doré Bible Illustrations*, Dover Publications, 1974.

Page 32: *Daniel in the Lion's Den* by Clark Kelley Price © Intellectual Reserve, Inc. Courtesy of the Church History Museum.

Page 33: *He Restoreth My Soul* © Walter Rane. For more information, visit www.walterrane.com.

Page 34: *Demetrius Inciting the Ephesians Against Paul*, from *The New Testament: A Pictorial Archive from Nineteenth-Century Sources*, Dover Publications, 1986.

Page 35: Peter Raising Dorcas from the Dead © Robert T. Barrett. For more information go to www.robertbarrett.com.

Page 40: *Elijah Contends Against the Priest of Baal* by Jerry Harston © Intellectual Reserve, Inc.

Page 41: *Mary's Visit to Elizabeth* by Carl Heinrich Bloch. Courtesy of Det Nationalhistoriske Museum på Frederiksborg, Hillerød.

Page 42: *The City of Enoch Translated* by Del Parson © Intellectual Reserve, Inc.

Page 44: *St. Paul at Ephesus* by Gustave Doré, *The Doré Bible Illustrations*, Dover Publications, 1974.

Page 45: *The Reconciliation of Jacob and Esau* © Robert T. Barrett. For more information go to www.robertbarrett.com.

Page 47: *Adam and Eve in the Garden* by Lowell Bruce Bennett © Intellectual Reserve, Inc.

Page 50: *The Grand Council* © Robert T. Barrett. For more information go to www.robertbarrett.com.

Page 52: *Paul Before Felix*, from *The New Testament: A Pictorial Archive from Nineteenth-Century Sources*, Dover Publications, 1986.

Page 54: *The Annunciation* by Carl Heinrich Bloch. Courtesy of Det Nationalhistoriske Museum på Frederiksborg, Hillerød.

Page 58: *Paul Preaching at Athens*, from *The New Testament: A Pictorial Archive from Nineteenth-Century Sources*, Dover Publications, 1986.

Page 60: *The Wise Men and Herod* by James Tissot.

Page 65: *Isaac Deceived by Jacob* by Frank Adams.

Page 66: *The Prophet Isaiah Foretells of Christ's Birth* by Harry Anderson © Intellectual Reserve, Inc. Courtesy of the Church History Museum.

Page 71: *James Writing His Epistle* © Paul Mann. For more information visit www.paulmannwesternart.com.

Page 74: *Inviting Him In* © Joseph F. Brickey. For more information, go to www.josephbrickey.com

Page 75: *Man of Galilee* © Joseph F. Brickey. For more information, go to www.josephbrickey.com

Page 79: *Jehovah Creates the Earth* © Walter Rane. For more information, visit www.walterrane.com.

Page 82: *The Living Christ* © Joseph F. Brickey. For more information, go to www.josephbrickey.com

Page 83: *In Humility* © Simon Dewey. Courtesy of Altus Fine Art. For print information, go to www.altusfineart.com.

Page 85: *Abide With Me* © Simon Dewey. Courtesy of Altus Fine Art. www.altusfineart.com.

Page 88: *Job* © Gary Kapp.

Page 89: *John the Revelator Shown a Heavenly City* by Innes Fripp.

Page 91: *John Preaching in the Wilderness* © Robert T. Barrett. For more information go to www.robertbarrett.com.

Page 93: *Jonah Is Cast Ashore* © Robert T. Barrett. For more information go to www.robertbarrett.com.

Page 94: *Joseph Interprets the Dream of Pharaoh's Servant* by Del Parson © Intellectual Reserve, Inc.

Page 95: *Annunciation to Joseph* © Joseph F. Brickey. For more information, go to www.josephbrickey.com.

Page 96: *Joseph's Brothers Tell Their Father of His Death* © Robert T. Barrett. For more information go to www.robertbarrett.com.

Page 98: *Judas Betrays Christ* by Ted Henninger © Intellectual Reserve, Inc.

Page 100: *I Am the Way* © Simon Dewey. Courtesy of Altus Fine Art. www.altusfineart.com.

Page 101: *Raising Lazarus* by Carl Heinrich Bloch. Courtesy of Det Nationalhistoriske Museum på Frederiksborg, Hillerød.

Page 102: *Christ Calling Levi Matthew* by Harry Anderson © Pacific Press Publishing Association, Nampa, Idaho.

Page 103: *The Flight of Lot* by Gustave Doré, *The Doré Bible Illustrations*, Dover Publications, 1974.

Page 108: *The Better Part* © Simon Dewey. Courtesy of Altus Fine Art. www.altusfineart.com.

Page 109: *Annunciation to Mary* © Joseph F. Brickey. For more information, go to www.josephbrickey.com.

Page 111: *Why Weepest Thou* © Simon Dewey. Courtesy of Altus Fine Art. www.altusfineart.com.

Page 112: *Mary Heard His Word* © Walter Rane. For more information, visit www.walterrane.com.

Page 115: *Melchizedek Teaching a Family* © Del Parson. For more information go to www.delparson.com

Page 118: *Hallowed Be Thy Name* © Simon Dewey. Courtesy of Altus Fine Art. www.altusfineart.com.

Page 121: *Moses the Lawgiver* by Ted Henninger © Intellectual Reserve, Inc.

Page 123: *Moses Parting the Red Sea* by Robert T. Barrett © Intellectual Reserve, Inc.

Page 125: *Naaman Cured of Leprosy* © Paul Mann. For more information visit www.paulmannwesternart.com.

Page 129: *Nicodemus Came Unto Him by Night* © Walter Rane. For more information, visit www.walterrane.com.

Page 135: *Paul Teaching the Athenians* © Paul Mann. For more information visit www.paulmannwesternart.com.

Page 136: *Peter Preparing to Write an Epistle* © Robert T. Barrett. For more information go to www.robertbarrett.com.

Page 138: *Peter's Denial* by Carl Heinrich Bloch. Courtesy of Det Nationalhistoriske Museum på Frederiksborg, Hillerød.

Page 139: *The Pharisee and the Publican* by Gustave Doré, *The Doré Bible Illustrations*, Dover Publications, 1974.

Page 142: *Phillip Teaching the Ethiopian Eunuch* © Robert T. Barrett. For more information go to www.robertbarrett.com.

Page 145: *Behold the Man* © Simon Dewey. Courtesy of Altus Fine Art. www.altusfineart.com.

Page 146: *An Atonement Sacrifice is Presented to the Priests* © Robert T. Barrett. For more information go to www.robertbarrett.com.

Page 148: *Isaiah* by Ted Henninger © Intellectual Reserve, Inc.

Page 155: *Paul's Arrival in Rome* by Julius Schnorr von Carolsfeld, *Treasury of Bible Illustrations Old and New Testaments*, Dover Publications, 1999.

Page 156: *Ruth Finds Favor with Boaz* © Robert T. Barrett. For more information go to www.robertbarrett.com.

Page 159: *If Anyone Thirst, Let Him Come to me and Drink*, from *The New Testament: A Pictorial Archive from Nineteenth-Century Sources*, Dover Publications, 1986.

Page 163: *St. Samson and Delilah* by Gustave Doré, *The Doré Bible Illustrations*, Dover Publications, 1974.

Page 164: *God Appears in a Night Vision to the Prophet Samuel* by Harry Anderson © Intellectual Reserve, Inc. Courtesy of the Church History Museum.